UNEXCEPTIONAL POLITICS

UNEXCEPTIONAL POLITICS

ON OBSTRUCTION, IMPASSE, AND THE IMPOLITIC

EMILY APTER

VERSO

First published by Verso 2018
© Emily Apter 2018

Images courtesy of William Powhida and Postmasters Gallery, New York

1 3 5 7 9 10 8 6 4 2

Verso
UK: 6 Meard Street, London W1F 0EG
US: 20 Jay Street, Suite 1010, Brooklyn, NY 11201
versobooks.com

Verso is the imprint of New Left Books

ISBN-13: 978-1-78478-085-2
ISBN-13: 978-1-78478-086-9 (US EBK)
ISBN-13: 978-1-78478-087-6 (UK EBK)

British Library Cataloguing in Publication Data
A catalogue record for this book is available from the British Library

Library of Congress Cataloging-in-Publication Data
A catalog record for this book is available from the Library of Congress

Typeset in Minion by Hewer Text (UK) Ltd, Edinburgh
Printed in the UK by CPI Group (UK) Ltd, Croydon CR0 4YY

Contents

Introduction: Unexceptional Politics   1

I.   Resistant to Political Theory
"Small P" Politics   21
Micropolitics   37
Microsociologies   53
Nanoracisms   67

II. Scenes of Obstruction
Impolitic   83
Disentrenchment   97
Interference   101
Obstinacy   113

III. Political Fictions
Political Fiction   139
Psychopolitics   145
Collateral Damage   155
Thermocracy   163
Milieu   177

IV. Economies of Existence
Schadenfreude   199
Managed Life   213
Occupy Derivatives!   231
Serial Politics   249

Acknowledgements   269
Index   271

Introduction: Unexceptional Politics

Overflowing the bounds of Realpolitik or informal politics, what I call *unexceptional politics* could be thought of as the material and immaterial stuff of politics that encompasses everything from government gridlock and dysfunction to political cunning (Machiavellianism in its modern historical mutations), from politicking (backroom deals, information trafficking, the petitions of local constituents, jousting and ousting) to Occupy or Maidan, with their neo-anarchist strategies of occupation, assembly, riot, strike, obstination (utopianism against all odds, resistance to primitive expropriation), interference, and creative leveraging.

Unexceptional politics, as an umbrella rubric, subsumes and exceeds micropolitics insofar as it is pointedly posed against the ideological exceptionalism enshrined in nationalist compacts and the American heritage of manifest destiny. It conceptually engages, in the form of dialectical resistance, the "state of exception," foundationally inscribed in theories of "the Political," from Thomas Hobbes to Carl Schmitt, from Hannah Arendt to Jacques Derrida and Giorgio Agamben. Thinking politics exceptionally, however—through states of emergency or sublations of political subjectivity—blocks the representation of what is unintelligible or resistant to political theorization, while thinking politics *unexceptionally* spools into explanatory structures of historical epic and of classical political theory, muddying their structural coherence, obfuscating mainstream political and diplomatic ends. This is politics that eludes conceptual grasp, confronting us with the realization that we really do not know what politics *is,* where it begins and ends, or how its micro-events should be called.

Claude Lefort laments the "no there there" view of statecraft that leaches out of decentralized structures of governance and systems of controlled information.

How, in fact, can we cling to the idea that politics invades every-thing? If there is no boundary between politics and that which is not political, politics itself disappears, because politics has always implied a definite relationship between human beings, a relationship governed by the need to answer the questions on which their common fate depends.[1]

If there is no demonstrable boundary between politics and the non-political, then how can we *not* accept the idea that politics invades everything? The problem, it would seem, lies with classical political theory and philosophy, whose language has a relatively limited vocab-ulary for describing the allness and everywhereness of political atmos-phere and milieu.

Hence the impetus to initiate a glossary of terms that have no ready standing in political theory, yet share something in challenging the assumption that "the Political" is always for tomorrow. Rather than treat politics ("small p," or "*la* politique") as nothing more than the fore-closure of the possibility of a critical politics, or a concession to what Ross McKibbin calls "what-works" politics, or a "realist" politics that is supposedly party-neutral and beyond ideology (though it is anything but), this vocabulary focuses instead on (1) terms for the political that have no standing in classical political theory, particularly in relation to psychopolitical forms of obstruction and impasse to direct action; (2) an "untheologized politics" "where there is no Homo Sacer"[2] (as argued

---

1   Claude Lefort, *Democracy and Political Theory*, trans. David Macey (London: Wiley, 1991).

2   Stathis Gourgouris, "Society Defended against Whom or What?," *New Philosopher*, May 25, 2013, newphilosopher.com. Gourgouris approves the term unexceptional politics because, in his own view, "democracy is precisely the regime that does not make exceptions, if we are to take seriously Aristotle's dictum of a politics where the ruler learns by being ruled, making thus the ruled simultaneously the ruler, in a determinant affirmation of an arche that has no precedent and no uniqueness but is shared by all. No exceptions." Gourgouris elaborates his own concept of an "anarchic politics" of "no exceptions" and in which nothing is sacred: "insofar as arche is unexceptionally shared by all and therefore lapses as a singular principle. Anarchy as a mode of rule—democratic rule par excellence—raises a major challenge to the inherited tradition of sovereignty in modernity." For Gourgouris, the challenge is to propel "left governmentality" into a new public space; in this space we would discover "unexceptional collective political action," happens

by Stathis Gourgouris, who has himself adapted my own coinage of "unexceptional politics"); (3) historical notions of politics as métier and praxis and (4) concept-metaphors for experiments in underachieved socialism, states of care, non-capitalized labor time, the recalculation of social interest, non-exclusionary franchise, the undercommons, and micropolitics.[3] As Roberto Mangabeira Unger has argued, "the illusion of the indivisibility of formative contexts," which has led to the belief that "all changes short of total revolution must amount to mere conservative tinkering . . . induces in its adepts a fatal oscillation between unjustified confidence and equally unjustified prostration."[4] The twin poles of unjustified confidence and unjustified prostration may admit of no supersession, but what we are given to work with by Unger—worth thinking about—is "divisible formative context." In my own thinking, this would be a micropolitics that foregrounds what Unger calls "disentrenchment." Its point of departure is the abrogation of any social compact that consigns whole sectors of the population to the status of "non-occupant of society" or "resource outcast."[5]

---

not just on election days, but every day, enacted by "unexceptional people" (i.e., those who are not professional politicians or members of the politically empowered classes). I agree with Gourgouris politically, but my own usage is applied descriptively, for political states of affairs, or blockage and obstruction, rather than prescriptively. I would therefore situate unexceptional politics squarely in the spheres of state function and the machinations of politicians rather than in projections of a new anarchy or left governmentality, regardless of their appeal.

3   Ross McKibbin, "What Works Doesn't Work," *London Review of Books* 30:17, 2008, 20–2. "The culture of the focus group does not, however, lead to an apolitical politics. On the contrary, it reinforces the political status quo and encourages a hard-nosed, 'realistic' view of the electorate that denies the voter any political loyalty, except to 'what works'. 'What works', though, is anything but an objective criterion: these days it is what the right-wing press says 'works'. The war on drugs doesn't work; nor does building more prisons; nor, one suspects, will many of the anti-terror laws. But that doesn't stop ministers from pursuing all of them vigorously. New Labour in practice is much more wedded to what-works politics than the Conservatives were under Thatcher, who was openly and self-consciously ideological."

4   Roberto Mangabeira Unger, *Social Theory* (London and New York: Verso, 2004),158.

5   Rob Nixon cites Rebecca Solnit's phrase "non-occupants of society" in his discussion of the politicization of what he calls "resource outcasts": "When people feel reduced (in Rebecca Solnit's phrase), to "non-occupants" of society, such discounted casualties—such resource outcasts—will have every incentive to make common cause against neoliberalism's disinheritance plot." Rob Nixon, "Neoliberalism, Genre, and 'The Tragedy of the Commons,'" *PMLA* 127:3, 2012, 598.

In lieu of a *theory* of unexceptional politics, I have made an effort to think politics *as it happens* in circumstances thrush with contingency and baffled institutional authority, on the left, on the right, and inside the mainstream or beltway. Hence, this idiosyncratic and by no means exhaustive glossary drafted in the face of a political environment—neoliberal Euro-America—severely pockmarked by obstructionism, obstinacy, the marketing of affairs and financial scandals, rude-boy tactics (incivility, tactlessness) and the submersion of political struggle in the vagaries of managerialism. Drawing on theorists of micropolitics (Foucault, Deleuze, Guattari), critics of the bourgeois novel (Jameson and Moretti), and critical thinkers who have mobilized political aesthetics (Lukács, Rancière, Badiou), I have experimented with distilling a vocabulary for the microphenomenology of political life. This has entailed investigating approaches to modes of politicking that, despite their formulaic or serial character, fit no precise rubric or institutional ascription. Hannah Arendt (in "On Violence") bemoaned the paucity of terminology in political science for distinctions among keywords like power, strength, authority, and violence and urged developing an ear for the logical grammar of their usage, their contextual circulation, and specific properties and attributes.[6]

I have taken Arendt's point to heart in designating certain glossemes as belonging to a currency of unexceptional politics, in listening for the logical contradictions and creative eruptions in political syntax, in looking at how politics is pictured in narrative scenography or anecdotally telescoped. Literature, and especially the political fiction of French authors from the Restoration to the Belle Époque—Stendhal, Balzac, Flaubert, Zola, Taine, Proust—allows me to consider narrative accounts of scams, seductions, backroom deals, and the kinds of diplomatic intrigues that dilute and diffuse "the Political," highlighting the elusiveness of the political event. It is the inchoate texture of the micro-event that preoccupies writers in the post-revolutionary period, a time marked by parallels to the present-day era, which is to say, by crises of governmentality, financial debacle, defeat in war, civil

---

6   Hannah Arendt, *Crises of the Republic* (New York: Harcourt Brace & Co., 1972), 142.

disorder, strikes and attacks, imperial expansionism, new strands of xenophobia, new forms of democratic leisure, and a burgeoning mass media fully participant in the spread of journalistic irony and political corruption.

From the beginning I was faced with the question of how politics, as a scene of maneuvers and an application of cunning, maps onto (or does not) formal, abstract models of political aesthetics; onto the workings of capitalist epic, democracy in language, the "revolution-ary" dimension of avant-gardism, comic forms of class struggle, modes of narrative realism, and tragic aporias of *communitas*. Meeting this challenge of a structural interpretation of politics soon proved impossible, but the abiding issue of politics and form, as framed in 1974 by Fredric Jameson's watershed study *Marxism and Form: 20th-Century Dialectical Theories of Literature*, were integral to the book's heuristic. Where Jameson focused on dialectics in structuralist aesthetics, I focused instead on the structurelessness of political atmosphere that suffuses what Jameson named the "political uncon-scious," as well as the "atmospheric walls," associated by Sarah Ahmed with internalized moods, that stratify social space and foreclose participation in community.[7]

This attempt to define the amorphous construct of unexceptional politics undertakes no systematic critique of theories of sovereign exception, which, recurring to Carl Schmitt's application of *Ausnahmezustand* to the Roman *justicium* and *auctoritas*, refer to the "state of siege" and "suspension of the rule of law." After all, this critique already exists, fully developed in the 1990s and early 2000s around the construct of the *sovereign decision*—defined as the excep-tional authority vested in the sovereign to institute a state of emergency—which has gradually taken over as the basis of Western models of the sovereign subject, or sovereignty subjectivized. Such theorizations of exceptionalism acquired renewed traction and impe-tus in the work of Giorgio Agamben, Jacques Derrida, Slavoj Žižek and Judith Butler (among others) during America's Iraq invasions, when the exercise of extralegal powers transformed the "state of

---

7   Sarah Ahmed, "Atmospheric Walls," *Feminist Killjoys*, September 15, 2014, Feministkilljoys.com.

emergency" and "extraordinary rendition" into routine political measures. The routinization of the state of exception continues to underwrite drone warfare, supranational border patrol, domestic police practices, and the surveillance abuses of the National Security Agency; taken together they constitute an "unexceptionalization" of illegal political intervention.

While exceptionalism may be an unexceptional feature of routinized war and staple of American jingoism, I would rather construe unexceptionalism less as the logic of "exception to the rule," and more as one of "just politics as usual," an attitude that inevitably shores up the status quo. Sidebars in the business of deal-brokering, sex scandals in the stalls of the national assembly, information-trafficking in diplomacy; all have formed the traditional stock-in-trade of pamphlets, caricatures and post-revolutionary political fiction. Their contemporary correlate may be found in media reportage and insider accounts of the political "Club" (as in Matt Bai's book *All the Truth is Out: The Week Politics Went Tabloid* [2014], or Mark Leibovich's *This Town: Two Parties and a Funeral—Plus Plenty of Valet Parking!—in America's Gilded Capital* [2013];[8] art (as in the satirical graphics of financial derivatives and corporate data by William Powhida); and in myriad films, comedy specials, and TV serials that take government back-offices as their settings.[9] What

---

8   A reconstruction of the erasure of Gary Hart as a 1987 presidential contender, caught lying about his affair with Donna Rice, *All the Truth is Out* is a contemporary pendant to Timothy Crouse's classic dissection of political journalism, *The Boys on the Bus* (1973). Leibovich's anthropology of Washington analyzes the self-perpetuating group of political professionals who serve as the "support sectors" of elected officials and who "never get voted out or term-limited." As Leibovich puts it, this "insider swarm" forms a "crucible of easy wealth, fame, forgiveness, and next acts . . . and has been known by various names: 'Permanent Washington.' 'The Political Class.' 'The Chattering Class.' 'The Usual Suspects.' 'The Beltway Establishment.' 'The Echo Chamber.' 'The Echo System.' 'The Gang of 500.' 'The Gang of 600.' 'The Movable Mess.' 'The Club.' 'This Town.'" Mark Leibovich, *This Town: Two Parties and a Funeral—Plus Plenty of Valet Parking!—in America's Gilded Capital* (New York: Blue Rider Press, 2013), 7–8.

9   See, for instance, the British sitcom *Yes, Minister!* (1980–82), Garry Trudeau and Robert Altman's ground-breaking mockumentary television series *Tanner '88* (1988), the Danish political drama *Borgen* (2010–13), and *House of Cards* (2013–present), as well as films like Armando Iannucci's film *In the Loop* (2009), a spin-off from the televised series *The Thick of It* (2005–12).

these books, films and serials depict so well is how the quirks of human personality—complacency, wounded narcissism, lassitude, bloody-mindedness, bureaucratic reflex—transfer to the workings of political institutions. Bureaucratic hurdles and legal obstruction are symptoms of human agency, such that simple words like "decrees," "signatures," and "contracts" become the currency of political logjams.[10] As Bruno Latour reads them:

> "What?" they exclaim. "How could this little obstacle have the power to stop us?" . . . On the one hand astonishing force, objectivity, on the other remarkable weakness. We feel that force every time we learn that, "because of a simple signature missing on the decree," the appointment of a bank director was blocked; or when we see that a dam construction project essential to the survival of a valley has been suspended owing to "a tiny defect in the declaration of public utility"; or that jobless workers have lost their rights "because they misread the contract that bound them to their employer"; or that one business was unable to acquire another "because of a legal constraint imposed by Brussels." But we feel the weakness every time we despair at seeing that the "legally justified" decision is not necessarily just, opportune, true, useful, effective; every time the court condemns an accused party but the aggrieved party has still not been able to achieve "closure"; every time indemnities have been awarded but doubts still remain about the exact responsibilities of the respective parties. With the law, we always go from surprise to surprise: we are surprised by its power, surprised by its impotence.[11]

The toxic combination of despair, grievance, doubt, and impotence lends psychic specificity to notions of obstructive "force," carried over to political speech in the guise of a special kind of impasse (a "category mistake" consisting in the accusation of lying "brought by a way of

---

10 On the obstructive role of bureaucratic rules and procedures in the maintenance of political structures of domination, see Béatrice Hibou, *La bureaucratisation du monde dans l'ère néolibérale* (Paris: La Découverte, 2012).

11 Bruno Latour, *An Inquiry into Modes of Existence*, trans. Catherine Porter (Cambridge, MA: Harvard University Press, 2013), 361.

speaking that claims for its part, *not* to pass through *any pass*"), or form of talk that goes nowhere. As Latour elaborates:

> There is nothing more fragmented, interrupted, repetitive, conventional and contradictory than political speech. It never stops breaking off, starting over, harping, betraying its promises . . . getting mixed up, coming and going, blotting itself out by maneuvers whose thread no one seems to be able to find anymore.[12]

In Latour's estimation the only counter is "the dissolution of coalitions of naysayers," so that "what was united disperses like a flock of sparrows, becomes a 'crooked movement.'"[13]

Perhaps all one can aspire to is "crooked movement" during a period in US political history when partisan obstructionism remains the order of the day. President Obama's election in 2008 precipitated a hard right turn in US politics, already in an archconservative place after two terms of the junior Bush presidency. By Obama's second-term election a culture of venomous incivility fanned by Tea Party extremism further encouraged the incessant posturing of the "party of no." Partisan voting blocks in Congress and the Senate, acting in lock-step, opposed all legislative and diplomatic initiatives, from routine committee member nominations, to nuclear nonproliferation agreements with Iran, to virtually any meliorist environmental legislation or gun control. The expansion of "conceal and carry" and "stand your ground" laws at the very moment of mass shootings; the increase in militias, border militarization, and incarceration without due process; the failure to prosecute police in the killings of black men, women, and children, along with the impact of movements associated with corrosive ideologies—"corporations are people," Citizens United, abortion restrictions, "right to work" attacks on organized labor, curtailment of public welfare, climate change denial—all contributed to the deathliness of obstruction. It goes without saying that governance at a standstill has only been further exacerbated in the era of Trumpism, where "the man in the white house sits, naked and obscene,

---

12   Ibid., 132, 133.
13   Ibid., 134.

a pustule of ego, in the harsh light, a man whose grasp exceeded his understanding, because his understanding was dulled by indulgence."[14] Legislative blockage is not only the chronic symptom of politics as usual, or the nasty aftereffect of government shutdown and paralysis (fortified by post-Brexit, new-populist cross-Atlantic mirroring to become what Balibar diagnoses as "a deep crisis of the *political institution*"), but also channels a lethal undertow, a death wish; it tolls the suicidal endgame for deliberative democracy.[15]

No longer persuaded that we can simply block blockage with its own blunt instruments (in the spirit of Wikileaks and Anonymous), I have channeled my critical ire (and profound political frustrations and fears) into compiling a lexicon whose terms, directly or indirectly, flow out of the conditions of political obstruction, impasse, and impolitic actions and speech. Bifocal by design, the book is organized, first, as an (albeit idiosyncratic) critical vocabulary of keywords that describe micropolitical phenomena for which classical political theory and political science have no precise names, and second, as a narrative about "the long Restoration" (the name of Alain Badiou's conservative sequence), whose through line extends from the French *monarchie censitaire* to configurations within early twenty-first-century capitalo-parliamentarianism.

To this end, I emphasize the character and range of "small p" politics, half of a dyad whose other half is "big P" Politics, or "the Political." "The Political," with emphasis on the definite article, has served as shorthand, especially on the left, for the refusal to accept the terms of politics on offer in the mediocracy. Though no uniform theoretical

---

14   Rebecca Solnit, "On the Corrosive Privilege of the Most Mocked Man in the World," *Literary Hub*, May 30, 2017, lithub.com.

15   Étienne Balibar, "'Populism' and 'Counter-Populism' in the Atlantic Mirror," *Open Democracy*, January 2, 2017, opendemocracy.net (original emphasis). The cross-Atlantic mirror effect enhances institutional paralysis and undoing on both sides, but in different ways. In Europe we are witness to the collapse of the parliamentary system, and a kind of contagious "ungovernability affecting one nation after the other (Britain, Spain, Italy, France . . .), which makes them easy prey for demagogic nationalistic discourses." In the United States, Balibar underscores the way in which "the declining power of the 'empire' is now shaking not only the 'social compact' to which it once gave an economic and patriotic basis, but also the constitutional edifice, despite its forming one of the oldest republican regimes in the world, with a remarkable system of 'checks and balances.'"

program is identified with it, the Political is commonly taken to mean the categorical rejection of capitalist triumphalism in a post-Wall era of global hypermarkets. As Alain Badiou explains in his chapter of *Metapolitics* titled "Against 'Political Philosophy,'" the Political delegitimates "plurality of opinion" in order to effect the "possibility of a rupture with what exists." It has been used as a catchall for modes of political thinking that are at once classical (Platonic, Kantian, Schmittian) and as yet unthought: a communism to come, a democracy relieved of applied ethics, an "inarticulable" subject of politics.[16]

I remain committed to these retreated forms of the Political, yet find myself at the start of a turning circle whose purview entails taking stock of politics in its messier, everyday guises. The abandonment of "small p" politics to pundits and members of the chattering classes risks putting theorists of "big P" Politics" out of action. By framing the Political in terms of that which is extraneous to or other to problems of statecraft, constitutionalism, and institutionalism, many thinkers have left undertheorized the formless force field of "smallest p" politics that keeps the system of capitalo-parliamentarianism in place and prevents emancipatory politics from taking place. This situation prompts a return to some of the classic writings on micropolitics by Michel Foucault, Félix Guattari, Pierre Bourdieu and Bruno Latour with an eye to building out a non-classical, non-canonical vocabulary of microphysical or molecular or non-transcendent disarticulations of power. Political fiction, with its exploration of psychopolitics, impolitic gestures, and idiosyncrasies of political intelligence, has also provided essential material for elucidating "small p" politics. And recent work on economies of existence have led me to highlight specific modes of financialization, managerialism, and calculated social relations as quintessential mediums of a "small p" political lexicon.

While the terms selected are occasionally neologistic ("thermocracy") or may involve an unconventional usage (the shift from substantive to adjectival inflections of "the impolitic"), they are chosen for their value as paleonymy—reworked old names that draw out recessed

---

16   Alain Badiou, *Metapolitics*, trans. Jason Barker (London and New York: Verso, 2005), 24.

political dimensions within ordinary language. Derrida associates paleonymy with the "extraction of a reduced predicative trait that is held in reserve" and considers it an instance of "the name *being maintained as a kind of lever of intervention* in order to maintain a grasp on the previous organization, which is to be effectively transformed."[17] It is precisely this heuristic of interventionist, paleonymic conceptual levering that one finds in the *Political Concepts* initiative, a loosely affiliated group of philosophers and theorists who produce an online journal. Typically the intellectual gambit involves reworking well-worn political vocabulary ("amnesty," "grandeur," "legitimacy," "consent," "equality"); or making-political parts of speech or minor words (prepositions, adverbs, adjectives), as in the juridical measure of "enough" when applied by the South African Truth and Reconciliation Commission (Jacques Lezra), the semantic traction of "blood" in contexts of theological vengeance (Gil Anidjar) or the neoliberal tincture of "development" within the politics of modernization (Gayatri Chakravorty Spivak). A similar way of working informs Alexander Kluge and Oskar Negt's idiosyncratic "An Atlas of Concepts (with interspersed stories)" which offers (for my purposes) a particularly rich and useful definition of "Obstinacy" [*Eigensinn*] as something plastically political: a "resistance to primitive expropriation" whose "elements continually construct themselves anew and grow out of such heterogeneous roots that the type of experience and resistance identified as OBSTINACY cannot be conceptually isolated."[18] Rather than the assumption of a predetermination of what does or does not count as a political concept, there is in such lexical experiments an effort to expand the scope of what demands political accounting or is considered politically significant. "Political" is taken to refer to the multiplicity of forces, structures, problems, and orientations constitutive of modes of existence and being-in-community. The concept of *political concept*, accordingly, becomes a way of endowing non-political vocabulary with political significance, and a way of thinking concepts not just as freestanding, transhistorical

---

17   Jacques Derrida, *Positions* (Chicago, IL: University of Chicago Press, 1981), 71 (original emphasis).

18   Alexander Kluge and Oskar Negt, *History and Obstinacy*, trans. Richard Langston et al. (New York: Zone Books, 2014), 390.

monoliths, but as time-sensitive and site-specific units of language. Barbara Cassin's notion of "philosophizing in languages" contributes to this view of political concepts as inflected by particularities of idiom, history and geopolitics.

Throughout the book, select terms are distilled from episodes that are themselves culled from scenes in novels, films or TV serials that fill in areas where political theory falls short. Such episodes typically feature intense lobbying; interests that are secured, only to be razed from memory by the arrival of ascendant agendas; opportunistic shifts of ideological position; flurries of bait and switch; and the traffic in personal information, mutual interest, earmarks, and palace intrigue. These are the effluvia constitutive of the anthropology of the opinion system and that render "what happens" historically unintelligible and politically unnameable. The debased foil of the Political, this micro, unexceptional politics is often barely perceptible, but it is *there* nonetheless, manifest at its most minute scale as a hum, a whisper, a mood, an atmosphere, a trade wind that sends particulates of ambition eddying around evanescent goalposts.

Unexceptional politics is an intangible milieu, but it may also be associated with distinct forms of political realism within political fiction; a political fiction that shares with postmodern fiction the loss of confidence in historical reality (and here we understand postmodernism in Fredric Jameson's sense of a movement made to order for "an age that has forgotten how to think historically"). Postmodernism, he notes,

> rattles at the bars of our extinct sense of history, unsettles the emptiness of our temporal historicity, and tries convulsively to reawaken the dormant existential sense of time by way of the strong medicine of lies and impossible fables, the electroshock of repeated doses of the unreal and the unbelievable.[19]

In the place of a grand theory of history, or the Romantic absolute, postmodernism presents us with a theater of mental machinations

---

19 Fredric Jameson, as cited in Perry Anderson, "From Progress to Catastrophe," *London Review of Books* 33:15, 2011.

and performative obstructions tailored to a society of calculation. In the place of a grand theory of the Political, it disseminates myriad political symptomologies that coalesce punctually around particularist names. One thinks here of Berlusconismo, which Paolo Flores d'Arcais associates with the destruction of critical independence brought about not by Fascism, but "through the creation of a *pensée unique* that blends conformism and commercial spectacularization, reducing culture to a form of consumption."[20] Berlusconismo is distinguished by its variety show effect and anthemic proclamations: with the Ministry of Love or Party of Love, featuring "rituals of enthusiasm worthy of Ceaucescu, replete with slogans and songs—'Thank heavens there's Silvio!'"[21] A political pasquinade, Berlusconismo resorts to the mawkish props of hair transplants and face-lifts, sexual boasting, and vulgar jokes to distract from the spectacle of counterfeit democracy.

By contrast, *Merkiavellianism* (an expression coined by Ulrich Beck in a much-circulated 2012 editorial in *Der Spiegel*, designed to put the world on guard against German Europe) is a sober affair. Beck attributed the Chancellor's effectiveness to "a tactical adroitness that might well be deemed Machiavellian," specifying that

> Merkel has positioned herself between the Europe builders and the orthodox adherents of the nation state *without* taking either side— or rather, she keeps both options open. She neither identifies with the pro-Europeans (whether at home or abroad) who call for binding German commitments, nor does she support the Euroskeptics, who wish to refuse all assistance. Instead, and this is the Merkiavellian point, Merkel links German willingness to provide credit with the willingness of the debtor nations to satisfy the conditions of German stability policies. This is Merkiavelli's first principle: on the subject of German money to assist the debtor nations, her position is neither a clear Yes or a clear No but a clear Yes and No.[22]

---

20   Paolo Flores d'Arcais, "Berlusconismo," *New Left Review* 68, 2011, 127.
21   Ibid., 129.
22   Ulrich Beck, "The Power of Merkiavelli: Angela Merkel's Hesitation in the Euro-Crisis," *Open Democracy*, November 5, 2012, opendemocracy.net.

For Beck, *Merkiavellianism* denotes the art of "deliberate hesitation," a method of coercion that turns on the constant threat of "withdrawal, delay and the refusal of credit." Merkiavelli's "trump card," said Beck, is actually a "siren call": "better a German euro than no euro at all."[23] Of all the leaders in Europe, Merkel has proved to be the most successful in navigating between a punishing austerity policy that violates democratic principle, and a "humanitarian" stance on refugees that puts the onus of responding to their dislocation on countries like Greece, Italy and Turkey. Navigating the posts between being feared and being loved, Merkel epitomizes the stance of what Beck called the "good-natured hegemon."

A particularist politics that could never be dubbed good-natured is now named *Trumpism*. It represents the endgame of politics as name-branding, as well as a type of the impolitic associated with "janking," a term connoting the art of dissing or offending, as in the game "the dozens," or rapping and slamming. "Janking off" describes Trump's incessant jibing and calumniating, specifically, the vicious, viral, Twitter vomit of his lamely derisive adjectives, weaponized as cyber-bullying. Trumpist janking derives its energy from hate speech, trolling, and verbal battery. It exults in forms of baiting reliant on ad hominem attacks on a person's heritage, race, gender, physical "rating," character, and body parts, or a worker's professional integrity (as when he vilified Chuck Jones, union leader of United Steelworkers Local 1999, who called out Trump for "lying his ass off" after Trump made specious claims about saving jobs at the Carrier plant in Indiana). No "average Joe," no former beauty pageant queen, no building contractor, no newscaster, no veteran, no journalist, no actor nor comedian is too unworthy of public interest to qualify for targeting by the Trumpist jank. The jank-off not only comes close to satisfying the risibility factor of the jank, but underlines the importance of scaling to the art of be*little*ment and to tumescent states of the ego in situations of political contest and phallogocentric competition.

Trump's denunciation of Washington's stalemate political culture with the phrase, "It is out of control. It is gridlock with their mouths," invents a strange figure of speech that, when one focuses on the mouth of the utterer, registers like a warning signal against *mouthing off.*

---

23   Ibid.

Mouthing off, wandering off script to some indefensible position that must be defended for lack of any other possible strategy, is the essence of jank, and it becomes consonant with a new meaning of the verb "to Trump," signifying quite literally the vagaries of disestablished politicking, or going rogue.

Derrida begins *Rogues* (Voyous) with a question that references La Fontaine's fable "The Wolf and the Lamb": "What political narrative, in the same tradition, might today illustrate this fabulous morality? Does this morality teach us, as is often believed, that force *'trumps'* law [que la force 'prime' le droit]?"[24] The verb form of *prime* in French contains the idea of "blocking," but also that of "adding to," "topping," accompanying *prime* in its use as a substantive to mean "bonus." Derrida's "que la force 'prime' le droit" suggests that force has the lead, surplus, or advantage over the law. His phrase echoes one attributed to Bismarck in the context of a speech delivered to the French National Assembly. It was taken to mean either that force breaks any laws that obstruct its course, or that force is the author of its own rule of law. Both senses are evident in La Fontaine's fable, in which the Wolf defies the natural laws of reality and makes up his own laws each time the Lamb raises a reasonable, evidence-based objection. "With that, deep into the wood/The Wolf dragged and ate his midday snack./So trial and judgment stood."[25] "Trumping" (close to *tromper*, to betray or act mistakenly) describes the strategy of brazenly upping the ante of the counterattack when you are patently at fault. The justice it recognizes belongs to the kangaroo court, where damages are routinely awarded to plaintiffs who make baseless allegations of libel and injury. *Trumpism* in this sense means justice flouted, and justice that panders to the caprice of the infant sovereign in the ego. Thin-skinned reactions to criticism or public displays of animosity and grievance are championed and fully claimed as the tactics of a winner at all costs. Trumpism brings to the public stage a performative incivility, taken in its full measure as a political concept designating extreme *impolitesse*— improper or uncivilized behavior, *un*civic-mindedness, bad manners,

---

24 Jacques Derrida, *Rogues: Two Essays on Reason*, trans. Pascale-Anne Brault and Michael Naas (Stanford, CA: Stanford University Press, 2005) (emphasis mine).
25 Ibid.

and displays of contemptuous mockery that destroy the fellow-feeling of spirited raillery. Trumpism calls up what Balibar discerns as the profound violence inherent in civil society, including the "modalities of subjection and subjectification" in *Sittlichkeit* (Hegel), such that civility is in fact little more than a response "to contemporary extreme violence from inside extreme violence."[26]

Trumpism inflates the dollar value of its patent with the trappings of wealth; with garish fashion redolent of the 1980s era of greed: tall buildings, gold fixtures, private jets, trophy wives. This plutocratic display is pumped up further by a litany of jankish hyperboles: "very, very best," "great," "tremendous," "huge," and so forth. While intended to provide ballast to the old doctrines of American exceptionalism, this bombast dissipates into vatic trumpetings. Trumpism—whose "ism" is keyed to populist autocracy—is identified with a rogue way of speaking that provides scaffolding for an absent political discourse. The proper name is tautologically performative, which is to say, Trumpism trumps public interest by facilitating the decampment of the citizen from the demos to media theaters of depolicitized life.

Trumpism lines up on axis with *Berlusconismo* inasmuch as both qualify as names for oligarchic name-branding, pasquinade, and the mastery of political special effects. In each case the proper name erects a fence—*a wall*—around a motley assortment of personality traits, bait and switch tactics, and, in the case of Trump and Berlusconi, crass publicity stunts that supply the playbook of political impasse. *Impasse* is perhaps the new watchword for the contemporary state of politics, at once unexceptional and diffusely traumatic. Lauren Berlant makes the argument that once trauma is conceived no longer as an exceptional event and "crisis ordinariness" takes hold as the norm, history becomes little more than an adjustment narrative in which difficulties are succumbed to or navigated. From this perspective, the extraordinary "always turns out to be an amplification of something in the works, a labile boundary at best, not a slammed-door departure. In the *impasse* induced by crisis, being treads water; mainly, it does not

---

26 Étienne Balibar, *Violence and Civility: On the Limits of Political Philosophy*, trans. G. M. Goshgarian (New York: Columbia University Press, 2015), 23.

drown."[27] Perhaps it is this sense of "small t" trauma that most effectively captures what is at stake in "small p" politics, from the ordinariness of exceptional crisis and the routinization of habitual politics, to
the micropolitics of molecular cultures implanted in the byways of
managed life.

---

27   Lauren Berlant, *Cruel Optimism* (Durham, NC: Duke University Press,
2011), 10 (emphasis mine).

I. RESISTANT TO POLITICAL THEORY

"Small P" Politics

Part of the difficulty, but also part of the interest, of trying to give definition to unexceptional politics derives from the opposition between the distinction in French between "*le*" and "*la*" *politique*: the Political versus politics, or polity versus policy. In his entry on "*le*" and "*la*" *politique* in the *Vocabulaire européen des philosophies: dictionnaire des intraduisibles* (Dictionary of Untranslatables: A Philosophical Lexicon), Philippe Reynaud observes that *la politique* in its most conventional translation to English, covers both "politics" and "policy."[1] Politics is commonly keyed to American pluralism—electoral politics, political participation, party formation, the recruitment of governing elites, and regime competition—whereas policy is taken to refer to strategies of state power. Reynaud stresses that the duality of politics and policy in English tends to get lost in French, where distinctions between state power (*commandement*) and deliberation, or between civic relations and strategic action, are more stringently maintained by the *le/la* divide.

Oliver Marchart reminds us that

> although the theoretical differentiation between "politics" and "the political" occurs for the first time in German political thought with Carl Schmitt, the habit of differentiating between these two concepts started in French thought as early as 1957, with the publication of Paul Ricoeur's essay "The Political Paradox."[2]

---

1   Philippe Reynaud, "(Le) politique, (la) Politique," in *Vocabulaire européen des philosophies: dictionnaire des intraduisibles*, ed. Barbara Cassin (Paris: Seuil, 2004), 963–6.

2   Oliver Marchart, *Post-Foundational Political Thought: Political Difference in Nancy, Lefort, Badiou, and Laclau* (Edinburgh: Edinburgh University Press, 2007), 4.

For Ricoeur, polity (*le politique*) denotes ideal political organization and historical rationality, whereas politics (*la politique*) refers to the empirical and concrete manifestations of this ideal sphere. Ricoeur factors temporality into the equation:

> Polity takes on meaning after the fact, in reflection, in "retrospection." Politics is pursued step by step, in "prospection," in projects; that is to say both in an uncertain deciphering of contemporary events, and in the steadfastness of resolutions ... From polity to politics, we move from advent to events, from sovereignty to the sovereign, from the State to government, from historical Reason to Power.[3]

In addition to foregrounding paradoxes embedded in political thought, Ricoeur underlines the familiar opposition between Machiavelli and Marx. "*The Prince*, he notes, showcases "the logic of means, the pure and simple techniques of acquiring and preserving power." It is on the basis of "this essential untruth, of this discordance between the pretension of the State and the true state of affairs, that Marx meets with the problem of violence." At stake is "a political mode of existence that combines the Marxist critique of alienation with the Machiavellian, Platonic and Biblical critique of power."[4] Here, Ricoeur would have us extend "polity" into politics by bracing together

---

Marchart is referring of course to Carl Schmitt's *Der Begriff des Politischen*, translated by George Schwab as *The Concept of the Political* (Chicago, IL: University of Chicago Press, [1927, 1932] 2007). A basic contention of the book is that the state (associated with "a specific entity of a people") is not equatable with "the Political," the latter a concept most often used adjunctively with morality, economy, politics and civil law." See Strauss, "Notes on Carl Schmitt." For concise and pointed elucidations of Schmitt's contestation of liberal decisionism, see Samuel Weber, "Taking Exception to Decision: Walter Benjamin and Carl Schmitt," *diacritics* 22:3–4, 1992, and Étienne Balibar's introduction "Le Hobbes de Schmitt, le Schmitt de Hobbes," in the French translation of Schmitt's *Der Leviathan in der Staatslehre des Thomas Hobbes: Sinn und Felhschlag eines politischen Symbols* (1938). Translated by Denis Trierweiler as *Le Léviathan dans la doctrine de l'État de Thomas Hobbes: sens et échec d'un symbole politique* (Paris: Seuil, 2002), 7–65.

3   Paul Ricoeur, "The Political Paradox," in *History and Truth*, trans. David M. Rasmussen (Evanston, IL: Northwestern University Press, [1965] 2007), 255.

4   Ibid., 257–60.

subjection and calculated maneuvers. This move runs parallel to Balibar's much later use of the term *politique* (devoid of any definite article) when glossing Schmitt's *Leviathan*. *Political*, taken both substantively and adjectivally, names the process by which the state of nature—essentially an anti-political force—becomes the state, straddling the rule of law (polity) and the police (politics).[5]

Though Ricoeur and Balibar reveal the fungibility of the distinctions among polity, politics, and the Political, it is clear that the theoretical gulf between politics and the Political widened considerably in the wake of bitter post-'68 schisms on the global left. Chantal Mouffe, for example, lays claim to the Political as a means of cutting loose discourses of the liberal subject from American-style pluralism. In *On the Political*, she defines the Political as "a space of power, conflict and antagonism" in contradistinction to Heidegger's "ontological essence of politics," or Hannah Arendt's "space of freedom and public deliberation."[6] Mouffe is interested in showing "how the rationalist approach dominant in democratic theory prevents us from posing the questions which are crucial for democratic politics." "My aim," she states, "is to bring to the fore liberalism's central deficiency in the political field: its negation of the ineradicable character of antagonism."[7] "In *The Concept of the Political* [1932]," Mouffe notes, "Schmitt declares bluntly that the pure and rigorous principle of liberalism could not give birth to a specifically political conception. Every consistent individualism must, in his view, negate the political since it requires the individual to remain the ultimate point of reference." What she proposes (following the examples of Arendt, Agamben, Derrida, Hardt, Negri and many others), "is to think 'with Schmitt against Schmitt,' using his critique of liberal individualism and rationalism to propose a new understanding of politics."[8] For Mouffe, to become operative "the Political" must recur to new social movements, political identities, and mobilizations of antagonism. The latter is more fully drawn out as "agonistics," to emphasize the discursive force of

---

5   Balibar, "Le Hobbes de Schmitt, le Schmitt de Hobbes".
6   Chantal Mouffe, *On the Political* (London: Routledge, 2005), 8.
7   Ibid., 9–10.
8   Ibid., 14.

antagonism: the demotic, colloquially articulated expressions of dissensus that serve to undercut consensus-driven interests, claims of inalienable right, and market values of competition.[9]

In *On the Shores of Politics* (Aux bords du politique), Jacques Rancière similarly targets neoliberal ideologues who trumpet "the end of political divisions and social antagonisms" under market capitalism, or who bemoan the "exhaustion of egalitarian and communal (mis)adventures."[10] Rancière is committed to identifying "a few paradoxes which may prompt us to reexamine not just philosophy's political role, but also the status of the peculiar activity which we call politics."[11] "Politics" here is "empirical politics," and traces back, via Plato's *Gorgias*, to maritime sovereignty and the sailor's ethical code of "profit and survival."[12] After maritime imperialism makes it to shore, it swells in scale, eventually occupying the cartographic and temporal expanse of infinitude. For Rancière, equality is the only countervailing force, qualified as the "Two of division"; that is, "a One that is no longer that of collective incorporation but rather that of the equality of any One to any other One."[13] Against empirical politics, against what he calls "the new 'liberal' dream of the weights and counter-weights of a pluralist society guided by its elites," Rancière endorses the old class struggle and the new "humanizing power of division."[14] They alone seem to have the capacity to make any politics (in terms that Rancière would be willing to call politics) visible. They

---

9 Chantal Mouffe, *Agonistics: Thinking the World Politically* (London: Verso, 2013), 137.

10 Jacques Rancière, *On the Shores of Politics*, trans. Liz Heron (London: Verso, 1995), 4. Originally published as *Au bord du politique* (Bordeaux: Editions Osiris, 1992).

11 Ibid., 4.

12 Rancière writes, "Athens has a disease that comes from its port, from the predominance of maritime enterprise governed entirely by profit and survival. Empirical politics, that is to say the fact of democracy, is identified with the maritime sovereignty of the lust for possession, which sails the seas doubly threatened by the buffeting of the waves and the brutality of the sailors. The great beast of the populace, the democratic assembly of the imperialist city, can be represented as a trireme of drunken sailors. In order to save politics it must be pulled aground among the shepherds" (*On the Shores of Politics*, 1).

13 Ibid., 32.

14 Ibid., 33.

alone seem up to the task of stripping democratic pluralism of its depoliticizing foils.

For Alain Badiou, the Political lives on in an emancipatory sequence most readily apprehended in the form of its retreat from "politics." In his 1984 broadside *Peut-on penser la politique?* (Can Politics Be Thought?) Badiou distinguishes the "evental" form of the Political from an easily dismissed politics of whatever happens to be "on the agenda—elections, parliament, presidency, trade unions, televised speeches, diplomatic visits and so on":

> Everyone knows that this is a disaffected scene, one that certainly sends out many signals of such a uniform nature that only an automated subject can be linked to them, a subject unencumbered by any desire . . . It is totally exact that the political finds itself in retreat and becomes absent, whence the interrogation as to its essence.[15]

The thinkability of the Political worthy of the name is positioned outside representative government and its institutions: "Politics will be thinkable only if it is delivered from the tyranny of number," oriented towards the hypothetical of "a proletarian capacity—of a politics that is not a politics of representation."[16] Rancière and Badiou have in common their rejection of ordinary democracy, understood to have euthanized political truths through the opinion system, the institutionalized manipulation of soft power, and the narcotic effect of consensus. As Badiou writes, "Democracy is never anything but a form of the State."[17] The grounds of their critique seem irrefutable, irreproachable. And yet, their republic remains for the most part elusive, invisible from within the situation, conceivable only from a possible-worlds perspective. In his *Second Manifesto of Philosophy* (a distillate of positions elaborated in *Logics of Worlds*), Badiou cycles through the four major truth procedures—experimental formal logics in mathematics and science, art, love, and emancipatory

---

15   Alain Badiou, *Peut-on penser la politique?* (Paris: Seuil, 1985), 68. Translated as *Can Politics Be Thought?* (London and New York: Verso, forthcoming). In citations of this text I use the Bosteels translation (manuscript draft).

16   Ibid., 88.

17   Ibid., 8.

politics—allowing that, under present conditions, they are blurred beyond recognition. The incursion of neuroscience, culturally relativist post-medium art, the boxing-in of love between familialism and libertinism, and incoherent political admixtures of economics, management, and police control have taken their toll.[18] Though the outlines of a new clarity of truths may be grasped—category theory with respect to the *matheme*, affirmation of the sensible with respect to art, an anti-statist International with respect to politics, non-heteronormative sexuality with respect to love (all of which renew the possibility of a "Platonism of the Multiple" and "a communism of the Idea)"—Badiou's truths are ultimately more "thinkable" as autonomous art, as poetry. The poem, he affirms

> is an exercise in intransigence. It is without mediation and thus also without mediatization. The poem remains rebellious—defeated in advance—to the democracy of audience ratings and polls . . . The poem has no nothing to communicate. It is only a saying, a declaration, which draws its authority only from itself.[19]

Nick Hewlett, criticizing the rare, exceptional status of the Badiouvian "event" or concept of change, raises the important issue of the extent to which Badiou's philosophical politics entails a distancing of the subject from material conditions, from the state of affairs that exists, from the status quo. He asks:

> Could we not in fact one day be faithful, in theory at least to a (far more egalitarian and socially just) status quo, rather than to a dramatic point of change? Why must fidelity necessarily be to a perhaps disputed and/or somewhat arbitrarily defined point of departure for what might become the status quo?[20]

---

18 Alain Badiou, *Second manifeste pour la philosophie* (Paris: Fayard, 2009), 135.

19 Alain Badiou, "What Does the Poem Think?," in *The Age of the Poets: And Other Writings on Twentieth-Century Poetry and Prose*, trans. Bruno Bosteels (London: Verso, 2014), 22.

20 Nick Hewlett, *Badiou, Balibar, Rancière: Re-Thinking Emancipation* (London: Continuum, 2007), 40.

Where Hewlett points out that the event in Badiou's system is insuffi-
ciently inoculated against lapsing into the status quo, one could extract
from this point another: the very fact that the event is susceptible to
becoming another status quo suggests that we should think of it
neither in terms of temporal exception, discrete break, hiatus, caesura,
or revolution, nor as a subtraction from the situation, but as myriad
micropolitical effects that might or might not induce the advent of an
emancipatory truth that historically rearranges worlds. We know that
advental truths—slaves are humans, all people are created equal,
women have rights, the proletariat exists, colonialism is unjust—have
been known to happen and to transform politics but they are not, I
would insist, detached from worlds of compromised materialities

While Hewlett asserts that Badiou "is in search of the highest
possible level of purity, which is as removed as possible from the
material," and that for him "this level of abstraction is achieved by
multiplicity as articulated by set theory," I would tend not to agree
that he is "removed from the material," but would argue that his
engagement with political materialities is of a selective order.[21]
Badiou's fidelity to the Idea, and to a position of militant resistance to
politics as theorized by classical political theory or political science,
leads him, on the one hand, to philosophy (from *Being and Event* to
Logics of Worlds), and, on the other hand, to polemical interventions,
as in his analysis of the Arab Spring (*The Rebirth of History*) or of the
excrescences of the Sarkozy regime (*The Meaning of Sarkozy*, a treatise on "depressive" politics").[22] In neither case are political

---

21   Ibid.
22   Alain Badiou, *De quoi Sarkozy est-il le nom?* (Clamecy: Lignes, 2007), 15,
translated by David Fernbach as *The Meaning of Sarkozy* (London and New York:
Verso, 2008). See also, *Sarkozy: pire que prévu . . .* [Sarkozy : Worse than We Feared]
(Clamecy: Lignes, 2012), 8. In this anti-electoral treatise, Badiou avows that, prior to
May 1968, as a young Socialist Party secretary, he quite enjoyed the rituals of
parliamentary politics with its "tortuous negotiations, vociferations, scattered
gatherings, the distant ties between secret meetings where real decisions are made
and public sparring, the defense of "programs" mounted for the occasion at hand,
the counting of votes, the ineluctable and painful result of the second round of
voting tipping the results in favor of a contemptible opponent." Badiou admits to
savoring the "culinary" pleasure of these novel-like encounters, in which the
narrative accents of France's subversive revolutionary heritage could be felt within a
fundamentally unchanging and conservative political order.

materialities extended to the fields of "small p" politics, which is to say, to applied ethics, rational choice, pluralism, constitutionalism, distributive justice, political realism or the kinds of quantitative sociological positivism predominant in political science. Badiou of course has his reasons for hewing to theories of the event, generic truths, and the rejection of consensus politics, but this hardly disqualifies questioning in his work that element of what Raymond Geuss (in reference to the Kantian ideal of rational agency) calls "empirical abstemiousness."[23] It is this abstemiousness that leaves one wondering how to breach the firewall between philosophy and so-called real politics, which, at least for Geuss, accounts for the failure of purely philosophical politics to deal with so-called real motivations and what actually happens.

"Big P" Politics implies, even if it does not prescribe, a refusal to accept the terms of homogenized opinion and engineered consent on offer in the mediocracy. Consistently *"le" politique* is summoned to delegitimate plurality of opinion, called on to effect the "possibility of a rupture with what exists."[24] Writing post-Maastricht, Philippe Lacoue-Labarthe and Jean-Luc Nancy formulated this position as "le retrait du politique." To "retreat the political" means calling for politics to be cognized otherwise—regrounded in an alternative semantics of equality, partitive being, singular community, distributive and social justice, deprivatization and the creative commons.[25] It is a concept of the Political as yet unthought: of a "time to come" (Negri's *l'avvenire*, constituted by a "phenomenology of revolutionary praxis")[26]; of "the coming community" (Agamben's coming being of the *quodlibet*, or "'whatever' being")[27]; of the communist hypothesis or a

---

23   Raymond Geuss, *Philosophy and Real Politics* (Princeton: Princeton University Press, 2008), 7.

24   Alain Badiou, "Against 'Political Philosophy'" in *Metapolitics*, trans. Jason Barker (London: Verso, 2005), 24.

25   Philippe Lacoue-Labarthe and Jean-Luc Nancy, *Le retrait du* politique (Paris: Galilée, 1983). Translated by Simon Sparks as *Retreating the Political* (London: Routledge, 1997).

26   Antonio Negri, *The Savage Anomaly: The Power of Spinoza's Metaphysics*, trans. Michael Hardt (Minneapolis: University of Minnesota Press, 1991), xx–xxi.

27   Giorgio Agamben, *The Coming Community*, trans. Michael Hardt (Minneapolis: University of Minnesota Press, 1993), 1.

"communism to come"; of democracy relieved of applied ethics; of inarticulable or impossible subjects of politics.[28]

Geoffrey Bennington develops a conceptually refined reworking of this "politics to come" in *Scatter 1: The Politics of Politics in Foucault, Heidegger and Derrida*. Bennington uses the tautology "politics of politics" to refer to something "persistently political" embedded in "rhetorico-political gestures which resist the suicidal tendency of exceptionalist political philosophy to end politics, or to end itself, by means of a redemptive moment or "decision to end all decisions."[29] He prepares this argument by emphasizing the untenability of any distinction between essential and inessential politics:

> I use the phrase "politics of politics" to try to capture the way in which politics is from the first *doubled up* in a way that the dogmatists and moralists denounce in proportion to their inability to understand it. Idioms beginning "the politics of . . ." are often used to describe a dimension of other activities thought to be nonessential to those activities . . . Like other activities, politics is thought to have an essential part (however it be defined—participating in the life of the *polis;* discussing, militating, deliberating, voting, enacting, and mandating the application of appropriate legislation, protesting, demonstrating, organizing) and an inessential "politics" or "politicking" (what in Washington is called "playing politics" and in Paris "la politique politicienne"). On this construal, *everyone*, including those most energetically and enthusiastically involved in it, eagerly denounces the politics of politics as a kind of corruption of what politics essentially is or should be, and everyone deplores the fact that politics seems increasingly bound up in its own politics in this way. On the other hand, "the politics of . . ." idiom often goes along with a more or less obscure sense that *something* political *is* in fact intrinsic to the activity being described and can have behind it the

---

28   "La politique ne représente nullement le prolétariat, la classe ou la Nation. Ce qui fait sujet en politique, quoique avéré dans son existence par l'effet politique même, y demeure inarticulable." Badiou, *Peut-on penser la politique?*, 87.

29   Geoffrey Bennington, *Scatter 1: The Politics of Politics in Foucault, Heidegger and Derrida* (New York: Fordham University Press, 2016), 241.

obscure conviction (which can range across the entire political spectrum from extreme left to extreme right) that in some significant sense "everything is political."[30]

Bennington forges a third way that lines up neither with the position that "only this is essentially political," nor with the position that "everything is political," but with the proposition that "*politics is always already the politics of politics.*"[31] This "always already" (retrospectively proleptic, *nachträglich*) politics is deconstructive and christened "scatter." Scatter subsumes what is "secretly at work from the start, from the ancient materialists to Plato and Aristotle and on through Bodin, Hobbes, and Rousseau to Kant and Hegel and beyond."[32] It disqualifies the possibility of any political philosophy setting itself apart from the fray of sophistics, legislative deliberation, or for that matter, politicking or political chatter (what Heidegger in *Being and Time* called *Gerede* [idle talk]).[33] And yet, insofar as politics speaks in specific idioms, or remains distinguishable as praxis, it stops short of being assimilated (as contamination or common property) into "everything." Instead, it "scatters" through the recursive effect of "distortion and deceit," moving from the *logos* into political sophistry, rhetoric, the noble lie, the expressive order of *pseudos*, possible error, dissimulation.[34] In its arrival at spurious truths and anacolutha (disrupted incoherence), "the politics of politics" harks back to Hannah Arendt's essay "Lying in Politics: Reflections on the Pentagon Papers," published in 1971, though newly resonant in the context of the 2016 election in the United States. During this period, fact-checking and trial-by-YouTube (and by Google) emerged as the political techne du jour, the informal court of appeals relied on in the face of spectacularly flagrant, exponentially elevated instances of public lying in political discourse and insidious infiltrations of fake news (not its Trumpist appropriational travesty: "fake news"), into

---

30   Ibid., 3.
31   Ibid., 4 (original emphasis).
32   Ibid., 4.
33   Ibid., 66.
34   Ibid., 4, 65–8.

mainstream media reportage.[35] Noting how the Pentagon Papers turned the political credibility gap into an "abyss," illuminating the fragility of facts and the proliferating modalities of "deception, image-making, ideologizing, and defactualizing," Arendt wrote:

> Truthfulness has never been counted among the political virtues, and lies have always been regarded as justifiable tools in political dealings. Whoever reflects on these matters can only be surprised by how little attention has been paid, in our tradition of philosophical and political thought, to their significance, on the one hand for the nature of action and, on the other, for the nature of our ability to deny in thought and word whatever happens to be the case. This active, aggressive capability is clearly different from our passive susceptibility to falling prey to error, illusion, the distortions of memory, and to whatever else can be blamed on the failings of our sensual and mental apparatus.[36]

Bennington extends Arendt's politics of lying to the "politics of politics," suturing deception to "the autoimmunity of the political, in a nonmoralistic way."[37]

In Derrida's ascription, autoimmunity is a variant of aporia (in Greek, literally "impasse," "puzzlement," "doubt"), identified by him in *Force of Law* not only with something "mystical" (related to Pascal's "mystical foundation of authority")[38], but also with the figuration of the impossible: the crossroads leading in mutually exclusive directions, the double bind, non-passage, the blocked transverse.[39] Derrida distinguishes among three types of aporia in *Force of Law*: First is the

---

35   "The internet-borne forces that are eating away at print advertising are enabling a host of faux-journalistic players to pollute the democracy with dangerously fake news items." Jim Rutenberg, "Journalism's Next Challenge: Overcoming the Threat of Fake News," *New York Times,* November 7, 2016.

36   Hannah Arendt, *Crises of the Republic,* 4–5, 44.

37   Bennington, *Scatter 1,* 280.

38   As Derrida illustrates: "A silence walled up in the violent structure of the founding act. Walled up, walled in because this silence is not exterior to language." Jacques Derrida, "Force of Law: The 'Mystical Foundation of Authority,'" trans. Mary Quaintance, in *Acts of Religion,* ed. Gil Anidjar (New York: Routledge, 2002), 242.

39   Ibid.

"the *epokhe* of the rule," aligned with a restitutive "fresh judgement" in the application of the law to the decision, such that the decision singularly reinvents the law in each iteration.[40] Second is "the haunting of the undecidable," in which "the *decision to calculate* is not of the order of the calculable." In this type, the deconstruction of "a determining certainty of a present justice" operates by virtue of an "'idea of justice' that is infinite, infinite because irreducible, irreducible because owed to the other—owed to the other, before any contract, because it has *come*, it is a *coming* [parce qu'elle est venue]."[41] Third is the aporia of obstruction, tied to a kind of madness brought on by a decision taken "in the night of nonknowledge and nonrule. Not of the absence of rules and knowledge but of a restitution of rules that by definition is not preceded by any knowledge or by any guarantee as such."[42] The pure performative of decision opens out to the *à-venir*, a space of "to come" that non-messianically harbors the emancipatory ideal (which Derrida, in direct tribute to the Enlightenment, insists will never be outmoded). This *a-venir* is carefully distinguished from the future, which in Derrida's view is simply another temporality of the present, where there can be no justice.

The aporia upholds what Bennington refers to as "sovereign" concepts (the concept *digne de ce nom*, "worthy of the name"), but it is also what defenestrates them:

> If they are to be worthy of their name (if we are to take them at all seriously as putatively sovereign, with all the solemn *dignitas* that sovereignty implies), [they will] always fall foul of aporias and paradoxes, succeed only in failing or in falling . . . their 'dignity' is therefore a little overblown in the metaphysical construal of them.[43]

Such phrases leave one to ponder the exceptionalism of "a space of 'to come'" and by extension of aporetic politics. Does the *à-venir* reside in a decision that is aporetic insofar as it is calculatedly incalculable?

---

40 Ibid., 251.
41 Ibid., 252, 254.
42 Ibid., 255.
43 Bennington, *Scatter 1*, 272.

Impossibly possible? Determinately indeterminate? Conditionally unconditional? Bennington indirectly responds to such queries when, after noting Derrida's admission (in *Rogues*) that the definition of "démocratie à venir" is coyly withheld, he refers it to the negative theology of the unnameable ("As if I had given in to the apophatic virtue of some negative theology that does not reveal its name").[44] Left with what he calls the "promissory dimension" of a deconstructive "democracy to come," Bennington gestures "abyssally" towards "the possibility of a complex kind of 'second-level' reinscription of dignity *itself* in its relation to its name, or in the 'worthy' relation anything whatsoever might have to its name," a possibility ascertainable in the "intimate" yet "potentially conflictual relation between the 'digne du nom' structure and the regulative Idea."[45] Immediately though, Bennington abandons the "regulative Idea" on Derrida's behalf, suggesting that too much "rule" lurks in the word "regulative," along with more of an "architectonic of Kantian critique" than Derrida would have allowed.[46] In the place, then, of a relation between scattered politics and the law, we have deconstructed regulation and a notion of the event that disrupts (courtesy of the indignity of the anacolutha) the fulfillment of sovereign teleology:

> An event worthy of the name would explode and scatter the name of which it is worthy, in being worthy of it. This eventness in general (in its singularity), openness to the coming of which seems in Derrida to be the only truly unconditional good, the "non-ethical opening of ethics," the very thing that will pry unconditionality away from sovereignty, is what affects the "digne de ce nom" structure in general with the structures of interruption and always-necessarily-possible indignity.[47]

"Scatter" ostensibly undoes the unconditionality of the sovereign name to create the conditions for an "unconditional good." Bennington

---

44   Ibid.
45   Ibid., 273, 274.
46   Ibid., 275.
47   Ibid., 276.

sets great store by a "demi-" qualification that supposedly modifies all of Derrida's "'unconditional' terms, including democracy." But, like other qualifications that "open up a space" or dissolve an impacted substantive or universal abstraction (truth, reason, ethics, metaphysics, theology, sovereign authority . . .), the half-unconditional condition subsides all too easily into another aporia, into a promissory *à-venir* that, if not exactly futural or messianic, returns us to states of suspension, or the long wait. Prospectivity becomes the condition of "a politics of politics," consigning us to wait for the "unconditional riposte to sovereignty in its narrower political sense," in a volume to come of *Scatter*.[48] We are left wondering how the aporetic structure of *à-venir* will actually perform politically, and whether, in the meantime, it might not be prudent to focus on how impasse and obstruction condition the political unconditionals of sovereign decision, states of emergency, exceptional power, or the stakes of an empty structure that Agamben, in reference to the state of exception from law, qualified as "a force of law without law."[49]

Though it might seem like an odd swerve to follow on a condensed lexicon of "politics" and "The Political" (passing through Arendt, Ricoeur, Balibar, Mouffe, Badiou, Nancy and Lacoue-Labarthe, Rancière, Derrida and Bennington), by cycling back to Bruno Latour, his commentary on Schmitt in *An Inquiry into Modes of Existence* warrants reference at this juncture because of the way it unexceptionalizes transcendent modes of the Political. Latour introduces the geometric figure of the curve or circle along which "little transcendences" are distributed, thereby circumventing the need for a Schmittian "exceptional man" charged with instituting sovereign decision above the law.[50] Latour's circle is *"exceptional at all points,"* and represents the collective as it coalesces around specific issues in real time.[51] Plotted on the curve is a "small p" politics that speaks in its own language, that defines distinct modes of acting or articulating politically that evolve and mutate. One could

48 Ibid.
49 Giorgio Agamben, *State of Exception*, trans. Kevin Attell (Chicago, IL: University of Chicago Press, 2005), 39.
50 Bruno Latour, *An Inquiry into Modes of Existence*, op. cit., 347.
51 Ibid., 348.

even say that Latour gives us something on the order of a *plastic politics*: an ontogenetics of political DNA comparable to what Arne de Boever, building on Catherine Malabou's notion of plasticity as an explosive/reparative capacity, calls "plastic sovereignty"; forms that retain "sovereignty's positive accomplishments." These include the skills of the professional organizer; non-vertical axes of agency; autopoeic transformation over and against "neoliberal flexibility"; and a "new experience of language."[52] A "plastic" approach to politics, from this perspective, might entail taking up anew elements of its DNA: terms that codify a concept of politics as professional métier (as in Cicero's *On Government*), or vocabulary that has fallen into desuetude (civility, civic virtue, the citizen subject).[53]

---

52   Arne de Boever, *Plastic Sovereignties: Agamben and the Politics of Aesthetics* (Edinburgh: Edinburgh University Press, 2016), 23, 28.

53   As rational citizenship seems to recede and become increasingly worth holding onto, as emancipatory politics risks being overwhelmed by the prospect of well-orchestrated conservative onslaughts unleashed on so many fronts at once; as the right to safe harbor—*le droit de cité*—is challenged by xenophobic border policy worldwide, and as racist harming, forcible entry raids, political exclusion, and the blanket killing of supsects with legal impunity, are normalized as routine policing, it is perhaps the "citizen" half of the dyad "citizen subject" that is most urgent to remake as a category of positive sovereignty. In recent years, the "subject" has been the focus of philosophical and critical attention, galvanizing debates around the relation of ontology to sovereignty, while the "citizen" has been more confined to political history and political science. "Citizen" is often freighted (especially within the familiar couplet "Man and Citizen") with the history of patriarchal suffrage and anthropocentrism. It harks back to the constitutional foundationalism of Madisonian democracy, that in its contemporary guises indexes a massive erosion of the checks and balances system of governance, a bankrupt majoritarianism epitomized by oligarchic donor networks, and (in the United States), a judicial coup titled "Citizen's United." The word "citizen" is more likely to be appended to the names of vigilante groups, antigovernment militias, Second Amendment advocates, border-enforcers, Confederate flag defenders, and all manner of hate-groups than to any grassroots progressive movement. In America today, "citizen" feels seriously compromised and appropriated by the alt-right.

Etienne Balibar's book *Citizen Subject,* though in no way presuming to protect the term "citizen," nonetheless goes some distance toward reinvigorating its political connection to the theory of the subject, especially across languages (his analysis ranges across "self," living substance, consciousness or *conscience, Dasein*, the subject of unconscious drives, the impersonal first person pronoun, the "I" in the "We"). Balibar notably traces a history of the subject arising from the Latin *subjectus*, ("brought under,") and *hypokeimenon* ("material from which things are made"), both of which are thought to underwrite a notion of *sujet* in Old French that in turn

It initiates and promotes thinking pragmatically *and* philosophically about the links between effective sophistical praxis and micropolitics.

---

gives on to the idea of a "person owing obedience." In English, as we know, "subject" functions first and foremost as a synonym for theme, subject matter, topic, issue, question, concern or point; for branches of knowledge or a discipline, or as a technical expression designating a state of being "subject to," in the sense of "being prone to, likely to be affected by, at risk of." And yet, even in English, this apparently neutral "being subject to" introduces the condition of conditions as such; of subordination, stipulation, jurisdiction and attributed power, all of which implicitly inscribe the trace of a sovereign will. The sovereign instance acts here as a silent partner to the subject of obedience. In considering the subject of obedience, in emphasizing how, since the beginning of the political history of Western Europe, "the time of *subjects* coincides with that of *absolutism,*" Balibar provides impetus for a de-absolutized vocabulary of sovereignty that gives rise to a new political concept of the "citizen subject." See, Étienne Balibar, *Citizen Subject: Foundations for Philosophical Anthropology*, trans. Steven Miller (New York: Fordham University Press, 2017).

Micropolitics

Micropolitics is an umbrella term covering a host of old and new political forms—"informal politics," "capillary politics," "the ungovernables," "radical incrementalism," "infrapolitics"—each of which proposes a politics measured in microdimensions.[1] Historically, the pivotal points of reference are found in the work of Foucault and Guattari, and to a far lesser extent, in that of Alexander Kluge and Oskar Negt. The latter two, though not considered here, coauthored *History and Obstinacy* (1981), which, like its predecessor volume

---

1 See publicity circular for the exhibition "The Ungovernables," New Museum Triennial, 2012, organized by Eungie Joo and Ryan Inouye. "Historically used as both a derogative colonial term to justify violent repression of the 'natives' ('These people are ungovernable!') and an affirmative call for civil disobedience ('We will make this country ungovernable!'), ungovernability is a double-edged sword that pursues a radical change in the everyday, but promises an upheaval that is not necessarily controllable. In terms of this exhibition, 'The Ungovernables' is meant to suggest both anarchic and organized resistance: protest, chaos, and imagination as a refusal of the extended period of economic, ideological, sectarian, and political conflict that marks the generation's inheritance. But the title also suggests a dark humor about this inheritance and the nonsentimental, noncynical approaches to history and survival it requires. Lingering in the present, artists in the exhibition embrace temporality and impermanence to explore new contingencies for an unknown future. 'The Ungovernables,' then, is about rejecting incorporation and monetization, recognizing heat, transforming potential, and offering possibilities while maintaining self-awareness."

See also, "Call for Papers: Radical Increments: Toward New Platforms of Engaging Iraqi Studies," Columbia University, April 24–25, 2015. "'Radical incrementalism' is a process wherein existing frameworks of knowledge are not paradigmatically changed but rather modified, extended, or repositioned to allow for new possibilities of application and action. Applying this conceptual framework, the conference encourages the creation of new platforms of engagement with the current Iraqi debacle, platforms that may generate a provisional meta-framework for the making of 'engaged theory' tailored specifically for the Iraqi case."

Public Sphere and Experience (1972), took "the microphysics of resistance" ("die Mikrophysik des Widerstands") as a crux of political and methodological orientation.[2] Microhistory (*microstoria*), became of course a signature term for a historical school associated with the work of Carlo Ginzberg, who, in a chapter of *Threads and Traces: True False Fictive*, presents a microhistory of the term "microhistory" before and after his own usage that contrasts it with constructs such as "local history," Richard Cobb's *petite histoire*, Fernand Braudel's *histoire événementielle*, Edoardo Grendi's *microanalysis* and Hayden White's "fragmentary" historiography.[3]

Foucault coined the expression "micro-physiques du pouvoir" (micro-physics of power) to designate modes of subjectivation and auto-regulation in the management of space and time. In *Discipline and Punish* (Surveiller et punir) the micro-physics of "cellular power," understood here quite literally with reference to the monk's cell, foregrounds the regulation of time within the monastic community. Religious orders were "the great technicians of rhythm and regular activities."[4] These ordering practices migrated to the army's "chronometric measurement of shooting" (based on precise correlations of body and gesture), and to protocols of time management, as the wage-earning class introduced a more "detailed partitioning of time" that normatively rewarded non-idleness or "exhaustive time," and equated wasted time with "moral offence and economic dishonesty."[5]

The concept of a "micropolitics of power" gives rise to the very notion of the disciplinary in its broadest Foucauldian ascription, as

---

2   According to Devin Fore, there are significant shifts of position on micropolitics between the earlier and later volumes. In *History and Obstinacy*, he maintains, "gone is the prominent role previously granted to the proletarian public sphere and to the proletariat itself as a subject of class resistance. Along with the revolutionary agent of history, the bourgeoisie has also exited, its monopoly on state power giving way in *History and Obstinacy* to more capillary and diffuse mechanisms of control and authority." See Devin Fore, "Introduction," Alexander Kluge and Oskar Negt, *History and Obstinacy* (New York: Zone Books, 2014), 16.

3   Carlo Ginzberg, "Microhistory: Two or Three Things That I Know about It," in *Threads and Traces: True False Fictive*, trans. Anne C. Tedeschi and John Tedeschi (Berkeley: University of California Press, 2012), 193–214.

4   Michel Foucault, *Discipline and Punish: The Birth of the Prison*, trans. Alan Sheridan (New York: Vintage, 1995), 149, 150.

5   Ibid., 150, 154.

Foucault's lectures at the Collège de France in the years 1972–73 (published under the title *The Punitive Society*) attest. Here, Foucault rehearses material that finds its way into *Discipline and Punish*, including the investigation of time management in the mid-nineteenth-century silk mill of Jujurieux, and the routines developed in early nineteenth-century correctional facilities. The "*surveil*-punish" couplet emerges here, and though it will be supplanted by terms with greater currency—sovereignty, biopower, and security apparatuses— it is an important carrier of the micropolitical into the larger structure of the disciplinary. Bernard Harcourt notes a passage from the lecture of March, 1973 where Foucault defines the *surveil*-punish couplet as an imposed "power relationship indispensable for fixing individuals to the production apparatus, for the formation of productive forces, and characterizes the society that can be called *disciplinary*."[6] What is key, for my purposes, is the notion of "fixing"; the fixative or adhesive that binds individuals to production apparatuses. It may only be an abstract idea rather than a material substance, but it reads out, Foucault suggests, when "microsociological research" is applied to structures of spatiotemporal organization. If we can determine the "fixing," we can accomplish something theoretically significant, from mapping genealogies of power to defining the disciplinary episteme as such.[7]

Microsociological research forms the basis for a "micro-physics of power" in *Discipline and Punish*, where Foucault writes of

> a new way of administering time and making it useful, by segmentation, seriation, synthesis and totalization. A macro- and micro-physics of power made possible not the invention of history (it had long had no need of that), but the integration of a temporal, unitary, continuous, cumulative dimension in the exercise of controls and the practice of domination."[8]

---

6   Bernard Harcourt, "Course Context," in Michel Foucault, *The Punitive Society: Lectures at the Collège de France 1972—1973*, trans. Graham Burchell (London: Palgrave Macmillan, 2015), 295.

7   Michel Foucault, *The Punitive Society: Lectures at the Collège de France 1972—1973*, trans. Graham Burchell (London: Palgrave Macmillan, 2015), 204.

8   Ibid., 160.

Micro-physics is no mere metaphor, then; it denotes a real physics of gesture and posture. In the measured hand movements of the military maneuver; in the hygienic brushing and rubbing rituals of self-care; in the spinal curvature of bodies hunched over the school desk; and in all manner of orthopedic conformity to the architecture of schools, hospitals and prisons.

Correctional architecture is treated as a medium of punitive micro-physics. Writing about Attica Prison in 1972 just one year after the riot, Foucault assigned significance to every element of the architectural infrastructure. Proceeding microphenomenologically, he zeroed in on aspects of spatial organization—like the action of a riot or prison escape—that remain unaccounted for by any totalizing frame:

> What struck me perhaps first of all was the entrance, that kind of phony fortress à la Disneyland, those observation posts disguised as medieval towers with their mâchecoulis. And behind this rather ridiculous scenery, which dwarfs everything else, you discover it's an immense machine. And it's this notion of machinery that struck me most strongly—those very long, clean, heated corridors that prescribe, for those who pass through them, specific trajectories that are evidently calculated to be the most efficient possible and at the same time the easiest to oversee, and the most direct. Yes, and all of this ends in those huge workshops, like the metallurgical one, which are clean and appear to be close to perfection.[9]

Foucault will admit that, before he visited Attica, his investigations of social exclusion were seated in abstractions. Now, his confrontation with the actual space of human warehousing, contoured by "bars everywhere," imparted vivid awareness of the disciplinary logic of the penal system that regards human subjects as if they were caged animals The microstructures of carceral surveillance encountered at Attica portend the for-profit prison industry in the United States that would reach full term through the impetus of privatization.

---

9 Michel Foucault and John K. Simon, "Michel Foucault on Attica: An Interview," *Social Justice* 18: 3, 1991, 26.

Ken Saro-Wiwa's novel *Prisoners of Jebs*, a bureaucratic dystopia, allows us to trace a line from Foucault to Achille Mbembe, which is to say, from the micropolitics of the prison-industrial complex to *necropolitics*, a term coined by Mbembe to designate regimes of death management. Jebs is a jail at Guantánamo Bay designed for pan-Africanist reformists:

> In the year of our Lord nineteen hundred and eighty-five, the Organization of African Unity decided in its accustomed wisdom to set up an elite prison on the Dark Continent. The reasoning was as follows: Africa needed political unity, and general unanimity. It had not been able to achieve these or anything like them after over twenty years of effort by Presidents and free men. It was felt that prisoners drawn from member-nations, locked up in a pollution-free environment and forced to think day and night about the problem of the continent and of each member-nation, would certainly usher in progress. The decision, not surprisingly, received unanimous approval. Each member-nation had a surplus of prisoners who ate too much food and embarrassed the big bosses. To offload them was sheer relief. The decision pleased the people of Africa because they reasoned that it was better to have living prisoners than dead ones, it being the fashion in those days to shoot prisoners and display their corpses in public.[10]

This send-up of African unity politics doubles as an exposé of the murderous logic of use-value that treats prisoner "surplus" as disposable material, and the caloric intake of the prisoner as a metric for profit-margin calculation. Saro-Wiwa's setting approximates the kind of "death-world" that Mbembe identifies with the necropolitical, and which is most commonly found in camps, migrant detention centers, labor colonies, prisons, quarantined townships and occupied territories.[11] In Mbembe's unnerving formulation, "politics is therefore death that lives a human life."[12] Necropolitics achieves its endgame in

---

10   Ken Saro-Wiwa, *Prisoners of Jebs* (Port Harcourt: Saros International Publishers, 1996), 1.

11   Achille Mbembe, "Necropolitics," *Public Culture* 15:1, 40.

12   Ibid., 14–15.

"zombification": "forms of social existence in which vast populations are subjected to becoming living-dead." These forms of existence create topographies of cruelty that blur the lines "between resistance and suicide, sacrifice and redemption, martyrdom and freedom."[13] Though it depends on a macro-scaled perspective of biopolitical organization, necropolitics is indistinguishable from micropolitics to the extent that both default to the calculus of managed life. In both micropolitics and necropolitics the subject is indissociable from temporal and spatial infrastructures of domination and subjective demolition.

In place of Foucault's biopolitics—a model built for structural diagnoses of discipline and, more specifically, for decortications of punitive society institutions—Félix Guattari introduces infrastructures of the unconscious in a field of libidinal potentialities. As Shigeru Taga has observed, the Foucault-Guattari relation remains relatively under-examined, and I would argue that elaborating that relation has bearing on how micropolitics, as a form of unexceptional politics, differs as a theoretical project from the unexceptional politics of "small p" politics.[14] Meeting and forming a friendship in the 1970s, Foucault and Guattari collaborated on projects sponsored by CERFI (Le Centre d'études, de recherches et de formation institutionelle) at the La Borde clinic with shared interests in medico-legal practices, regimes of care, and micropolitics.[15] In this context, we can see how Foucault's "microphysics of power" would serve as the fulcrum of Guattari's "micropolitique du désir," conceived in the struggle against oedipal hierarchization, and emergent as a medium of schizo-analysis, group subjectivity and discursive reprogramming.

Guattari's essay "Microphysique des pouvoirs et micropolitique des désirs" (Microphysics of Power/Micropolitics of Desire), first

---

13   Ibid., 39–40.

14   To wit, Simone Bignall's discussion of micropolitics in "Postcolonial Agency and Poststructuralist Thought: Deleuze and Foucault on Desire and Power," *Angelaki* 13:1, 2008, 127–47.

15   Shigeru Taga, "Foucault and Guattari au croisement de la théorie du micro-pouvoir et de la psychothérapie institutionelle," *Usages de Foucault*, ed. Hervé Oulc'hen (Paris: PUF, 2014). Guattari wrote about his ties to Foucault in *Les années d'hiver: 1980–85* (Paris: Les prairies ordinaires, 2009).

published in 1986, was initially delivered as a conference paper in Milan at a colloquium devoted to the work of Foucault. A close reading of Foucault's 1970 inaugural lecture at the Collège de France—*L'ordre du discours* (Orders of Discourse)[16]—Guattari introduced a "problematics of analytic singularity" based on unworking homogeneity within a logos-driven discursive field.[17] Foucault had opened this text with the fantasy of discourse shorn of institutional checks—free of decisionism, susceptible to chance, indefinitely open, calmly transparent—only to have the voice of the institution countermand the fantasy in the voice of an oppressively benevolent, superegoic guardian.[18] In standing up to the discursive guardian, Foucault, Guattari suggests, takes aim at universal mediation on the grounds that it elides "the reality of discourse." He concurs with Foucault in maintaining that discourse has been historically privileged in a vision of the logos bent on "everywhere elevating singularities into concepts, finally enabling immediate consciousness to deploy all the rationality in the world."[19] Foucault insists that the logos is "really only another discourse already in operation," a way in which "things and events insensibly become discourse."[20] This logocentric discursivity contains all manner of exclusions and internal procedures—classification, ordering, semiotic distribution, logics of coherence—that patrol and authorize what is expressible. Unbinding the singularities of things and events from a logos powered by the drive to universal knowledge and universal truth entails dissolving grammatology's structural foundationalism. Foucault, Guattari notes, produces a

> very distinct conception of the statement as no longer representing a unity of the same sort as the sentence, the proposition, or the

---

16   Translated by Robert Swyer as "The Discourse on Language," in *The Archeology of Knowledge* (New York: Pantheon Books, 1972).

17   Felix Guattari, "Microphysics of Power/Micropolitics of Desire," trans. John Caruana in *The Guattari Reader*, ed. Gary Genosko (London: Blackwell, 1996), 178.

18   Michel Foucault, *L'ordre du discours* (Paris: Gallimard, 1971), 9.

19   Guattari, "Microphysics of Power," 178.

20   Ibid.

speech-act. Consequently, the statement, for Foucault, no longer functions on the authority of a segment of a universal logos leveling out existential contingencies. Its proper domain is therefore no longer simply that of a relation of signification, articulating the relationship between signifier and signified, nor of the relation of the denotation of a referent. For it is also a capacity of existential production (which, to use my terminology, I call a diagrammatic function). In its mode of being singular, the Foucauldian statement is neither quite linguistic nor exclusively material.[21]

Guattari endorses Foucault's treatment of the statement not as a structure but as "a function of existence." Foucault's emphasis on the contingent *mise-en-existence* of signification, and its reliance on the interaction of semiotic, denotative and pragmatic functions within discourse, alerts him to "the rifts of discourse, that is, the ruptures of meaning in the ordinary language of scientific discursivity."[22] What counts for Guattari is how Foucault reterritorializes the linguistic unit of the statement, and by extension, the subject. No longer conceivable as "an irreducible point of escape from the systems of relations and representation," the subject of language is replaced by a "process of singularization" that "comes to exist as a collective assemblage of enunciation."[23] The impact of Foucault's ungrounding of discursive foundationalism is not restricted to intervening in the processes by which a social body is subjectivated; it extends to opening the enunciative field to an expansive "micropolitics of existence and desire."[24]

Guattari's analytic of singularity abandons the practice of honing words to an irreducible essence, as well as that of suturing knowledge to iconic concepts. What is at stake is a procedure that dismantles hierarchies of value within grammar. Predicates and propositions are unseated; loci of power within syntax and diction are denaturalized within discursive reason; acts of language that secure what Foucault

---

21   Ibid.
22   Ibid., 179 (translation modified).
23   Ibid., 180.
24   Ibid., 181.

characterized as the "government of individualization" are desubjectivized. Paraphrasing Foucault's *Archeology of Knowledge* Guattari
projects the discursive field as an "intentionality without subject"
proceeding from "collective surfaces and inscriptions." Micropolitics
is here identified with an inter-lingual relationality associated with the
active deindividuation of grammar. Guattari's deprivileging of the
pronominal "I" harks back to Gilbert Simondon's notions of prepersonal quanta and transindividuation.

What kind of depersonalized grammar would this be? It is found
in schizo-language. In his translator's introduction to *Schizoanalytic
Cartographies*, Andrew Goffey warns Anglophone readers that the
text's language will strike them as baroque jargon sourced from
psychoanalysis, philosophy, ecology and informatics.[25] Goffey will
insist, however, on working through this difficulty, treating it as central
to Guattari's project of stretching discourse beyond the limits of intelligibility, to the breakout points where words open onto deterritorialized planes of expression.

Guattarian micropolitics imagines orders of relationality that
enable language to be seen as a new materialism. This takes us back to
Foucault's evocation of discourse "in its material reality as pronounced
or written thing," which is to say, a thing fraught with danger insofar
as it harbors simmering "struggles, wounds, dominations, and
subordinations."[26] For Guattari, this discursive materialism can result
in such a state of war, but it can also be a revolutionary medium that
redistributes enunciation, matter, and existence on a flat plane. In this
context, discursive singularity anticipates Bruno Latour's investigation into modes of existence as well as multiple tendencies within
object-oriented ontology in which objects, including linguistic objects,
literary objects, or texts that become the object of translation, are fully
vested as existents.

Guattarian micropolitics adopts Foucault's focus on discursive
subjectivation, but transposes its micro to the molecular. In *La
Révolution moleculaire* (1977), abridged in the English translation

---

25   See "Introduction," Félix Guattari, *Schizoanalytic Cartotographies*, trans.
Andrew Goffey (London: Bloomsbury, 2013), xvi–xvii.
26   Foucault, *L'ordre du discours*, 10.

(The Molecular Revolution: Psychiatry and Politics), molecular networks of lateral links connect everything: fascism, desire, and even cookery. Molecular micropolitics is invoked to document how fascism permeates every kind of activity and social organization: from the passivity and complacence produced in response to machinic violence; to everyday forms of fascism in the family, on the shop-floor, in the trade-union hall or in any place where "local tyrants and bureaucrats of all sorts perform hysterical antics and paranoid double-dealing."[27] *Molecular Revolution* gives rise to political praxis insofar as it denounces libidinal economies that fuse oedipal organization to state structure, and promotes initiatives "to remove select areas of science, art, revolution and sexuality from dominant representations."[28] The micropolitical subject of this resectorization takes on a more robust existence as the "infra-individual" in *Lignes de fuite* (Lines of Flight). More vector or "trans" function than subject of ontology, the infra-individual crosses unconscious desires with bodily attributes, material orders of expression with semiotic ones.[29] Infra-individuals are the micropolitical subjects of social movements; at once popular and transversal (bi-polarized in schizo-analytic terms), they transgress the boundaries of privatized individualism securitized by law under oedipal capitalism.

A molecular micropolitics of desire is integral to the Guattarian vocabulary of anti-psychiatry, geophilosophy, chaosmosis, information theory and schizoanalytic cartography. Arguably it is really the *only* politics at issue in Deleuzean/Guattarian notions of deterritorialization, rhizomatic arboreality, minor literatures, and the hyphenated group-subject. Its imprint was palpable in post-'68 collectives and *groupuscules* pursuing creative practices at the juncture of poetry, punk, theater, plastic arts, theory, anarchism, ecology and anti-psychiatry. A constant among these experimental group-subjects was the desire to channel the therapeutic demiurge into

---

27 Félix Guattari, *Molecular Revolution: Psychiatry and Politics*, trans. Rosemary Sheed (London: Puffin, 1984), 225.

28 Ibid., 100.

29 Félix Guattari, *Lignes de fuite: Pour un autre monde de possibles* (La Tour d'Aigues: Éditions de l'Aube, 2011), 15, 241.

modes of theatrical and political existence, be it a politics of care, a principle of *disponibilité* (availability) and *acceuil* (unconditional welcome), a resolve to live in immediacy rather than in bankable intervals of postponed gratification, or a recognition of small acts, unrecompensed gestures, and unidentified modalities of experience.[30] Many small-group adherents apprenticed in the institutional psychotherapy of Guattari and Jean Oury, who welcomed at La Borde a host of intermittent residents who sojourned in the clinic as patients, staff, students or a combination of all three. An underlying ethic was the constant renewal of the clinic itself, echoed in Oury's injunction to "remake the therapeutic group, at all times" ("refaire le club thérapeutique, tout le temps"). Remaking included the physical labor of rebuilding environments of habitation. Oury sought to transform architecture into something other than a *"renfermerie"* (space of enclosure)—a current that was, in his view, exacerbated in the 1960s by the Brutalist style of concrete and glass walls that afforded no respite from surveillance. In an essay on "architecture and psychiatry" published in 1967, he called for the reconstruction of community according to simple steps: find a space with enough rooms to shelter people in precarity; explore materials; build through bricolage.[31]

Oury's spatiotemporal therapies are reprised today by the Invisible Committee (Comité Invisible) in their call for a blockade on infrastructure, considered to be the "mise en forme de la vie qui est le ravage de toute forme de vie" (modes of life-formation that wreak havoc on every form of life).[32] Small groups implanted in unprepossessing, semi-abandoned places—town edges, rural redoubts, graveyards for retired machines—attest to ongoing experiments in micropolitical living that take inspiration from past countercultural settlement movements—what Felicity Scott, in *Outlaw Territories*, groups under the heading "Woodstockhome." Scott's examples include the Open Land movement communes of Morning Star and Wheeler Ranch in

---

30 Olivier Apprill, "Vivre avec la folie," *Chimères* 84, 2014, 7.

31 Jean Oury, "Architecture et psychiatrie," *Recherches* 6, 1967, republished in *Journal de la Quincaillerie* 6, 2014.

32 Comité invisible, *À nos amis* (Paris: La fabrique, 2014), 87.

Northern California during the late sixties, and the Hog Farm Tent City in Stockholm of the early seventies, both dedicated to experiments in environmentalist living. Throughout the book, an implicit question hovers: what is the relevance of these communes to the politics of now? An answer can be gleaned from Scott's opening quote from the Invisible Committee's 2009 manifesto *The Coming Insurrection,* which indicts the conglomerate of global organizations responsible for the current state of the environment as "the vanguard of disaster."[33] Scott, it would seem, is advocating for an insurgent architectural practice that has little to do with building types and more to do with a futural militant ecology. Her study complements McKenzie Wark's eco-militant treatise *Molecular Red: Theory for the Anthropocene,* which, as its title suggestions, harks back to the Guattarian revolution, and to molecular micropolitics in its appeal to a "Carbon Liberation Front."

Wark's invocation of a Carbon Liberation Front echoes the Invisible Committee's neo-communist ecopolitical exploits. In 2005 the Invisible Committee, shepherded by the philosopher/Situationist/ activist Julien Coupat, established itself in a farmhouse in the Corrèze region of southwestern France. Though the collective would be accused as the "Tarnac Nine" of terrorist activity by the Sarkozy government in 2009, and prosecuted by the French anti-terrorist division as an anarcho-autonomist cell suspected of plots to sabotage train lines and global summits, it was officially acquitted for lack of evidence. Signing itself *Tiqqun,* a Hebrew term for repair, resurrection and healing, the group published *Theory of Bloom,* a poetical pamphlet that nominated James Joyce's Leopold Bloom (alongside Melville's Bartleby and Robert Musil's "man without qualities") as the figurehead of outliers and social outcasts. Bloom, as both character and principle, was hailed for his stigma-inducing sexuality as a "prisoner of the non-sensual sexualization [*Ulysses*] is riddled with."[34] In his suffering and embodiment of "radical insufficiency" (Agamben), Bloom allows for

---

33   Felicity Scott, *Outlaw Territories: Environments of Insecurity/Architectures of Counterinsurgency* (New York: Zone Books, 2016), 9.

34   Tiqqun, *Theory of Bloom,* trans. Robert Hurley (Berkeley: LBC Books, 2012), 28.

the burgeoning of a theory that recruits eco-activists for an environ-mentalist Commune.

The Invisible Committee belongs to a loosely associated network of communities that survive in the interstices of the society of calcu-lation and are occasionally characterized as manifestations of the contemporary groundswell for new utopias. Visiting the railway town of Vénéray-les-Laumes in summer 2015, I stumbled on one such collective at La Quincaillerie du Moulin, a building that had been boarded up for years and was gradually being reclaimed from the spiders, room by room, by Alexis Forestier and a group of friends and visitors. A bridge that cuts off this village siphons traffic from the giant regional supermarket ("Super U"), to feeder roads for the motorway. La Quincaillerie lowers under the bridge, a redoubt cham-pioning a site marked by dwindling residents and closed businesses. Forestier reclaimed this rambling factory compound, turning its outbuildings into spaces for performance and film projections, art ateliers and workstations, and hideaways for reading and sleeping. The place corresponds, as one visitor put it, to the dream of "the perfect palace of a peasant intellectual" ("le palais idéal d'un intellec-tual paysan").[35] Oneiric and eccentric, La Quincaillerie offers a refuge of hospitality: the furniture is scavenged; the front door remains open; tea and coffee are on the table; books on psychotherapy, philos-ophy, literature, and anarchism are ready for consultation by whom-ever. A woman with CDs to donate appears, followed by an expatriate British farmer. An actor tends the garden. It is this rhythm of coming and going, casual interruption and encounter, that makes of the site what the group called, in the first issue of their journal, a "place for making living possible," a kind of habitat factory ("un lieu de fabrique et d'un habiter possible").[36] Formerly, Forestier had collaborated with Jean Oury at the La Borde clinic while running through a range of hybrid métiers that included architecture, farming, ethnomusicol-ogy, psychotherapy, writing, and theater. He had helped found a community of "degree zero social alienation" called "Les Endimanchés"—a name meaning "Sunday best," in homage to

---

35 René Solis, "Divague à l'âme," *Libération*, January 12, 2015, liberation.fr.
36 *Journal de la Quincaillerie* 1.

nineteenth-century workers' movements who were inspired by Paul LaFarge's right to laziness.[37] Like the multiple phalansteries with which it is informally connected, La Quincaillerie dedicates itself to making creative time continuous with work time. There is the work of industrial archeology, the recycling of machine parts and old photographs of early technology, and the coordination of avant-garde performances. On the program were Dada's *Cabaret Voltaire*, plays by Brecht, Beckett, and Müller, and a philosophical promenade by bicycle (titled "Changer la vie") featuring octogenarian sculptor André Robillard, who lives in and out of psychiatric facilities. Each activity was infused with a distinct spirit of place emanating from the local stream, the factory remnants, and the depopulated streets. Like a scene excerpted from Romantic landscape poetry, the site, as its journal attests, aspires to being a "sojourner's way station" ("construction précaire d'une aire de séjour").

These forays into provisional homesteading and environmentalist autonomism, spearheaded by molecular *groupuscules* who take their cue from the Imaginary Party, come off, to be sure, as utopian adventures that, in their indifference to political institutions, are far removed from the arenas of ordinary politics. Though at risk of being dismissed or disparaged as alternative lifestyle politics, it is a molecular commune, a community of micro-affects and solidarities that corresponds politically to what Slavoj Žižek, reviewing Wark's *Molecular Red*, characterized as "weird domains which are NOT part of our experiential reality, from quantum oscillations to genomes." For Žižek, we are dealing with a

> molecular level so low that it is imperceptible not only to "molar" big politics or social struggles but also the most elementary forms of experience. It can only be accessed through "high" theory—in a kind of self-inverted twist, it is only through the highest that we get to the lowest.[38]

---

37   For an important discussion of "the politics and ontology of living labor," see Jason Read, *The Micro-Politics of Capital: Marx and the Prehistory of the Present* (Albany: SUNY Press, 2003).

38   Slavoj Žižek, "Ecology against Mother Nature: Slavoj Žižek on *Molecular Red*," *Verso blog*, May 26, 2015, versobooks.com.

Molecular micropolitics, whether we agree or not with Žižek's contention that it can only be accessed through high theory, infiltrates mainstream politics through its global dispatch of geophilosophic subjects;
subjects who have their ear low to the ground, their attention trained
on life beside the bridge.

Microsociologies

Micropolitics, historicized as an offshoot of the French anti-psychiatry movement, and repurposed for molecular politics is worlds apart from microsociology, a professionally recognized subset of the academic discipline of sociology. Its early practitioners—Erving Goffman, Harold Garfinkel, George Herbert Mead, R. D. Laing—had diverse interests and specializations that included group psychology, the social anthropology of ethnicity, behavioral codes within everyday life, social theory and social work. Posed against macrosociology, which instrumentalizes structural laws of behavior in the comparative social sciences (and whose magi were Talcott Parsons, Robert Merton and Paul Lazarsfeld), microsociology, conventionally understood, emphasized "up close and personal" humanist approaches to social interaction.

Within this subfield, Bourdieu stands out as an iconoclast, not just because he maintained suspicion towards the humanist heuristics of microsociological analysis, but more importantly because his major topics had a political origin. From his work on colonial violence and ethnosociology, to distinction and the social critique of judgment, to *habitus* and the structures of class domination, to economies of symbolic and cultural capital, to precarity of employment, and worldly suffering—each area bore the mark of an at-hand political situation, of a personally experienced political engagement.

The son of a postal worker in rural southern France, Bourdieu rose through the system of competitive exams to become a star Parisian academic, all the while experiencing a profound alienation from the corps of professional educators to which he belonged. In his *Sketch for a Self-Analysis*, he described his lifelong feeling of inner desolation, despair and solitude, relieved only by phrases and conversations in novels that granted access to other worlds and the chance, as Flaubert put it, "to live every life" ("vivre toutes les vies").[1] His escape from the normative constraints imposed by *homo academicus* was obtained only by throwing himself into fieldwork that began in Algeria with the ethnography of Kabylian villages, researched while a conscripted soldier during the Algerian War.

To define Bourdieu as a microsociological thinker is not an easy task, since he had no theory of micropolitics and did not employ the term in his writings. His approach to class stratification and group segmentation had little in common with that of Guattari and Foucault. Guattari's recourse to desire, the unconscious and schizo-language was anathema to Bourdieu, like the language of psychoanalysis more generally.[2] He shaped his view of sociology around analyzing "what psychoanalysis dismisses as secondary or insignificant."[3] He was closer to Foucault inasmuch as their projects are situated at the conjuncture of philosophy and the social sciences, even if Bourdieu complained that Foucault remained too faithful to the classical discipline of post-war French philosophy. Both dismantled structures of domination and state power in politically marked spaces. In Bourdieu, décor and architecture form part of an animated picture of public and private life, in contrast to Foucault's factories, hospitals and prisons, which often loom as the impersonal statuary of institutional *dispositifs*. In Bourdieu's concept of *habitus*, the place of habitation always leaves its imprint on the animacies of lived life. In his earliest work on the Kabylian house, he breaks open the typology of the plan with descriptions of the everyday duress of survival under conditions of colonial war. The same painstaking method of analysis was applied to the dissection of his own paternal *habitus:*

Housed with his family in an apartment that came with the job but lacking the most basic comforts (for a long time water had to be

---

1   Pierre Bourdieu, *Sketch for a Self-Analysis*, trans. Richard Nice (Chicago, IL: University of Chicago Press, 2008), 71, 66.

2   This view is disputed in an article by Jean-François Fourny and Meaghan Emery, but their case, in my view, is not particularly persuasive. See "Bourdieu's Uneasy Psychoanalysis," *SubStance* 93, 2000, 103–12.

3   Pierre Bourdieu, *La Misère du monde* (Paris: Seuil, 1993), 717.

fetched from the public fountain), he was tied to a grueling schedule, from Monday morning to Saturday evening and from six in the morning when the post van came and the mail was collected, until the accounts were balanced, often late at night, especially when the end-of-the-month accounts had to be finalized; he kept his own garden, bought and sawed his firewood, and the slightest purchase— a Lévitan-style bedroom suite that my mother and he had made for them in Nay[4]

Bourdieu's subjects are never as anonymous as Foucault's, but seated in a nexus of character types, as in a novel. The characters are distinguished in time and place by motivations, intentions and social anxieties that crystallize in ways of speaking and living (translated infelicitously in English as "lifestyles"): "I spent hours listening to conversations, in cafés, on pétanque or football pitches, in post offices, but also at society receptions, cocktail parties or concerts."[5] In his work, conversation is the carrier of microsociologies whose surprising contents can often shift the course of research. In his *Sketch for a Self-Analysis*, he describes how an offhand remark made by his mother precipitates an epistemological revolution in his understanding of sociology:

It was no doubt a banal remark of my mother's, which I would not even have picked up if I had not been alerted to it ("they've become very 'kith and kin' with the X's now that there's a Polytechnicien in the family") that, at the time of my study of bachelorhood, triggered the reflections that led me to abandon the model of the kinship rule for that of strategy . . . It is only at the cost of a veritable epistemological conversion, irreducible to what the phenomenologists call the épochè that intrinsically non-pertinent lived experience can enter into scientific analysis.[6]

---

4 Bourdieu, *Sketch for a Self-Analysis*, 85.
5 Pierre Bourdieu, *Distinction: A Social Critique of the Judgement of Taste*, trans. Richard Nice (Cambridge, MA: Harvard University Press, 1984), 7.
6 Bourdieu, *Sketch for a Self-Analysis*, 65.

The phrase "kith and kin" spurs Bourdieu to rethink how class complicities transform the laws of kinship in the marriage system, prompting him, in his study of the peasant community of Béarn, to train his gaze on the unmarried and the unmarriageable. From there, a vista opens into the "ethnography of ethnography," which entails understanding "how social experience that seems to have no value can be converted into capital."[7]

The novelist Annie Ernaux, drawn to casual dinner table conversation as a rich source of microhistory that could be used as the raw material of autofiction, recognized her debt to Bourdieu's listening techniques and powers of material ethnography, particularly as they informed the composition of her novel *Les Années*. She noted Bourdieu's observations on how people in business and the professional classes project self-importance, assigning weightiness to their own words, angling their expressions, and asserting their bodies in social space.[8] In *Distinction* this critical regard led to a portrait gallery of workers shown touching their machines or blending in with their workstations.

Distinction expands the vocabulary of class analysis by using large data samples to multiply and complicate the definitions of class identities. No consumer preference or facet of daily life is too trivial to be tallied and interpreted. Bourdieu's subjects acquire density as subjects when they are shown eating, socializing, and choosing hairstyles, cosmetics, and footwear ("blue dungaries, town shoes, moccasins, sneakers, dressing gowns, lumber jackets," et cetera).[9] "To save washing up," we learn, a woman in a middle-class household distributes dessert,

> on improvised plates torn from the cake-box (with a joke about "taking the liberty" to mark the transgression) . . . The soup plate, wiped with bread, can be used right through the meal. The hostess will certainly offer to "change the plates," pushing back her chair

---

7   Ibid. 65.
8   Annie Ernaux, "*La Distinction*: oeuvre totale et révolutionaire," in *Pierre Bourdieu: l'insoumission en héritage* ed. Édouard Louis (Paris: PUF, 2013), 35.
9   Bourdieu, *Distinction*, 201.

with one hand and reaching with the other for the plate next to her, but everyone will protest.[10]

Much of this information seems superfluous: do we need to know that the soup plate gets wiped with a piece of bread? But this is precisely how Bourdieu proceeds. Miniscule gestures are recorded because they are socially meaningful in ways that resist facile decoding. The improvised cake-box plate signifies nothing in particular, but its function, as a jazz variation in the composition of a social life, is all-important in unpacking the structural workings of class formation.

Challenging the very notion of *culture* as a term predicated on the suppression of "lower, coarse, vulgar, venal, servile" attitudes, Bourdieu, in *Distinction*'s postscript, redeems "vulgar" critiques of so-called "pure" critique. Vulgarity, which smacks of "vulgar Marxism," has for Bourdieu the felicitous effect of importing ordinary language into sociology; a rebuff to scientific jargon and academic circumlocution. Édouard Louis associates Bourdieu's resistance to discursive professionalism with the theoretical construct of "insubmission" ("l'insoumission en héritage"). The French education system is the incubator of submission to systems of inherited privilege and class triage. So Bourdieu must attack it at the level of disposition formation, and to this end he homes in on

the ordinary choices of everyday existence, such as furniture, clothing, or cooking, which are particularly revealing of deep-rooted and long-standing dispositions because, lying outside the scope of the educational system, they have to be confronted, as it were, by naked taste, without any explicit prescription or proscription, other than from semi-legitimate legitimizing agencies such as women's weeklies or "ideal home" magazines.[11]

Bourdieu treats marketing research—as found, for example, in the Luxury Trade Directory, which itemized upper-class animals,

10   Ibid., 195.
11   Ibid., 77.

children's clothing labels, fireworks, astrologers, hairdressers, clinics, florists, furs and haute couture—like a score that arranges relations between "the reputation of a person and the social image of a thing."[12] If Bourdieu painstakingly annotates the minutiae of taste (providing an anachronistic time capsule of French consumer products and cultural pastimes of the 1970s), it is because at this level recognition occurs. Recognition is the mechanism that orders the database; allowing objects or lifestyles unequally distributed among social classes to be attributed to specific classes. Bourdieu's inclusion as appendix 4 of the "parlor game" called "Associations" uses the results of a 1975 survey that invited the public to tally French politicians to consumer objects or pastimes, such that we find the assignment of "skiing to Giscard, and boxing or rugby to Marchais, the top hat to Giscard, and the cap, emblem of the rowdy urban populace to Marchais, and the beret, symbol of the placid working man, to Mitterrand; the Rolls Royce to Giscard."[13] Games like this one prove crucial to understanding the hypnosis at work in "small p" politics, where triggers of subliminal class association not only produce cathexis with a given candidate, but also institute regimes of irrational choice that override policies or party platforms that may be in the voter's self-interest.

Bourdieu converts the material of political parlor games and market research into a tool of social critique, just as he converts his own class insecurities into a critical microsociology of insecuritization and precarity:

> Only slowly did I understand that if some of my most banal reactions were often misinterpreted, it was often because of the manner— tone, voice, gestures, facial expressions, etc.—in which I sometimes manifested them, a mixture of aggressive shyness and a growling, even furious, bluntness, might be taken at face value, in other words, in a sense too seriously, and that it contrasted so much with the distant assurance of well-born Parisians that it always threatened to give the appearance of uncontrolled, querulous violence to reflex

---

12   Ibid., 557.
13   Ibid., 558.

and sometimes purely ritual transgressions of the conventions and commonplaces of academic or intellectual routine.[14]

The willingness to transgress academic professional protocols brings Bourdieu to a method based on sympathy—"sympraxis"—that will orient his future research and political activism. In "Job Insecurity is Everywhere Now," a chapter of *Acts of Resistance: Against the Tyranny of the Market* (1998), Bourdieu deplores how neoliberal Europe exploits economic crisis to destroy the welfare state, undermine collective responsibility and introduce a psychology of "blame the victim" to justify "the destructuring of existence." This is a condition that deprives workers of temporal structures and subjects them to "the deterioration of the whole relationship to the world, time and space."[15] Casualization creates suffering by putting the future into question, thereby sapping the energy and confidence required for collective resistance. With insecuritization comes a vocabulary ranged along a spectrum from fragility to robustness, in which expressions like "on the way down," "hanging by a thread," and "bad investment" refer to vulnerable persons rather than to the state of the economy.

Written in the heat of the transportation worker strikes that brought Paris to a standstill in 1995, *The Tyranny of the Market* builds a language of precarity that Bourdieu had already begun to compile in *La Misère du monde* (The Weight of the World, 1993), a project undertaken with a twenty-seven-member research team in the 1980s and early 1990s.[16] In *La Misère du monde* Bourdieu and his group interviewed people of varying social sectors whose economic situations had worsened during the Socialist-sponsored neoliberal turn, including laid-off workers, concierges, inhabitants of the *banlieue*, ruined farmers, night-workers, people with disabilities, the mentally unstable, contingent teaching faculty, and women and elderly people living

---

14   Bourdieu, *Sketches for a Self-Analysis*, 89.
15   Pierre Bourdieu, *Acts of Resistance: Against the Tyranny of the Market*, trans. Richard Nice (New York: The New Press, 1998), 82.
16   On the analysis of precarity in the French context, see "La déconstruction du monde du travail," in Luc Boltanski and Éve Chiapello, *Le nouvel esprit du capitalisme* (Paris: Gallimard, 1999, 2011), 317–76. Translated by Gregory Elliott as *The New Spirit of Capitalism* (London and New York: Verso, 2007).

in social isolation. The word *misère* in the French title is especially charged, signifying poverty in the strict economic sense, as well as in spiritual, moral and philosophical senses (Pascal's "misery" of man without God). Miserableness, ordinary suffering, work settings that have become uncertain places of employment—these associations come through in chapter headings like "The Old Worker and the New Plant," "The Shop Steward's World in Disarray," "The Temp's Dream." The overtranslated English title, *The Weight of the World: Social Suffering in Contemporary Society*, highlights the psychic collateral damage of unemployment: depression, lassitude, loneliness, world-weariness, the sheer difficulty of living.[17] "We are offering here the accounts that men and women have confided to us about their lives and the difficulties they have in living those lives," Bourdieu announced in his opening remarks.[18] Bourdieu makes a point of privileging personal testimony over the specialists' diagnoses. "As I was listening," he writes, in an entry,

> everything also became natural to me, so present in their words and their actions was the "inert violence" in the order of things, the violence inscribed in the implacable wheels of the job market, the school market, racism (also present within the "police forces" that are, in principle, supposed to repress it), etc., I did not have to force myself to share in the feeling, inscribed in every word, every sentence, and more especially in the tone of their voices, their facial expressions or body language, of the obviousness of this form of collective bad luck that attaches itself, like a fate, to all those that have been put together in those sites of social relegation, where the personal suffering of each is augmented by all the suffering that comes from coexisting and living with so many suffering people together.[19]

"Inert Violence," "feeling inscribed in every word," "coexistent suffering"; these terms of sympraxis are calibrated as non-quantitative

---

17   Pierre Bourdieu et al., *The Weight of the World: Social Suffering in Contemporary Society*, trans. Priscilla Ferguson (Stanford, CA: Stanford University Press, 2000).

18   Ibid., 3.

19   Ibid., 64.

metrics of social precarity and must be trained for, listened to, and channeled. It is only through extreme attention to detail that precarity can be phenomenologially calibrated as a boxed-in lifeworld. Stéphane Beaud writes about a temp worker laid off from his job at the Peugeot plant in 1991. Alain's principal activity is sitting,

> in a tiny room that seems as if it has been invaded by objects: a big black and white TV set up on a chair facing the bed, a cassette tape recorder on the table, a small refrigerator next to the sink. The walls are covered with posters from films and hard rock groups.[20]

Why does it matter that the TV is black and white? That the refrigerator is next to the sink? That the walls are covered in posters? As in a film or literary work these concrete particulars are registered not simply to impart atmosphere to the vignette of cramped quarters. They register a mode of subjectivated existence, a phenomenology of what it is like, to adopt the Heideggerian turn of phrase, to be "poor in world."

Microsociological case studies in *The Weight of the World* double as a form of poignant storytelling, doing their best to avoid the traps of miserabilism, objectification, or the genre of hardship narrative so readily appropriated by marketers. Christian Salmon has documented the way in which empathy-inducing storytelling techniques are readily transformed into "sales techniques" ("narrative branding") and strategies enabling companies "to manage emotional flows and affective investments, and to organize the world of sense-perceptions."[21] The lesson here is that microsociology cuts politically both ways, instilling attunement to subtle modalities of subjectivation, precarity and suffering, while lending itself to being co-opted as a toolkit for managing emotional labor. Arlie Russell Hochschild, in her classic study *The Managed Heart: Commercialization of Human Feeling* (1983), tracked in the airline industry what happens "when private capacities for empathy and warmth are put to corporate uses . . . when

---

20 Ibid., 282–3.
21 Christian Salmon, *Storytelling: Bewitching the Modern Mind*, trans. David Macey (London and New York: Verso, 2010), viii.

worked-up warmth becomes an instrument of service work," and when "emotive dissonance" arises from the pressures of "maintaining a difference between feeling and feigning."[22] In measuring the differential in production of a "work smile" and a smile, Hochschild identifies the particular forms of capital produced by engineered displays of motivational enthusiasm or pleasure in work. This forced, capitalist grin lines up with what Frédéric Lordon, writing in a Spinozist vein, associates with the coerced joy factor, embodied by the mask of alienated emotion coached and cooked to proclaim the love of the master. It is tantamount, for Lordon, to a violence committed on the conatus ("the desiring force at the root of all interests").[23] The production of masks of expression/oppression thus joins other salaried forms of domination that, in Lordon's estimation, constitute Bourdieu's greatest theoretical achievement.

The Weight of the World is built to resist commercial appropriation, but this did not prevent the storytelling embedded in its case histories from furnishing the material for a commercially successful film—the Dardenne brothers' Oscar-nominated *Two Days, One Night*. Made in 2014, years after the Bourdieu volume appeared, the film is loosely based on the case of Hamid, a CGT (General Confederation of Labor) representative at the Peugeot auto plant in Sochaux. It was filmed near Seraing, a small industrial town in Belgium that was the epicenter of steel production and the site of a bitter general strike from 1960–61. Thus it traces a long history of contingent labor and the proliferation of precarity across multiple sectors, with specific analogies drawn between the 1880s (when workplace deregulation and a general disaffection with unions gave a special advantage to management) and the era of financial crisis post-2008. In the Bourdieu volume, Hamid's case history (titled "The End of the World") tracks how employees in a particular section of the plant come to endorse a petition to terminate a putatively underperforming coworker (who happens to be a veteran union member) whom they believe has cost

---

22   Arlie Russell Hochschild, *The Managed Heart: Commericalization of Human Feeling* (Berkeley: University of California Press, 1983, 2003), 89–90.

23   Frédéric Lordon, *Willing Slaves of Capital: Spinoza and Marx on Desire*, trans. Gabriel Ash (London and New York: Verso, 2014), 15.

them their bonuses. When Hamid fails to obtain the votes needed to protect the employee's job, he falls into depression, unable to process how profoundly the foundations of worker solidarity and social justice have been shaken.[24] In the Dardennes' film adaptation, the point of view is shifted to that of the fired worker—a woman called "Sandra" who returns from a medical leave at a Belgian solar panel factory to discover that she has been made redundant. In exchange for their vote in favor of the layoff, her coworkers are promised a bonus of 1,000 euros. When Sandra pleads her case with the boss, she is faced with an infernal proposition: she can retain her job only if, in the span of a single weekend, she can convince the majority of her coworkers to relinquish their premiums. Thus begins, as one reviewer put it, the "low-rent labors of Hercules in which the original tasks are replaced by the locked door, the secret ballot and the bottle of Xanax on the bathroom shelf."[25] Sandra's ordeal consists of dragging herself door to door, ambushing her colleagues, and abasing herself as she confronts them with their own shame at having sold her out. The outlines of this parable of Capital versus Work are filled in by close-ups of Sandra's creased, exhausted face, the heaviness of her gait as she gets in and out of the car between visits, the expelled sigh of despair, and the anguished relays of looks between herself and her colleagues. Some pull away; others express anger and outrage at her discomfiting presence. Ariane Nicolas observes,

> The fact that personal interest is all-powerful ("sovereign" as Frédéric Lordon would say), doesn't explain where to put the cursor: "I really need this money," repeat those who will vote no. To pay for a child's tuition, to renovate the terrace, to make up for the loss of a second income . . . in short, "everyone has their reasons," even if, with the same base salary, some seem to be able to pass up the bonus and others not.[26]

24   Bourdieu et al., *The Weight of the World*, 323.
25   Xan Brooks, "*Two Days, One Night* review—small-town tale with a universal punch," *Guardian*, August 24, 2014, theguardian.com.
26   Ariane Nicolas, "Deux jours, une nuit: Marx revisité par les frères Dardenne," *France TV blog*, May 23, 2014, blog.francetvinfo.fr.

The humanity shown by the compassionate fellow workers does nothing to mitigate structural exploitation, that is, the predication of finance capitalism on the expendability of employees.

Sandra's body is carefully monitored by the camera, weakening each time she comes into physical contact with the abusive foreman, with the workers whose jobs will continue on as before, and with the legions of other bodies—the surplus labor—that stand at the ready whenever there is a redundancy or a strike. Sandra's downward spiral is documented through scenes of progressive abjectification. She is shown in close-up writhing on the bed covers, gasping for air through a car window, crumpling up in tears before the bathroom mirror, running the gauntlet of hostile looks as she walks past her coworkers, and wallowing in the realization that her existence is "nothing at all."

As the chronicle of a person's fall into precarity, *Two Days, One Night*, like *The Weight of the World*, invites being read alongside Judith Butler's *Precarious Lives*, or her coauthored *Dispossession: The Performative in the Political*. The latter, a dialogue with Athena Athanasiou, elaborates the premise that "the differential ways of allocating precarity, of assigning disposability, are clearly aims and effects of neoliberal forms of social and economic life."[27] "Precaritarization" is identified as a "process of acclimatizing a population to insecurity. It operates to expose a targeted demographic to unemployment or to radically unpredictable swings between employment and unemployment."[28] Invisibilization is the result of economic dispossession, itself based on a system of possessive individualism whereby property ownership is privileged as the measure of personhood, ontic value and political agency. Precarity, they maintain, arises too from the unequal distribution of legal protection, as laws protective of the basic welfare of citizens are dismantled while others are put in place to safeguard privileged sectors and corporate entitlements. This legal distributive injustice is only reinforced, as Simon During suggests, by capitalism's reinscription of Christian sin, Hobbesian fear, and Lockean uneasiness: "The secular notion that uneasiness and

---

27 Judith Butler and Athena Athanasiou, *Dispossession: The Performative in the Political* (Cambridge, UK: Polity, 2013), 20–1.

28 Ibid., 43.

instability are primary to human existence is kept alive under capitalism since it is a mode of production that, in effect, invests in insecurity, which therefore reaches a certain fulfillment in today's global precarity."[29]

The politics of precarity, underwriting the microsociological case studies of *The Weight of the World,* as well as *Tyranny of the Market,* anchors Bourdieu's call, launched during the Mitterrand years to the consternation of the Socialist Party, for a "gauche de gauche" (a Left worthy of the name) that would resist being in thrall to American-style neoliberalism. Microsociology is, in this sense, a motivated political praxis, integral to the struggle against austerity politics, redundancy politics, casualization politics—in short, any politics arising from a sovereign economy that turns precarity into capital, a derivative, or somebody's bonus. To *be* a microsociologist is to fight this politics of involuntary servitude. Bourdieu's approach: sympraxis; his task: to strike, vigilantly, against indifference to the disposability of the contingently employed and the dissolution of structures of social solidarity; his method: to assign concrete particulars to modes of subjectivation. As in Étienne de La Boétie's *Discours de la servitude volontaire* (The Discourse of Voluntary Servitude), which in Lordon's view parses "bodies moved by conatuses of affect," so *Distinction,* along with the narratives archived in *The Weight of the World,* breaks down monolithic abstractions (domination, precarity) into microsociologies of capital traced to the most mundane pursuits, anodyne object-choices, and modes of behaving microsociologically.[30]

---

29 Simon During, "Choosing Precarity," *South Asia: Journal of South Asian Studies* 38: 1, 2015, 22. For During, the reasons for choosing "precariat" are found in Amit Chaudhuri's novel *The Immortals.* Chaudhuri's depiction of a jumble of classes made precarious by the vagaries of global capital is compelling not because it "scandalises the demand for those kinds of distributive justice that aim to ameliorate or justify insecurity and poverty, or to service marginalized identities, or both," but rather because it "is not bound to the demand for social improvement and justice." Precarity, for During, generates affective connection precisely because it "has no merely political solution" (37).

30 Frédéric Lordon, *Willing Slaves of Capital,* xii, 113.

Nanoracisms

In his "Introduction to Frantz Fanon: Provincializing Nietzsche (13/13)", Bernard E. Harcourt exhorts us to forget Nietzsche (using Nietzsche *contra* Nietzsche, as only Nietzsche might commission his own, nihilistic self-forgetting); to provincialize Nietzsche in line with Dipesh Chakrabarty's injunction to provincialize Europe (*Provincializing Europe: Postcolonial Thought and Historical Difference* [2000]); and to think the times—the strange tragedy of our raced actuality, the violent untimeliness of the dawn of a new Confederacy shored up by openly racist policy—with and through the medium of a singularly Fanonian theory and praxis of *ressentiment*, flush with Fanon's ambivalent, self-critical dialectics of blackness (*négritude*).[1] This last point comes to the fore in the chapter of *Black Skin, White Masks* on "The Negro and Psychopathology," where Fanon approvingly cites Gabriel d'Arboussier's denunciation of Sartre's existentialization of generic black suffering, which d'Arboussier calls out as the "dangerous mystificatory aspect" of "theories of negritude." "The objection is valid," writes Fanon; "It applies to me as well . . . Against all the arguments I have just cited, I come back to one fact [une évidence]: *Wherever he goes, the Negro remains a Negro* [Où qu'il aille, un nègre demeure un nègre]."[2]

How to overcome the impasse of the black man's overdetermination as a nonbeing because of his color, his occluded self-sovereignty,

---

1   Bernard E. Harcourt, "Introduction to Frantz Fanon: Provincializing Nietzsche (13/13)," *Nietzsche 13/13 blog,* January 11, 2017, blogs.law.columbia.edu. This entry accompanied the January 19, 2017 session of the "Nietzsche 13/13" seminars with Emily Apter, Homi Bhabha and Brandon Terry.

2   Frantz Fanon, *Black Skin White Masks*, trans. Charles Lam Markmann (New York: Grove Press, 1967), 172, 173. Originally published as *Peau noire, masques blancs* (Paris: Seuil, 1952), 139, 140.

the condition of his foreclosed access to universal humanity? In Fanon's clinical foray into the philosophy of a new subject there was recourse to Nietzsche from the start. The Zarathustran man of affirmation, poetically captioned as a "*yes* that vibrates to cosmic harmonies" ("*oui* vibrant aux harmonies cosmiques"), occupies a universe that must become a universe of the black man too, even at the price of cauterizing the historic black subject, cutting him out of himself, severing him from his antinomies and his agonistics.[3] As scholarship on Fanon's library confirms (with reference to passages that Fanon underlined in his copy of Charles Andler's *Nietzsche, sa vie et sa pensée* [1921]), Fanon seized on the necessity of the transvaluation of suffering infused with Nietzschean terms of normative right, specifically, the right to civilization and to life.[4]

A temporally situated Fanon—inside the Nietzschean cosmic chronotope (and thus beyond the time frame of Euro-philosophy's unconditional priority), yet within the perdurable, generic time signature of the so-called "evidence of blackness" (a raced psychopolitics today inflected by Black Lives Matter and the advent of a presidential biopolitics steeped in white supremacism)—helps frame and bring into focus emergent languages of ethicopolitical militance and vigilance. These languages have produced marked terms of anti- and decolonial struggle, drafted for an early twenty-first-century age of assaults on civil liberties, black citizens' rights (including but obviously not limited to voting rights), and economies of existence that refuse to reduce racial difference to "bare life." Particular attention will be devoted to several psychopolitical constructs that could be said to sublate aspects of Nietzschean *ressentiment* and/or Fanonian "reactivity" at the contemporary pass.[5] The first is Achille Mbembe's post-Schmittian take on the "politics of enmity," *retournement*, and juridical humanity, which reworks, through a Fanonian psychiatrized lens, the relation between violence and colonial force of law in the context of racist structures of securitization and anti-migration. The second is

---

3   Ibid., *Black Skin, White Masks*, 6; *Peau noire, masques blancs*, 8.
4   Jean Khalifa, "La bibliothèque de Frantz Fanon," in Frantz Fanon, *Écrits sur l'aliénation et la liberté* (La Découverte, 2015), 592.
5   "There is always resentment in a *reaction*." Fanon, *Black Skin, White Masks*, 222.

Mbembe's notion of "nanoracism," which stands as a politically nuanced alternative to the institutionally proliferating and highly problematic term "micro-aggression" (whose performative effects vary wildly depending on illocutionary context and the subject-positioning of speakers and addressees). The third is Alexander G. Weheliye's concept of *habeas viscus*, a term denoting "sociogenic imprints on 'the hieroglyphs of the flesh,'" "pornotroping" as depravation, and what he calls, critically building on Deleuze, "racialized assemblages." A central concern undergirding this discussion: how might we think with Fanon to *re*think the micropolitics of racist psychopolitics, especially at the historical conjuncture of militarized policing and the rhetoric of the new Confederacy?

Achille Mbembe builds his book *Politiques de l'inimitié* (2016) (The Politics of Enmity) around the problem of "Schmittian enmity-amity," in which *inimitié* (enmity) is calqued on *amitié* (friendship). The ambivalent relation between enmity and friendship, carefully deconstructed by Derrida in *Politiques de l'amitié* (Politics of Friendship) extends to homophonically related terms such as *inimité* (inimicalness, inimitability, matchlessness) and *intimité* (intimacy, proximity). The spine of Mbembe's book lists the title erroneously as *Politiques d'inimité*, which translates roughly as "incomparable politics," prompting the suggestion that this slip is not entirely wrong; Mbembe may in fact be addressing what is inimical to politics—its peerless capacity to mask hostilities as acts of friendship and goodwill, its ability as a medium to foment and circulate hostilities of every stripe and scale.

Inimitié, which gained traction in the eighteenth century as a synonym of enmity implying targeted charge at a person or collectivity, is akin to *ressentiment*, particularly its French ascription as untranslatable from the French. Both terms are premised on the *objet a*, a causative object-desire exterior to the subject that entrains loving the enemy, desiring the enemy as oneself. For Nietzsche, this neighbor-loving is the trap of the noble (Christian) man against whom the man of *ressentiment*, "whose soul squints," must gird himself. Enemy-desire must be used against itself, resisted through a politics of concentrated hate that leaves its traces, as Mbembe sees it, in apartheid, fantasies of extermination, hate speech, logics of suspicion, conspiracy theories, anxiogenic formulas of the "War on Terror," and a host of other symptoms of paranoid democracy and racist ethnonationalism. Under such conditions, to be, as it were, deprived of enemy (qua subject-substance rather than any particular enemy), becomes the worst punishment, tantamount to removing pretexts for negative disinhibition.[6] The hallmarks of *ressentiment* associated by Nietzsche with slave morality—envy, insecurity, frustration, defensiveness, guilt, weakness, *mesquinerie* (nastiness, the nursing of petty grudges against perceived slights)—are thus recouped as permits for the maintenance of a politics of *inimitié*. If hostility must be preserved at all costs, *ressentiment* functions as a prophylactic that wards off the privative consequences of comity, peace, compassion and care. By means of this inverse reasoning, a logic of defensive instrumentality—enshrined in the obsession with securitization—is privileged as the overriding principle governing juridical humanity. Its manifest symptoms include the unilateral justification of deportation, collateral damage, world policing, and mass incarceration, all of which allow hostile phantasms to thrive and multiply.[7]

Ressentiment inscribes the possibility of backlash, reverb, and recursivity in its very prefix. The "re" of "re-feeling" redounds to the affective subject, with self-transformation and self-destruction equally possible in the becoming. *Ressentiment*, in its Nietzschean associations, resonates with *return* ("eternal return," *retournement* as in life-changing, transformative experience, being turned; from Deleuzian anti-dialectics, the will to power as infinite *devenir*); with *recurrence* (structural violence, cyclical repetition, OCD, colonial mimicry, auto-immunity, Mbembe's planetary *à rebours* identified with necropolitical inversions of human value, ecopolitical regress)[8]; and with *reversal* (Christian love, *renversement* as in the Deleuzian critical reversal, the differential element from which the value of values issues forth). All these effects are registered in Mbembe's enmity politics even if he does

---

6   Achille Mbembe, *Politiques de l'inimitié* (Paris: La Découverte, 2016), 69–70. All translations from this work are my own.

7   Ibid., 76–7.

8   Ibid., 17.

not explicitly name *ressentiment* as the catalyst. They inform his descriptions of pathogenic modes of reactivity and structures of regression. And these structures lead back to Fanon, who, in *Black Skin, White Masks*, is concerned with working through the devastating effects of *ressentiment* on the black psyche. Fanon devoted many pages to dissecting the black subject's "pathological sensitivity" (what he dubbed "affective erethism"); desire for vengeance; his or her morbid, will-sapping fixation on past injuries; or the painful realities of black on black *ressentiment* (named as such), as when Guadeloupian blacks become the object of resentment on the part of Martinican blacks for trying to pass as Martinicais, or the hatred of Senegalese solders by Antilleans.[9] Such infraracisms were and remain easily marshaled as psychopolitical technologies through which societies of control divide communities of color.

The concern with countering the self-defeating recursivity of *ressentiment* brought Fanon to strategies for "breaking the cycle" that included "going beyond comparison," and going beyond the "Negro as comparison" (where the "Negro" is the yardstick of nonbeing against which white humanity is measured and through which the measure of black humanity is erased).[10] As Bernard Harcourt reminds us,

> The idea, it seems, is to get beyond notions of superiority and inferiority. Not to respond that black culture is in fact superior or equal to European culture; but to overcome the comparison itself. To get beyond these moral judgments. Not to refute them, not to invert them, to get over them entirely—as if they never existed.
>
> Not to invert. "In our view," Fanon writes, "an individual who loves Blacks is as 'sick' as someone who abhors them." The idea is to break the cycle, not continue it. To get beyond it, not to replicate it:
>
> "Our sole concern was to put an end to a vicious cycle. Fact: some Whites consider themselves superior to Blacks. Another fact:

---

9 Fanon, *Black Skin, White Masks*, 28. "Pathological hypersensitivity" and the reference to Fanon's term "affective erethism" are borrowed from Anthony Appiah's foreword to the Richard Philcox translation of *Black Skin, White Masks* (New York: Grove Atlantic, 2008), ix.

10 Ibid., 211.

some Blacks want to prove at all costs to the Whites the wealth of the black man's intellect and equal intelligence. How can we break the cycle?"[11]

For Fanon, the stakes of breaking the cycle (or "vicious circle") embedded in the dialectics of *ressentiment* point to a sublation that might today be associated with "woke" racial consciousness.[12] In Mbembe's book, by contrast, there really is no moment of critical awakening, or structure of sublation. *Ressentiment* is baked into modes of being in the political present; it is a persistent feature of enmities that are themselves identified with self-destructive practices of biopolitical annihilation, autophagy, baffled revolutionary telos, the continuous reproduction of sadomasochistic social relations and inferiority-superiority complexes whose contemporary narcotic form is nanoracism. Mbembe chillingly identifies nanoracism as a modern pastime. Where before there were outlets such as public games, circuses, palace intrigues, cabals and gossip, now there is nanoracism, a sick *divertissement*, a narcotic version of racial prejudice reliant on poisonous compounds that induce tetanized stupor, paralysis and contracted sociality. Nanoracism—traceable to Fanon's pharmacy—proliferates in the guise of "miniscule madnesses" ("folies miniaturisées") distributed through systems of social existence in dosed portions of neurosis, psychosis, and erotic delirium.[13]

For Mbembe, nanoracism, whether identified with the lived experience of people of color or with expressions of white domination, has become a common denomination of planetary enmity. In this picture, politics is a psychopolitics, characterized by a reactivity typically ascribed to persons. This approach to the Political allows Mbembe, much like Fanon and Nietzsche before him, to diagnose state violence through the lens of subjectivized history (not personified history, but history comprised of agents in the process of being reactively subjectivated). Mbembe will chart the dynamics of injury and hate within social microcosms and global networks of nanoracism, mapped as

---

11   Bernard E. Harcourt, "Introduction to Frantz Fanon."
12   Fanon, *Black Skin, White Masks*, 217.
13   Mbembe, *Politiques de l'inimitié*, 113.

countless discharges of negative affect within force fields of brute sensualism and capitalist lubricity.[14]

Interestingly, one important characteristic of nanoracism is its indifference to scale: the smallest gestures can trigger great trauma, thus placing quotidian *blessures* on the same plane as world-historical catastrophe. Micro-aggression and genocide, though not proportionally equivalent or similar in kind, become at times structurally interchangeable within an omnibus system of stress disorders that perforce introduce a certain ethical relativism. This relativism makes it impossible to rationalize trauma within ethically coherent systems of retribution and redress; it presupposes and posits an extra-juridical subject of injury that is stranded, irrecuperable even by nosological standards. Nanoracism thus renders virtually impossible the conversion of focused, soul-destroying, pathogenic rage and suffering into self-determination. It arguably impedes, to borrow Joseph F. Lawless's terms of the Deleuzian-Nietzschean paradigm, the shift from the "active-reactive" to the "affirmative-negative" mode, whereby negation proves foundational to an emancipatory becoming.[15] Rather than tarry with the negative (that is, with Nietzsche), Mbembe returns us to a Hobbesian state of nature in which the most one can hope for is a return to the unfinished Fanonian project of politico-existential psychiatry forged in the crucible of militant anticolonialism. For Mbembe, I would argue, the poisoned chalice of the Fanonian *pharmakon* contains a pessimistic politics of "inimities" specific to the contemporary global condition, which is to say, characterized by intractable iniquities and inequities at levels both great and small. As nanoracisms proliferate and gather momentum, they prepare the ground for a new Confederacy, itself shored up by the defensive and ultimately self-defeating political calculation that took hold in the Obama administration when it was presumed that any ownership of the "black agenda" would, as Attorney General Eric Holder put it, produce "a reaction in the larger community that would have prevented

---

14   Ibid., 87.
15   Joseph F. Lawless, "La Storia dei Mascherari—Nietzsche, Deleuze, and the (Un)masking of Subjectivity," *Nietzsche (13/13) blog*, December 6, 2016, blogs.law. columbia.edu.

the things you wanted to do."[16] The result, by the end of Obama's second term, was a forestalled black agenda and the unimpeded political ascendency of white nationalism.

Where Mbembe updates Fanonian psychiatric politics for a politics of psychosexual enmity—writ large in white hegemony's curtailing of black civil liberties, in policing apparatuses of security societies, and in international juridical institutions tailored to the latest forms of ethnonationalist racism—Alexander G. Weheliye makes the clinical Fanon newly relevant to contemporary critical race studies. Though he does not engage with the psychiatric writings directly (many were, until recently, unpublished or discredited on account of their controversial support for electroshock treatment and subordination of psychoanalysis to neuropsychiatry), Weheliye arguably sources his concept of *habeas viscus* from Fanon's theories of dermal subjectivation.

Fanon's 1951 thesis, "Altérations mentales, modifications caractérielles, troubles psychiques et déficit intellectual dans l'hérédo-dégénaration spino-cérébelleuse," commences with an epigraph attributed to Nietzsche's *Zarathustra* (but which in fact hails from an early version of *Ecce Homo* and is only partially cited).[17] Nietzsche's full phrase was "Ich will das höchste Misstrauen gegen mich erwecken: ich rede nur von *erlebten* Dingen und präsentiere nicht nur Kopf-Vorgänge" (original emphasis), which may be freely translated: "I seek to arouse the greatest suspicion against myself: I only speak of things I experienced and don't just present processes of the head." Fanon cites only the second part of the sentence: "Je ne parle que de choses vécues et je ne représente pas de processus cérébraux" (literally parsed as: "I speak only of things lived, and I do not represent cerebral processes").[18] The allusion here to "choses vécues" resonates in the title

---

16   Eric Holder, as cited by Michael D. Shear and Yamiche Alcindor, "Finding his Voice on Race," *New York Times*, January 15, 2017, 1.

17   Frantz Fanon, "Altérations mentales, modifications caractérielles, troubles psychiques et déficit intellectual dans l'hérédo-dégénération spino-cérébelleuse: A propos d'un cas de maladie de Friedreich avec délire de possession," in *Écrits sur l'aliénation et la liberté*, 168.

18   Friedrich Nietzsche, *Kritische Studienausgabe*, as cited by Jean Khalifa, "Fanon, psychiatre révolutionnaire," in *Écrits sur l'aliénation et la liberté*, 147.

of a 1951 essay published in *Esprit*—"L'expérience vécue du moi," later reprised as a chapter title in *Black Skins, White Masks*—in which "l'expérience vécue" was famously mistranslated by Charles Lam Markmann as "the fact of blackness." According to the interpretation offered by Ronald A. T. Judy, the expression "lived experience" had an ambiguous status in Fanon—with tension, first, between "the factual" as "in-itself, independent of consciousness" and the factual as "in-itself-for-consciousness"; and second, between factuality and "lived-experience," where the latter is taken to designate no objective event, but "a reality" or "process in which objects acquire their status as such for-consciousness."[19] Regardless of how we read the finer points of *vécue*, whether "in-itself" or "for-consciousness," the arc that leads from the Nietzschean *erlebten Dingen* to the Fanonian variants of *chose vécue* and *l'expérience vécue* brings us to a concept of material-subjective ontology linking Fanon's thesis to his career-long ambition to invent sociotherapies grounded in lived life and responsive to racial difference (rather than focused, as was neuropsychiatry at the time, on brain lesions). The thesis served as a dress rehearsal for Fanon's introduction of the problem of black alienation into white neuropsychiatry, and on this point, it is relevant that Fanon's first title for *Black Skin, White Masks* was "An Essay for the Disalienation of Blacks." This early work cast aside ethnopsychiatric *idées reçues*— notions of "primitive mentalities," or "dependency complexes"—that were nothing more than racist constructions congealed into History. "History," Fanon wrote in his thesis, "is little more than the systematic valorization of collective complexes." ("Nous montrerons alors que l'Histoire n'est que la valorization systématique des complexes collectifs.")[20] To negate the valorization of this History, he borrowed from Karl Jaspers a notion of historicity as "immanent reality," which fosters the examination of instances of subjectivation in real time. This heuristic may well have led Fanon to the epic discovery—precipitated by the interpellation "Tiens, un nègre!"—of the triplex "racial

---

19   For an analysis of this mistranslation, see Ronald A. T. Judy's essay "Fanon's Body of Black Experience," in *Fanon: A Critical Reader*, eds. Lewis R. Gordon et al (Oxford: Blackwell, 1996), 53–4.

20   As cited by Jean Khalifa, "Fanon, psychiatre révolutionnaire," *Écrits sur l'aliénation et la liberté*, 140.

epidermal schemata"; a self in three places: "occupying here, moving toward the other, and not there, because rendered transparent, opaque, disappeared." ("J'occupais de la place. J'allais à l'autre ... et l'autre évanescent, hostile mais non opaque, transparent, absent, disparaissait.")[21]

George Yancy underscores the portent of this discovery for theories of corporeal subjectivation. Commenting on the powerful invocation that closes *Black Skin, White Masks*—"My final prayer: O my body, make me always a man who questions!"—Yancy observes that Fanon "appeals to something that is beyond abstract political rights discourse. He appeals to his own body, something concrete and immediate. Fanon asks of his body not to allow him to be seduced by forms of being-in-the-world that normalize violence and dehumanization."[22] What Yancy identifies is the all-important category of the Fanonian soma: integral to Weheliye's construct of *habeas viscus*, it is an order of inscription that concentrates on racial subjectivation at every level of embodiment, extending the referential range of flesh to include viscosity, blood, saliva, taste, streams of life, intestinal viscera, and neurochemistry. Deferring to Fanon, and in tune with Silvia Wynter, Weheliye writes,

> Since the being of nonwhite subjects has been coded by the cultural laws in the world of Man as pure negativity, their subjectivity impresses punishment on the neurochemical reward system of all humans, or in the words of Frantz Fanon: "My body was returned to me spread-eagled, disjointed, redone, draped in mourning on this white winter's day" ... Political violence plays a crucial part in the baroque techniques of modern humanity, since it simultaneously serves to create not-quite-humans in specific acts of violence and supplies the symbolic source material for racialization.[23]

---

21   Fanon, *Black Skin, White Masks*, 90; *Peau noire, masques blancs*, 112.

22   George Yancy, "The Perils of Being a Black Philosopher," interview with Brad Evans, *New York Times,* April 18, 2016, nytimes.com.

23   Alexander G. Weheliye, *Habeas Viscus: Racializing Assemblages, Biopolitics, and Black Feminist Theories of the Human* (Durham, NC: Duke University Press, 2014), 28. Weheliye cites the Richard Philcox translation of *Black Skin, White Masks* (New York: Grove Atlantic, 2008), 93.

Working off of Hortense Spillers's phrase "hieroglyphics of the flesh," Weheliye conceives of flesh as something that supersedes legal notions of body as container of an individuality to which the subject is entitled:[24]

> If the body represents legal personhood qua self-possession, then the flesh designates those dimensions of human life cleaved by the working together of depravation and deprivation. In order for this cruel ruse to succeed, however, subjects must be transformed into flesh before being granted the illusion of possessing a body.[25]

The crux of depravation and deprivation, the conjoining of sexuality and political violence (crucial to Fanon's diagnostics of colonial violence), compose what Weheliye dubs the "pornotrope," localized in titillating sadomasochistic fantasias of rape and beating that produce surplus enjoyment from afflictions centered on the captive body. Though such enactments may pass under the moral cover of consciousness-raising and political good intentions, the effects of objectification, dehumanization and alterity, induced by the spectacle of violence, rebound, and in doing so they reproduce cycles of race violence. Pornotroping is rampant in literary and visual stagings of slavery; as Weheliye notes, hardly any "imagining of slavery exists without at least one obligatory scene of gratuitous whipping, branding, boiling."[26] On this point, we can fast-forward through a history of cinema from D. W. Griffith's 1915 *Birth of a Nation*, to blaxploitation films of the '70s, to Haile Gerima's *Sankofa* (analyzed in some detail by Weheliye), to, most recently, Quentin Tarantino's *Django Unchained*, Steve McQueen's *Twelve Years a Slave*, and Nate Parker's *The Birth of a Nation*. Each instance of the genre harks back to examples cited by Fanon—*Strange Fruit* and *Uncle Remus*—in which the black subject is portrayed "as the keeper of the impalpable gate that opens into the realm of orgies, of bacchanals, of delirious sexual sensations"; and in

---

24 See Hortense Spillers's groundbreaking essay "Mama's Baby, Papa's Maybe: An American Grammar Book" *Diacritics* 17 (2): 64–81.

25 Ibid., 39.

26 Ibid., 97.

which he or she acts as an incentive to white fantasies of masochism that involve "going to 'houses' in order to be beaten by Negroes."[27]

Pornotroping locates "deviant sexuality and slavery beyond the reach of liberal democracy" and condemns slave flesh to the serial reproduction of "elusive" desubjectivations.[28] "What the pornotrope contributes to the theorization of modern sociopolitical subjectivity," Weheliye argues, "is its freeing and setting in motion of the viscous deviances—the detours, digressions, and shortcuts that authorize violence as a vital layer in the attires of modern sovereignty."[29] Taking on the Deleuzean-Guattarian notion of "assemblage," Weheliye indentifies pornotroping as a scopically driven "racializing assemblage" denoting "black suffering in enslavement and beyond."[30] "Assemblage" is a productive category for Weheliye in part because of its departure from Deleuze and Guattari, for whom the term referred to neutral bodies contoured by the hydraulics of forces and flows. He writes,

> By asking neither how racialized impurity is articulated within a given adjudication of racial categories (or what counts as racial hybridity and what does not) nor whose interests are served by the adjudication of racial categories, Deleuze and Guattari foreclose the conceptual reflection of the ways racialization and different axes of domination cooperate in founding racializing assemblages.[31]

Once micropolitical assemblage is literally "*fleshed out* in law" it supplies the terms necessary to comprehend the reproduction of "the curse of color." Weheliye thus gives voice to a renewed Fanonism, with *habeas viscus* featured as the locus of a raced micropolitics grounded in political violence: "an articulated assemblage of the human (viscus/flesh) borne of political violence, while at the same time not losing sight of the different ways the law pugnaciously adjudicates who is deserving of personhood and who is not (habeas)."[32] "Contrary to

---

27   Fanon, *Peau noire, masques blancs*, 177.
28   Weheliye, *Habeas Viscus*, 110.
29   Ibid., 112.
30   Ibid., 110, 116.
31   Ibid., 37.
32   Ibid., 16.

bare life and habeas corpus," Weheliye stipulates, habeas viscus "does not have as its prerequisite the comparative tabulation of suffering, the suspension of racial caesuras in the state of exception, or the transcendence of the flesh."[33] As it moves away from a juridical/biopolitical model of life (specifically, the implicit equation of life and law in Agamben's notion of "bare life"), *Habeas viscus* harks back to the soma evoked in *Black Skin, White Masks*; emulsifying its bulwarks of *ressentiment*, its imagos of corporal punishment, humiliation and enmity sociogenically scored on the body and the psyche of black humanity. The book sets in motion *enfleshed* grammars of freedom and *viscous deviances*—"the detours, digressions, and shortcuts that authorize violence as a vital layer of the attires of modern sovereignty"—positioning them inside rather than outside politics, where "practices, existences, thoughts, desires, dreams and sounds" persist "in the law's spectral shadows."[34]

---

33   Ibid., 39.
34   Ibid., 112, 137, 132. my italics. On the mobilization of "viscous" politics see too, Gilles Châtelet, *To Live and Think Like Pigs: The Incitement of Envy and Boredom in Market Democracies*, trans. Robin Mackay (New York: Sequence Press, 2014).

II. SCENES OF OBSTRUCTION

Impolitic

Impolitic, whether used as an adjective or, neologistically, as a noun ("the impolitic"), hardly stands out as a high-performing political concept or premier Untranslatable on the order of the *citoyen-sujet*, *partisano*, subaltern, party hack, "unpolitical man" (as in Thomas Mann's 1918 *Betrachtungen eines Unpolitischen*, [Reflections of an Unpolitical Man]), or *Der Untertan* (the title of Heinrich Mann's 1914 novel, rendered as "patriot," "loyal subject," or "man of straw"). But in the way that I am interested in marking it, "impolitic" becomes a supremely political term for the messy space between policy and political theory, and for speech that conveys extreme incivility from inside political institutions. It is necessarily positioned in dialectical relation to the *politic*, itself historically grounded in the "manner" of Aristotle's teaching protocols; those technes of *phronesis* (practical reason, regimes for what is useful for living) that Thomas Pangle discerns in the "sinuously instructive path" of Aristotle's "public theo-rizing about political practice" in the *Politics*:

> We cannot learn the most important lessons the philosopher seeks to teach, about both political theory and political practice, and about the fraught relation between theory and practice, unless we maintain a constant attentiveness to the politic and exemplary *manner* in which he reaches out to, and enters into dialogue with, potential students—who he knows to be of varying abilities and needs, and embedded in or contending with divergent and clashing regime-contexts.[1]

---

1   Thomas Pangle, *Aristotle's Teaching in the* Politics (Chicago, IL: University of Chicago Press, 2013), 1.

Building on the psychodynamics of "manner" in the context of "public theorizing" and "clashing regime-contexts," I would argue that "impolitic," rendered as a substantive, is called up for its potential to articulate relations between micropolitics and psychopower that are both resident in and outside of classical political theory and political philosophy. It refers to the political uses, on both the right and the left, of insolence, impertinence, discourtesy, truculence, tactlessness, and intractability as well as a particular skill in the art of timing the political.

The Tea Party playbook richly illustrated the first sense of the impolitic during the Obama years. Consider, for instance, South Carolina House Representative Joe Wilson's "You lie!" shouted out during a 2009 speech by President Obama; Missouri Representative Todd Akin's campaign-killing reference to "legitimate rape"; presidential candidate Mitt Romney's "47 percent" reference to a putatively freeloading portion of the electorate, captured on video at a Florida fundraiser and virally disseminated by *Mother Jones* magazine; Romney's clueless reference to "whole binders full of women"; House Speaker John Boehner's sour impassivity and "activist doing" of doing nothing; Texas Senator Ted Cruz's comparison of Obamacare to Nazism, fourteen-hour filibuster on the Senate floor, and facial expressions of contempt aimed at Chuck Hagel during the nomination hearings for defense secretary. Frank Bruni's description of Cruz offers a thumbnail of the impolitic politician:

> He's an ornery, swaggering piece of work. Just six weeks since his arrival on Capitol Hill, he's already known for his naysaying, his nitpicking and his itch to upbraid lawmakers who are vastly senior to him, who have sacrificed more than he has and who deserve a measure of respect, or at least an iota of courtesy . . . Ted Cruz typifies the knee-jerk belligerence that blots his party.[2]

"Impolitic" signifies *not* politic; contrary to, or wanting in policy; unwise; imprudent; indiscreet; inexpedient; undiplomatic, as in, an

---

2   Frank Bruni, "The G.O.P.'s Nasty Newcomer," *New York Times*, February 15, 2013, nytimes.com.

impolitic ruler, law, or measure. Edmund Burke emphasizes measure: "The most unjust and impolitic of all things, unequal taxation."[3] We might today speak in such terms of a grossly impolitic budget sequestration or, in a more general way, of impolitic economic divergences and laws of averages based on standard deviation in statistics and probability theory.

In the British tradition, "impolitic" connotes the obverse of tact, itself assigned renewed political focus by David J. Russell as he examines how the English essayist Charles Lamb helped define "a tactful social style," in terms of "a democratizing 'feel[ing] [one's] way'" posed against "the Utilitarians' democratizing transparency and privileging of method."[4] Lamb, Russell argues, was concerned with

> the conditions of possibility for a sociability in which no party is diminished and in which multiple ways of life may thrive. To this end, tact proposes less knowing forms of kindness; it resists the codification of social laws and the pinning of individuals to fixed meanings. It is an ethic of the ad hoc, continually rereading and rewriting the social.[5]

By the end of the first half of the nineteenth century, however, tact became in Russell's view a form of the Political, transitioning in meaning from "*politesse* to politics." An improvisatory, pragmatic art of workaround and managed spontaneity, tact is valued for a reactivity that optimizes semiotic cues produced in social situations. Tact "allows metaphor to stay on the move, [and] prevents meaning from congealing into a coercive demand for concession to a single consensus."[6] In its modern, utilitarian guise, tact came to reject soft diplomacy and empathic social feeling. It hewed to a Benthamite model of discursive indifference and impersonality, according to which (and I again quote Russell), "social and political 'sanction' could remain neuter ... [and]

---

3 *Webster's Revised Unabridged Dictionary*, ed. Noah Porter (Plainfield, NJ: MICRA, Inc., 1996), 736.
4 David J. Russell, "'Our Debt to Lamb': The Romantic Essay and the Emergence of Tact," *English Literary History* 79:1, 180.
5 Ibid., 180.
6 Ibid., 185.

everyday language . . . [could be] purged of its unfortunate accretions of value hierarchies."[7] Bentham, he reminds us, even "proposed replacing common words that were loaded with emotional and social bias with more neutral counterparts."[8] The impolitic, placed in this historical context, would be conceivable as a politicized tactlessness that shares with tact the need to negotiate the zone between Romantic *Gefühl* and utilitarian functionalism. At once a mechanism for regulating tactlessness and an instrument for desublimating the latent insecurity underwriting even the most casual, routine political transactions, the impolitic also qualifies as a crucial constituent of what Roberto Esposito characterizes as "the immunitary logic of the 'democratic game.'"[9] In his discussion of threats to individual boundaries in an "anthropological frame . . . dominated as it is by the principle of fear and the persistence of insecurity," Esposito contends that "politics itself ends up resembling an art of diplomacy that conceals a relationship of natural enmity in courteous forms of etiquette, tact, and civil behavior."[10]

The impolitic, whether identified with the dialogic controls of self-governant rhetoric (Aristotle's *politic*), or the destabilizing effects of unruly political speech or incivility (Plato), is sharply distinguished from Esposito's ontologically driven theory of the "impolitical" (*l'impolitico*). Esposito's "impolitical" foregrounds the unrepresentable in politics as we know it. Departing from Thomas Mann's *Betrachtungen eines Unpolitischen* (Reflections of an Unpolitical Man), which projected an image of Germany beyond the conflict between socialism and liberalism, as well as from Simone Weil's concepts of "decreation" and "immanence" ("pure being and nothing more"), Esposito situates *l'impolitico* in that which remains obstinately other to politics, in that which refuses politics elevated to the level of values. Moving beyond Carl Schmitt's critique of the depoliticizing effect of modernity on institutions (the polis's loss of legitimacy as the theologized modern state becomes detached from substance and organized around empty claims), the category of *l'impolitico* embraces a

---

7   Ibid., 201.
8   Ibid.
9   Roberto Esposito, *Terms of the Political: Community, Immunity, Biopolitic*, trans. Rhiannon Noel Welch (New York: Fordham, 2013), 39–40.
10   Ibid., 40.

counter-theory and a counter-history of modernity; not in the sense of an impossible return to what was before, but in the sense of a radical questioning of the Political—a confrontation of the Political with its aporetic origin in *communitas*. Between a theological conception of politics as the salvation of humanity and a purely technical, administrative conception, Esposito, in *Categorie dell'impolitico* (Categories of the impolitical) refers to a different possibility which certain authors of the twentieth century—from Elias Canetti to Simone Weil to Georges Bataille—were able to grasp, though not to define precisely.[11] Unassimilable to all forms of depoliticization or antipolitics, the perspective of the "impolitical" constitutes the strongest, most radical (and exceptional) modality in which politics can be thought, in a phase where all the traditional terms—liberty, community, power— seem to have lost traction.[12] In his *Nove pensieri sulla politica*, Esposito reaches for a Bataille-inflected injunction: "Place the limits of the political at the center, and exit thus from the pregiven suppositions of political philosophy."[13] If this sounds a bit like the familiar argument about the unrepresentability of democratic principle (whether in the guise of juridical equality, or delegation of power), that is because it is: the "impolitical" is identified as an aporia, as non-sense, or as a limit condition that describes why democracy will always be incomplete; it is an infinite incompleteness positioned as the complement to a myth of organic community. Whereas, as Étienne Balibar has pointed out, Schmitt exposed the crisis of political representation, or the representability of political community as an end of secularization and as the neutralization of the Political, Esposito reclaims this negation.[14]

Drawing on Nietzsche and Bataille, Esposito retrieves the negation or nothingness at the heart of normative politics, which depends

---

11   Roberto Esposito, *Categories of the Impolitical*, trans. Connal Parsley (New York: Fordham University Press, 2015).

12   Roberto Esposito, *Categorie dell'impolitico* (Bologna: Il Mulino, [1988]1999).

13   Ibid., 13. See too, Andreas Kalyvas's attempt to reinperate, via Schmitt's creative constitutent power, a "politics of the extraordinary" capable of refounding radical democracy. *Democracy and the Politics of the Extraordinary* (Cambridge: Cambridge University Press, 2008).

14   Étienne Balibar, "Qu'est-ce que la philosophie politique? Notes pour une topique" in *La proposition de l'égaliberté* (Paris: PUF, 2010).

on mystified expressions of value and totality. Esposito follows Nietzsche in seeking to suspend the absolutes that guarantee hierarchies of value and authorize biopolitical models of autoimmunity. He assigns a special role to the *munus* ("understood as the law of reciprocal giving or donation") in immunization.[15] The common *munus* in *communitas* is the "empty spot around which community takes form . . . like a 'nothing in common,' calling into question the subjective logic of the presupposition: rather than being presupposed, the subjects in common are exposed to that which deprives them of their status as such."[16] While Esposito's *l'impolitico* extends the promise of *communitas* defined by amity, living-with, a concept of the subject as *in-dividu* (which is to say, *in-dividuation* and the surrender of all pretension to totality), its constant return to the "nothing" in what is common causes it to veer towards an ascetic worldliness remote from "any really existing mode of politics, whether communist or fascist, liberal or anarchist" (as Bruno Bosteels has noted)—or, I would add, from the sphere of unexceptional politics.[17]

In *Living Thought: The Origins and Actuality of Italian Philosophy*, Esposito positions *l'impolitico* as that which exposes the ontological

---

15   Roberto Esposito, *Living Thought: The Origins and Actuality of Italian Philosophy*, trans. Zakiya Hanafi (Stanford, CA: Stanford University Press, 2012), 256.

16   Ibid.

17   Bruno Bosteels, *The Actuality of Communism* (London and New York: Verso, 2011), 224. Bosteels characterizes the withdrawn aspect of Esposito's *impolitico* as an "ultrapolitical" position discernible in the "impasse" between being political and thinking politics. He writes, "The ambition, in a certain sense, is neither apolitical nor anti-political but rather ultrapolitical: more radically political, in any event, than any really existing mode of politics, whether communist or fascist, liberal or anarchist . . .

Paradoxically, this radicalization is enabled by the very same impasse from which the impolitical seeks to escape, namely, the fact that, because of 'the increasing differentiation between politics and thought,' politics as such can no longer be thought, if ever this was possible in the first place, from within politics. To the contrary, what is needed to think politics is a minimal distance, a step back: precisely the step marked by the added prefix. Esposito thus can speak of 'the dialectic between "political" and "impolitical,"' whereby "impolitical" means neither an apolitical or antipolitical attitude but rather the space of a form of thinking from where alone, by contrast, the sphere of politics could be thought,' for indeed 'the place from where to think politics cannot itself be political. It must remain separate and delayed with regard to real politics, and it must be safeguarded as such, in its "modern impoliticity," especially in critical situations such as the present'" (224).

negation at the heart of political efficiency: "Devoid of an ontological foundation and any transcendental finalities, political action is flattened into a technical ability to simply manage what is in existence."[18] But then, the category becomes more ambivalent, serving as "both the critical counterpoint to this entropic movement and its silent witness."[19] The impolitical embodies an irresolvable contradiction:

> By not allowing itself to take on a positive form—which would make it an alternative or opposing entity to the reality of politics—on the basis of its own negative status, it ends up affirming what it should be differentiating itself from. From this point of view ... when the impolitical tends to infinity, it coincides with the same political realism that was taken to its most radical form by Machiavelli ... Contrary to all political philosophies of a normative type, the impolitical adopts the Machiavellian point of view of those who recognize no reality other than the effectual one of the conflict between powers and interests.[20]

Here we see the "impolitical" used as a synonym for a "realism" (called Machiavellian), a realism that recurs to struggles between life forces of power, and to the vanishing subject of politics. Esposito associates this with the "mundanization" of the subject, a political subject that sets off the *mundus* in *munus*; that is, it exemplifies a phenomenology of existence, or brute force of living, attuned to a commons of the political scene (the refractive, agonistic, dissensual space of the polis, or Pnyx, the site of monthly assembly and opening to direct action) and capable of transforming existing structures of biopolitical autoimmunity.

From Esposito's concept of the "impolitical," a pulsing exercise in "living thought," propelled along by the "positively inexistent locus" of the Nietzschean "'nothing [nulla]'—or 'no,'" we extract something specific for a future use of the term "impolitic," namely, the tempo and rhythmic unbalancing of contrarian articulations.[21] French

---

18 Esposito, *Living Thought*, 224.
19 Ibid.
20 Ibid., 225.
21 Ibid.

definitions of *l'impolitique* emphasize timing in the art of political calculation: imprudence, the inopportune, injudiciousness. From the literary dictionary *Littré* come the notions of bad governance and defective sovereignty: "*impolitique*: adj. Qui est contraire à la bonne, à la saine politique, soit dans le gouvernement d'un État, soit même dans la conduite privée. Une conduite, une démarche impolitique" (that which is contrary to good, healthy government, whether state government or private conduct. A conduct, an impolitic demeanor). "Une démarche impolitique," an impolitic conduct, runs the gamut from social fumbling to the "the most radical gesture," as typified by the Situationist scandal in which the Lettrist Serge Berna, dressed as a Dominican priest, entered Notre Dame during Easter mass and read a passage from Nietzsche on the Death of God or, more recently, by Pussy Riot's viral video "Punk Prayer—Mother of God, Chase Putin Away!" A strongly impolitic way of doing politics connotes gestures of refusal, non-cooperation and civil disobedience. It mobilizes a tactics of tactlessness that encompasses the right to offend and the rude-boy maneuvers of rogues and *voyous*. It assaults conventions of *bienséance*, good taste, and liberal tolerance with obscene gestures and nasty retorts. It points to instances of violent *disaffiliation* or disidentification with a community, a *habitus* of citizenship, a select political estate, a given set of identitarian affiliations.[22]

In Alain Badiou's hypertranslation of Plato's *Republic*, Thrasymachus and Glaucon perform the impolitic as a reactionary mode of pugilistic *ressentiment*. Thrasymachus denigrates Socrates as a sycophant and "idiotic hairdresser" ("un coiffeur débile").[23] He cuts him off, dismisses his responses as Socratic verbiage, and subjects him to profane insult: "As far as I'm concerned, if your nurse had done a better job of wiping you, your asshole wouldn't be as full of shit as your speech."[24] Glaucon's onslaughts are less crude, but more destabilizing.

---

22 See Étienne Balibar's discussion of Hegelian *Sittlichkeit*, in *Violence and Civility*, 112–14.

23 Alain Badiou, *La République de Platon* (Paris: Libraire Arthème Fayard, 2012), 53.

24 Ibid., 57. Translation my own. For a variation, see Susan Spitzer: "It's just that, in my opinion, your nanny ought to do a better job wiping your bottom if it's as shitty as your argument!" Alain Badiou, *Plato's Republic. A Dialogue in 16 Chapters*,

His skepticism registers as a "surprise attack" that catches Socrates off guard:

— So, Socrates, since I approve of your account of the innumerable benefits of our communism, let's not discuss it any further. Let's focus the whole argument now on the two unresolved issues. One: is such a system of government possible? Two: if so, where, when, and how?

Socrates, caught off guard, set his glass down:

— My goodness! he exclaimed. That was some surprise attack you just launched on my argument! Don't you ever grant extenuating circumstances to someone who's hesitant? From the start of our discussion I just barely escaped the devastating effects of a theoretical tidal wave concerning my feminism; I drowned in another about the family; and now here you are—granted, without realizing it—unleashing the most enormous and dangerous of all tidal waves of this sort against me! Once you've witnessed it, you'll be more than willing to grant me extenuating circumstances. You'll understand my hesitations, my fear not only of putting forward such an extremely paradoxical idea, but of completely defending it as well.

— The more you try to dodge the issue, the less likely we'll be to put up with your not telling us how our fifth system of government can come about in reality. Stop wasting our time: speak![25]

What Badiou gleans from Socrates' adversaries are modes of discursive *impolitesse* whose traits are incivility, brutality, mockery, defensive posturing, a refusal to listen, and autocratic impatience. These attitudes acquire a political and theoretical currency that surpasses their narrative value as descriptions of obstructionism. Dialectically, they produce the counter-figure of a Socratic Bartleby ("I would prefer not to"), who effects a detourned "strategy of refusal" (the expression is Mario Tronti's) that forecasts an autonomist politics of organized passivity: waiting, stymied work orders, and an assembly absent its organizational *dirigeants*.

---

trans. Susan Spitzer (New York: Columbia University Press, 2012), 25.
25   Alain Badiou, *Plato's Republic*, 163.

The impolitic functions ambivalently as the modus operandi of the disciplined militant and the bumptious ideologue. George W. Bush laced his speech with calculated insults that often came packaged in the form of insult, gaffe, or amphiboly, the last, a structure of ambivalent syntax that naturalizes logical fallacies and double binds within a singular grammar. Here is W. defining the impolitic in utterances that may be characterized as passive-aggressive, willfully tone-deaf amphibolies:

> Our enemies are innovative and resourceful, and so are we. They never stop thinking about new ways to harm our country and our people, and neither do we. (Washington, DC, August 5, 2004)
>
> For every fatal shooting, there were roughly three non-fatal shootings. And, folks, this is unacceptable in America. It's just unacceptable. And we're going to do something about it. (Philadelphia, PA, May 14, 2001)
>
> You know, one of the hardest parts of my job is to connect Iraq to the war on terror. (interview with CBS News's Katie Couric, September 6, 2006)

What makes these comments politically compromising is not so much that they allow us to hear a political unconscious speaking (and they certainly do), but that they present language as a potentially AWOL medium. The spectacle of "unsafe sense"—runaway meanings, the impossibility of securing language festering at the heart of global projects of securitization—provokes complex affective responses: a mélange of hilarity, giddiness, anger, contempt and anxiety. Here the impolitic denotes that uncontrollable aspect of speech acts constitutive of a consequential, if rarely acknowledged, dimension of what sociologist Anthony Giddens terms the "risk society."

The British film *In the Loop*, directed by Armando Iannuci in 2009, satirizes just how high the stakes of this risk are in politics. During a radio interview, the inexperienced cabinet minister Simon Foster makes the off-the-cuff remark that war in the Middle East is "unforeseeable." His political handler, the Scotsman Malcolm Tucker, desperately moves to rectify Foster's faux pas, but the comment is picked up by a warmongering American official, and Foster only digs himself deeper into a hole after he is invited to Washington.

> Simon Foster MP: [On radio] Well, personally, I think that war is unforseeable.
> Malcolm Tucker: [Listening to the radio] Sam! Sam!
> Eddie Mair: [On radio] Unforseeable?
> Simon Foster: [On radio] Yes.
> Malcolm Tucker: No, you do not think that! Sam, I'm going to have to go to International Development and pull Simon Foster's fucking hair.
> [. . .]
> Malcolm Tucker: [To Simon Foster] In the words of the late great Nat King fucking Cole: unforseeable, that's what you are.

Foster's stumble—an interesting one insofar as the very word "unforsee-able" names the structure of impolitic speech—triggers the mechanism of damage control. Malcolm will turn his full thymotic fury on his charges, raining down torrents of invective laced with puns and macaronic barbs. Malcolm is activated as a war machine; and though his job is to resecure language and protect the political status quo, his own particular billings-gate is socially destabilizing. It unleashes a democratizing disrespect toward social hierarchies; it treats everybody equally badly:

> Malcolm Tucker: [On mobile phone] Okay, okay, go ahead and print "unforseeable". See when I tell your wife about you and Angela Heaney at the Blackpool conference, what would be best? An email, a phonecall, what? Hey! I could write it on a cake with those little silver balls: "Your Hack husband betrayed you on October the fourth and congratulations on the new baby." . . . Yeah, maybe it's better to spike it. Yeah, fuckety-bye.
> [. . .]
> Judy: It's a scheduled media appearance by this department's secre-tary of state and therefore falls well within my purview.
> Malcolm Tucker: Within your purview? Where do you think you are, in some fucking regency costume drama?! This is a govern-ment department! Not a fucking Jane fucking Austen novel!

Simon Foster: [Interrupting] Malcolm.

Malcolm Tucker: Allow me to pop a jaunty little bonnet on your
purview and ram it up the shitter with a lubricated horse cock![26]

When Simon Foster displays his political ineptitude with the answer
about war being "unforseeable," he reveals how bound up the impolitic is with political timing: the moment of *kairos*, where, in a split
second, political liability and hazard are assessed, the future is divined,
and the game is either won or lost. Reason of State, in these terms, is
Machiavellian, involving the ability to take the correct measure of the
situation or seize on accidents of experience. This exercise of political
intelligence is not confined to a flash idea or moment of intuitive
genius; it is more like a hyper-consciousness, sixth sense, or canniness
that is refined into a technique of opportunistic self-management. The
"politic" impolitical subject, in this case, demonstrates the ability to
extract maximum utility from unforeseen admixtures of happenstance and self-awareness.

Stendhal may be credited with inventing, in the nineteenth century,
a form of Machiavellian political fiction that made this kind of psychological acumen flush with Reason of State. *The Charterhouse of Parma*
offers an x-ray of this pyschopolitical ratiocination in the character of
Count Mosca, counselor to the Prince of Parma, Ranuce Ernesto IV.
In one brief passage we are schooled in logistical thinking as applied
to the conquest of a younger woman. Mosca is shown turning a sudden
onrush of timidity—registered as a hesitation on the stair—to personal
advantage:

"I cannot," the Count mused, "spend more than half an hour in her
box, recent acquaintance as I am; were I to remain longer, I should
be making a spectacle of myself, and thanks to my age and worse still
to this damned powdered hair, I should have all the attractions of the
old fool in the *commedia dell'arte*." But a further reflection made up
his mind for him: "If she were to leave that box to visit another, I
should be paid as I deserve for the greed with which I am hoarding
such pleasure." [*je serais bien récompensé de l'avarice avec laquelle je*

---

26   *In The Loop, Wikiquote*, en.wikiquote.org.

méconomise ce plaisir] He stood up to go down to the Countess's box, when all of a sudden he felt no further desire to present himself there. "Ah, now here's a pretty mess!" he exclaimed, laughing at himself and stopping on the stairs. "An impulse of authentic timidity —it's been twenty-five years since I've experienced such a thing."

He entered the box with a certain effort of will, and taking advantage, as a man of intelligence, of what had just occurred to him, ["profitant en homme d'esprit de l'accident qui lui arrivait"] he made no effort to seem at ease or to be clever by telling some entertaining story; he had the courage to be shy, he employed his wit in revealing his disturbance without being ridiculous. "If she takes it amiss," he told himself, "I'm lost for good. So! Timid with powdered hair which would be gray without it! But it's all true, so it can only be ridiculous if I exaggerate the fact or boast about it."[27]

In the original French, phrases like "je serais bien récompensé de l'avarice avec laquelle je m'économise ce plaisir" or "profitant en homme d'esprit de l'accident qui lui arrivait" bring out the economistic and actuarial calculations of political intelligence. Mosca extracts profit from the risk of depriving himself of pleasure. He gambles successfully on his own fear that his loss will be another's gain. He games his own psychopolitical system, and in this way, assumes the mantel of the supremely politic subject, avatar for the society of rational choice.

Thus far the impolitic, as I am defining it, has been loosely identified with a *démarche*—a way of proceeding, walking, or talking characterized by impoliteness, tactlessness, speaking out of turn, ill-timed or well-timed *kairos*, and obstructed thought. But one might also associate it with the attitude of cynical reason, identified by Peter Sloterdijk with the figure of a modern Diogenes, at once an outlier and a "lone owl (*kynic*), provocative stubborn moralist, creating mocker, a biting and malicious individualist who acts as if he needs nobody and who is loved by nobody because nobody escapes his crude unmasking

---

27 Stendhal, *The Charterhouse of Parma*, trans. Richard Howard (New York: The Modern Library, 1999), 97–8.

gaze uninjured"—and at the same time, an "intellectual ascetic" (a philosopher like Wittgenstein) who wants

> to force the carelessly garrulous world to repent, this world to which logic and empiricism do not mean ultimate revelations, and that, unaffected in its hunger for "useful fictions," continues to behave as if the sun does, in fact, revolve around the earth and as if mirages of "imprecise" thinking are, in fact, good enough for our practical life.[28]

The point here is to upgrade the impolitic to the status of a political concept that names the principle of political obstruction flowing out of stymied legislative bodies, pointless point-scoring in the mediocracy, attitudes of "kynicism" and theories of political retreat. It also has the function of drawing attention to the way in which throwaway lines and the glancing arrows of the quarrel throw political destiny off course.[29] The impolitic is a term applicable to the instrumentalization of the unforeseeable, which lurks in the recesses of ratiocination or in uncivil exchange. It serves as an all-over rubric for political intelligence applied to the tactics of tactlessness; to irruptions of the political unconscious (missteps, gaffes, amphibolies); and to punctual calculations of statecraft encompassing *kairos*, psychopolitical power leveraging, and profit extraction from the situation at hand. It refers to a divisive politics of grandstanding and interference-running designed to bring history to a standstill. And yet, as a political concept, it also describes procedures of disentrenchment that open up places of entry for inhabitual modes of thinking politically.

---

28 Peter Sloterdijk, *Critique of Cynical Reason*, trans. Michael Eldred (Minneapolis: University of Minnesota Press, [1983] 1988), 35.

29 Jean-Claude Milner, *Pour une politique des êtres parlants: Court traité politique 2* (Paris: Éditions Verdier, 2011), 7, 9.

Disentrenchment

Disentrenchment, as the political-legal theorist and Brazilian politician Roberto Mangabeira Unger marks it, is less dependent than the impolitic on the cunning appropriation of instances of untimeliness and unforeseeable happenstance. In *False Necessity: Anti-Necessitarian Social Theory in the Service of Radical Democracy* (1987), part of a wider project titled *Politics: A Work in Constructive Social Theory,* disentrenchment speaks on behalf of small acts of creative leveraging and answers to Unger's belief in the powers of cumulative gains in emancipation. As a way of doing politics, disentrenchment is yoked to "negative capability"—a concept originally coined by John Keats to designate a state or perception that empties out individual ego through a complete aesthetic orientation to the external object world. Negative capability is politically enlisted to break the patterns of routine deal-making, power-brokering, and lobbying that limit imagination and political experiment: "We must crack the routines of practical life open to the recombinational activity of practical reason," he writes in *False Necessity*; "Practical empowerment requires institutions and preconceptions that permanently weaken social divisions and diminish the arbitrary, recalcitrant just-thereness of our social orders."[1] For Unger, disentrenchment is the best hope against the extreme necessitarianism of contemporary institutions of governance hobbled by their inability to produce either "a credible theory of transformation" or a "persuasive account of the remaking of formative contexts."[2]

---

1   Roberto Mangabeira Unger, *False Necessity: Anti-Necessitarian Social Theory in the Service of Radical Democracy* (London and New York: Verso, [1987] 2004), 283.
2   Ibid., 349.

Like the impolitic, disentrenchment proves capable of scrambling political programs and flouting conventions of appropriateness. Disrobing social life as a masquerade of natural fact (revealing it to be a malleable political artifact), it reinvigorates what Unger calls the "cultural-revolutionary politics of role-jumbling," opening a space for improvisational experience.[3] It breaks down statecraft's immunity to disturbance while sustaining interventionism in the arena of "small p" politics. For Unger, whose background includes a role as a founding member of the Brazilian Democratic Movement Party and a stint in the second administration of Luiz Inácio Lula da Silva, this entails entering the fray of political institutions and debates around closed options, reform cycles, the private-rights complex, the advantage of "not fitting," "routine without reason." The goal is to reawaken what Unger calls, in a very old-fashioned formula that in many ways seems newly resonant, "the senses of spirit."[4]

As a social theory of progressive political democracy that seeks out where and how politics opens up to shifts of position, disentrenchment shares certain aspects with Alberto Moreiras's signal notion of *infrapolitics*. Grounded in the realization that "real politics is not where it says it is, or rarely," infrapolitics mobilizes displacement, small moves of position on the map that de-essentialize concepts of the Political.[5] Infrapolitics marshals leftovers, traces of "factio-temporal experience" that are extra to political determinations.[6] It brings to the "disaffected scene of postpolitics" a repertory of destabilizing operations that erode biopolitical structures from within.[7] As Bruno Bosteels observes, Moreiras "introduces a kind of intimate fracture, a dedomestication, or a point of internal exodus," drawing on a subtractive language of exit, ousting and retreat (*éxodo* [exodus], *ajuste* [adjustment], *desalojo* [ousting, expulsion], *arretramento*

---

3   Ibid., 285, 293.
4   Ibid., 570–2.
5   Alberto Moreiras, Alejandra Castillo et al., "A Conversation with Alberto Moreiras regarding the Notion of Infrapolitics," *Transmodernity*, July 2014, 144, 147.
6   Ibid., 150–3.
7   Bruno Bosteels, "Politics, Infrapolitics, and the Impolitical: Notes on the Thought of Roberto Esposito and Alberto Moreiras," *The New Centennial Review* 10:2, 2010, 205–6, 226.

[withdrawing], *retiro* [retreat]).[8] Unger's notion of disentrenchment diverges from infrapolitics insofar as it refuses withdrawal and retreat. It is closer to Massimo Cacciari's complex notion of the "Unpolitical," which evolved from a Nietzschean concept of political nihilism to a construct of "impracticable" utopia (*intransitabile utopie*: intransitabile, impassible), and from thence, to the practicable politics of a new federalism (based loosely on Cacciari's experience as mayor of Venice and long years serving in the Italian and European parliaments).[9] Cacciari's "unpolitical," though often derided on the left as a failed political praxis, shares with disentrenchment the prospect of a philosophized political *techne*, a *techne* that renews traditions of jurisprudence, as well as programs of planning and projects delimited by geographic localism.

Disentrenchment, as defined by Unger as a challenge to the "exorbitant stability" of politics in the routinized social world, similarly sets store by the untapped resources of jurisprudence, planning and canonical social theory. One important technique for enabling disentrenchment to occur involves re-marking the conventional vocabulary of politics, not with a "new theory" terminology, but with phrases that shift political meanings around, all the while retaining the force and flow of legal reasoning. Unger invites us to imagine, for example, what it would mean to undermine "recalcitrance" (newly marked as a political concept), to unfulfill "self-fulfilling ideas about social life," or to destabilize infrastructure within formative contexts. Throughout *False Necessity*, disentrenchment leans on the vocabulary of architectonics to make the case for weakening foundational assumptions that bind collectivities, group interest, social possibilities, privileges and access to governmental power. When Unger posits that "a reconstructed, practicable version of the petty bourgeois alternative to the dominant industrial style must break down the stark contrast between task-defining and task-executing activities" with the help of the

---

8   Ibid., 226. See also, Alberto Moreiras, *Línea de sombra: El no sujeto de lo politico* (Santiago: Palinodia, 2006).

9   Massimo Cacciari, *The Upolitical: On the Radical Critique of Political Reason*, trans. Massimo Verdicchio (New York: Fordham University Press, 2009). See Alessandro Carrera's introduction, where he discusses the translator's choice of "Impractical Utopia, in English, for the Italian Intransitabili utopie" (9).

non-passive worker, he marshals metaphors of structural engineering and building science.[10] Even the hyphens are functional in this way, mechanically separating the habituality of doing from the definition-ality of tasking. To reimagine what a task is proves to be essential to challenging rational choice as the predominant model of political theory in neoliberal economies.

Disentrenchment proposes a mode of applied politics that retools the language of practical wisdom (*phronesis*) as a spiritual utilitarian-ism that resists turning into normative statecraft. To disentrench, then, is to undertake the disarrangement of social relations, the recu-peration of nonintentional agency (recognizing the hidden potential of unorganized willings), and the imagination of non-foreordained institutions of governance.[11] Unger would have us move the trench through an anti-necessitarianism that pins its hopes on modest gains and gradualist changes in processes of governmentality (typically dismissed as contemptible, reformist compromise or co-optation). His reinscription of social theory refuses to abide the prostration of individual agency to the exigencies of routinized life and labor, enjoin-ing the powers of negative capability to free collective agency from fabricated structures of causality. Unger reclaims "small p" politics for a politics of "small practices" that tap into the resources of poiesis. He heralds a disentrenched vocabulary of politics from *within* institu-tions of governance, a language that—almost surreptitiously—exceeds the bounds of closed lists and closed systems of political thought.

---

10   Unger, *False Necessity*, 257.
11   Ibid., 259–319.

Interference

In his death penalty seminar, Derrida expatiates on the legal rationale offered in Plato's *Laws* for Socrates' condemnation to death, focusing on this passage:

> If he [the ambassador] seems to have returned corrupted, let him keep company with no one, neither young man nor old, in his pretense of wisdom; if he obeys the rulers, let him live as a private citizen; if not, let him die, if he is convicted in the law-court for illicit interference in education and the laws.

Derrida observes:

> The council, the syllagos, receives visitors, consultants, observers, experts returning from abroad where they went to study the customs and laws of other countries. Well, if one of them comes back spoiled or corrupted, if he continues to make a display of his false wisdom, to refer willy-nilly to foreign models and if he does not obey the magistrate, "he shall have sentence of death (tethnatô) if the court convicts him of illicit interference in any matter of education or legislation (peri tēn paideian kai tous nomous)" *Laws* 952d. Once the court of justice has proved that he is intervening wrongly, on behalf of the foreigner, in the formation of the youth and the formation of the laws, he is punished with death.[1]

---

1   Jacques Derrida, *The Death Penalty*, vol. I, trans. Peggy Kamuf, ed. Geoffrey Bennington et al. (Chicago, IL: University of Chicago Press, 2013), 7. Originally published as *Séminaire: La peine de mort*, vol. I, ed. Geoffrey Bennington, et al. (Paris: Éditions Galilée, 2012), 31. The French edition of the *Laws* cited is Platon, *Les Lois*, Libre XII, 951d, *Oeuvres complètes*, trans. and ed. Auguste Diès (Paris: Les Belles Lettres, 1956), 61.

In addition to revealing how the stranger—and by extension the teacher-translator—when held responsible for imparting foreign ideas becomes criminalized, this moment in Plato's *Laws* illuminates core principles of Athenian democracy, political justice and legal custom. The phrase *peri tēn paideian kai tous nomous*, which focuses on the infraction of "illicit interference," or "intervening wrongly," refers to a political subject who, on the one hand, ignores the virtue of political usefulness and behavior of the proper citizen (extolled by Thucydides in the funeral oration of Pericles), and, on the other hand, traduces the ideal of aristocratic non-interference conventionally associated with Odysseus when (as Plato recounts in a myth told by Er in the final book of the *Republic*) his soul chooses to be reborn into a life without public involvement (as "one lying off somewhere that had been neglected by the others").[2]

A footnote by Peggy Kamuf, the translator of Derrida's death penalty seminar, indicates how the Greek phrase becomes a translation flashpoint: "In this quotation, Derrida has significantly modified the published French translation by substituting *d'ingérance illicite* [rendered here as 'illicit interference'] for *de s'immiscer* ['interfering'; A. E. Taylor translates: 'meddling']." The Penguin edition of the *Laws*, translated by the British classicist Trevor J. Saunders, also has "meddling."[3] "Meddling" connotes the character of the busybody, whose latter-day equivalent might be the lobbyist or the quasi-seditious politician; consider Speaker John Boehner's smug defense of his interference in foreign policy with his invitation to Israeli Prime Minister Benjamin Netanyahu to speak to a joint session of Congress,

---

2   In the final book of the *Republic* (narrated, Socrates says, by someone named Er), the souls are choosing the lives in which they will be reincarnated: "[Er said that] by chance the soul of Odysseus had drawn the final lot of all the souls and went forward to make its choice. Remembering the desire for honour of its many former toils it went about its search carefully and for a long time, looking for the life of a man, a private citizen and *apragmôn*, and found only one lying off somewhere that had been neglected by the others, and seeing it said that it would have done the same thing even had it drawn the first lot, and chose that life with delight." Plato, *Republic* 620c–d.

3   Derrida, *The Death Penalty*, 7. The more recent translation by Luc Brisson and Jean-François Pradeau, has "se mêler". *Platon, les lois* (Paris: Garnier-Flammarion, 2006), vol. II, livres VII à XII.

by claiming that it was necessary because, when it comes to terrorism, the president [Obama] "is trying to act like it's not there."

Meddling does not fall not wide of the mark of the French verb *s'immiscer* (to get mixed up in, to fiddle with), selected by Plato's French translator Auguste Diès in the edition used by Derrida. But Derrida wants to ramp up with something stronger than "meddling." As Kay Gabriel informs us, "the Greek word that Derrida re-translates as *ingérance illicite* is πολυπραγμονῶν, *polupragmonôn*, from which πολυπράγμων, *polupragmôn*, the figure of the "busybody," is derived. This busybody runs active interference, to the point of threatening Athenian justice—and thus making sense of the moment in Plato's *Republic* (433a) where Socrates defines justice as "to do one's own task and not to *polupragmonein*."[4] While the *Republic* may run counter to the civic ideology of Athenian democracy, it remains evident that *polupragmonein* is a condemnable offense. It violates the principle of usefulness by implying political involvement in all the wrong ways: it's an impediment to the exercise of power, and, at worst, it exposes power's arbitrary basis. *Ingérance* captures the full thrust of the negative, referring to those who force themselves on the polity. Obstruction of justice, sedition, government shutdown; all these threats to the demos issue from such a term. In its broadest ascription *ingérance* spans *dirigisme* (top-down administration, state autocracy, as in *ingérance étatique*); political inoperability (*désoeuvrement, blocage,* direct action, the politics of *autonomia*); and the impact of the *pharmakon,* the parasitic host, which, introduced into the system, functions like interferon, a compound of protein molecules released by host cells to block viral replication, whose harmful side effects include the triggering of autoimmune disorders.

From the gaps and jumps in translation, from the effort required to reconstruct what is not translated, a greater appreciation of the politics of interference comes to the fore. I think of it as a political theory of the impolitic crossed with subversive pedagogy—itself arising directly out of translation trouble that, on a purely linguistic level, is of course a form of interference with texts, laws of grammar and logic, protocols of the Political, and grooved ways of thinking, articulating, and socially comporting.

---

4   Kay Gabriel, email correspondence, December 28, 2014.

Translation trouble is worth delving into as a means of theorizing political interference. Departing from Derrida's retranslation from the French of Plato's Greek phrase, we thus move full throttle into what it means to run interference, from (as in football) blocking players from the opposing team to secure a way through for the ballcarrier which, when applied to politics, might take the form of aides throwing themselves in harm's way in order to distract public attention from shady maneuvers by their superiors); to procedural acts of parliamentary obstructionism; to tactics of civil disobedience including die-ins, cyber-attacks and data intercepts; to catastrophes of autoimmunity. Each of these political takedowns can be connected to education—specifically, to Socrates' dialogic pedagogy and skepticism towards the educational status quo. As a teacher, Socrates is a *polupragmôn* par excellence, even if, as the *Republic* attests, he is on record opposing interference in affairs of state.

Barbara Cassin has an expression for this translation trouble. She calls it "philosophizing in languages."[5] In the ensemble of her writings on the Pre-Socratics and the Sophists, she developed the construct of the *intraduisible*, "the Untranslatable," to point up the instability of meaning and sense-making, the equivocity of homonymy and amphiboly, the performative dimension of discursive sophistic effects, the risks and rewards of "consistent relativism."[6] Cassin gives herself over to a praxis that involves relinquishing the hold of words and conceptual networks, and engaging fully with the symptomologies that emerge when we keep on (not) translating. For Cassin, what follows from this point is entrance into the labyrinth of Lacanian sophistry, a psychoanalytic doxography in which non-sense is an incontrovertible core of signifying practices that elicit rhetorical workarounds.[7] Psychoanalysis becomes a linguistic process philosophy, present and perpetual.

---

5 Barbara Cassin, "Preface," "Philosophizing in Languages," trans. Yves Gilonne, *Nottingham French Studies* 49:2, 2010, 18.

6 For an overview of her writings in English, see Barbara Cassin, *Sophistical Practice: Toward a Consistent Relativism* (New York: Fordham University Press, 2014).

7 See Barbara Cassin, *Jacques le sophiste: Lacan, logos et psychanalyse* (Paris: EPEL, 2012).

Following Cassin, I have defined "the Untranslatable" not as the name of a concept, but as a dual practice of theoretical interference and workaround; as a praxis of cognizing philologically, deconstructively and politically. The starting point consists of particularities of translational resistance that account for a text's singular unreadability, an effect duly noted, in the case of the Plato's *Laws* for example, by translator Trevor Saunders:

> Plato's Greek in the *Laws* is difficult: emphatic yet imprecise, elaborate yet careless, prolix yet curiously elliptical; the meaning is often obscure and the translator is forced to turn interpreter. How should such an extraordinary text be rendered into English? Any translation which preserved every note of the original would be doomed to failure more surely in the case of the *Laws* than of almost any other classical text: it would be quite unreadable.[8]

The Untranslatable imposes an exigent relation on the translator; it makes impossible demands, bringing the translation to the brink of failure, or brooking that failure in translations that never materialize.

In his review for the *London Review of Books* of the *Dictionary of Untranslatables: A Philosophical Lexicon*, Christopher Prendergast took issue with the notion of the Untranslatable. Noting that the English editors (myself, Jacques Lezra and Michael Wood) chose to foreground the term in the main title, whereas it appeared in the subtitle in the original French edition, Prendergast (like David Bellos, Lawrence Venuti, and other noted critics in the translation field) deemed the Untranslatable to be a red herring:

> This is a term that conservative fundamentalists like; it puts up barriers and ring-fences cultures. What's it doing here? A short (and uncharitable) answer is: not very much. Apter claims that 'it is by no means self-evident what "untranslatability" means'. But that is far from being self-evidently the case. "Untranslatable" normally means exactly what it says: that which cannot be translated. Cassin wants to

---

8 Plato, *Laws*, trans., introduction by Trevor J. Saunders (London: Penguin, 1970), 39.

deny this: "'untranslatables" in no way implies that the terms in question . . . are not and cannot be translated'. In no way? One possible answer to that is: in every way. There does seem to be here a confusion between the untranslatable and the untranslated. The former is essentialist all the way down (which is why fundamentalists like it), an absolute blockage on transmission. The untranslated is an altogether more open and porous category. It has to do more with difficulty than impossibility ("difficulty" and "difficult" recur often in the actual work of the volume), although not typically of the same order of difficulty as that faced by the translator of poetry (Valéry described this as dancing in chains) or of paranomastic prose (*Finnegans Wake*, while it has been translated into several languages, remains basically untranslatable into anything other than what it itself is made of, "Eurish").[9]

While it should be acknowledged that much of what the Untranslatable does concerns the navigation of what Prendergast characterizes as "hits and mis-hits, convergences and divergences, continuities and breaks, incomplete and imperfect translation, or even plain vanilla translation," he fails to take account of its distinctive "abilities" (to borrow Sam Weber's analysis of the role of the persistent suffix -*barkeit* [-ability] in Walter Benjamin's notions of reproducibility, translatability, et cetera). Not a reified essence of linguistic singularity, nor a simple remainder, it refers to how concepts assimilate ways of speaking and being and how ways of speaking and being interfere with concepts. And while the Untranslatable might well be taken as proscriptive, its force of interdiction is hardly reducible to a defense of fundamentalism, universal dogma, political absolutism or censorship. Rather, it operates like interferon, affirming the presence of *Unverständlichkeit*, un-understandability, unintelligibility, and inoperability. The political Untranslatable, in this sense, is what disables the workings of instrumental language, ushering in the "foreign" on a plurilingual surge and injecting the language of the street into the system of the laws.

---

9   Christopher Prendergast, "Pirouette on a Sixpence," *London Review of Books* 37:17, 2015, 35–7.

Experimenting, then, with doing things with political Untranslatables, one is led to further theorize interference within micropolitics. Consider how the word "occupy"—freighted with the connotations of colonial occupation and violent resource extraction in economically vulnerable regions of the planet—was interfered with by "Occupy Wall Street." Something similar happened to the phrase "blocchiamo tutto," which appeared on a Turin wall in 2012 as part of the tag, "Il potere è logistico. Blocchiamo tutto!" (Power is logistic. Let's block everything), a phrase taken as a declaration of war on infrastructure by a range of militant small groups.[10] "Zone" in French has a similar trajectory; normally associated with zones of detention, camps or dangerous neighborhoods, it was transfigured by the acronym ZAD (*zones à défendre*) into a synonym for squatting in fallow property or for actions against environmentally damaging construction projects (which resulted not long ago in the killing of Rémi Fraisse, who was protesting the construction of a dam at Sivens). Consider too, *Maidan*, the Ukrainian term for central square. As Timothy Snyder wrote in the *New York Review of Books* shortly after the Kiev uprising,

> What does it mean to come to the Maidan? The square is located close to some of the major buildings of government, and is now a traditional site of protest. Interestingly, the word *maidan* exists in Ukrainian but not in Russian, but even people speaking Russian use it because of its special implications. In origin it is just the Arabic word for "square," a public place. But a *maidan* now means in Ukrainian what the Greek word *agora* means in English: not just a marketplace where people happen to meet, but a place where they deliberately meet, precisely in order to deliberate, to speak, and to create a political society. During the protests the word *maidan* has come to mean the act of public politics itself, so that for example people who use their cars to organize public actions and protect other protestors are called the *automaidan*.[11]

---

10   Comité invisible, *À nos amis*, 81.
11   Timothy Snyder, "Fascism, Russia, Ukraine," *New York Review of Books* 61:5, 2014.

Maidan in its philology connects Arabic, Greek and Ukrainian notions of public politics. It is site-specific, yet connected transpolitically to places of assembly and occupation all over the world where insurrection erupted: Syntagma Square, Tahrir, Taksim, Madrid's Puerta del Sol, Zucotti Park, Ogawa Plaza in Oakland. It designates a particular instance of competing nationalisms in eastern Europe (Putin's envoy officially denounced "the nationalist-revolutionary terrorist *Maidan*"), as well as strategic solidarity among regionally, ethnically and religiously conflictual groups. It is a lodestone of language politics, as well as a breakout scene of sexual politics, with feminists and LGBT volunteers well represented at hospitals and emergency hotlines. The sexual politics are a particularly important feature of *Maidan*'s untranslatability: for as we know, gay-bashing in Russia is part of a Kremlin-backed effort to galvanize anti-European Union factions—and to force groups that might otherwise be strongly critical of Western neoliberalism into becoming aligned with it. The *Maidan* political map is configured unpredictably according to its case-sensitive retranslation. Keywords are always inflected by language, but most dictionaries of philosophy tend to forget the politics of translation in adopting transhistorical approaches to concepts.

The transiting of *Maidan* and "occupy" to unfixed forms and sites of global interference, ranging from resistance to oligarchic repression to anticapitalist pushback, reminds us that political glossaries and lexicons have a historic role in opposition politics. I have in mind the glossary that Althusser's English translator Ben Brewster appended to *For Marx*. Terms like *alienation, epistemological break, conjuncture, consciousness, contradiction, humanism, ideology, dialectical materialism, practice, problematic*, and *theory* project an encapsulated political program, and it is perhaps for this reason that Althusser gave them close attention. "Thank you for your glossary," he wrote to Brewster; "What you have done is extremely important from a political, educational and theoretical point of view . . . I return your text with a whole series of corrections and interpolations (some of which are fairly long and important, you will see why)."[12] After noting the genealogy of

---

12   Louis Althusser, *Reading Capital: The Complete Edition* (London and New York: Verso, [1965] 2016), 323.

"break" and "problematic," from Gaston Bachelard's early coinage of "epistemological break," to Georges Canguilhem's unsystematic usage, to Michel Foucault's Althusserian appropriation, he underscored the importance of "correction."

Althusser's political activation of theory in the form of an "interfered with" glossary of his own critical lexicon brings to mind Alain Badiou's philosophical lexicon of riot and uprising in *The Rebirth of History* (Le réveil de l'histoire), his response to the Arab Spring. Badiou proceeds through a tripartite typology. The first term, "immediate riot," is defined as a tumultuous assembly of the young, characterized by weak localization and a lack of distinction between universalizable intention and random rage, between demonstrating and pillaging. The second is "latent" or "pre-political" riot, marked by a qualitative extension outward from the local. The example he gives is the emergence of a single slogan endorsed by disparate voices, "Mubarak, clear off!" "Thus is created," Badiou affirms,

> the possibility of a victory, since what is immediately at stake in the riot has been decided ... The movement can persist in anticipation of a specific material satisfaction: the departure of a man whose name—a short while before taboo, but now publicly condemned to ignominious erasure—is brandished.[13]

The third term is "historical riot," and it is closest to reaching the bar of what Badiou recognizes as an event. The event is really an advent, the emergence of an "intervallic period" that reboots the revolutionary sequence by nullifying the "natural harmony between unbridled capitalism and impotent democracy."[14] For the riot to become historical, it must become political, which is to say, come to embody the "subjective sharing of an Idea," and demonstrate that *"The inexistent has arisen."*[15] It must, as it turns out, run interference in the affairs of state. Badiou reprises Mao's injunction issued during the Cultural

---

13   Alain Badiou, *The Rebirth of History: Times of Riots and Uprisings*, trans. Gregory Elliott (London and New York: Verso, 2012), 35.
14   Ibid. 38, 40.
15   Ibid., 56. Italics in the original.

Revolution: "Get involved in the affairs of state!"[16] But he remakes it into a slogan for the new times of insurrection via fragment 2 of René Char's *Feuillets d'Hypnos* where one line rings out as a rallying cry: "Don't linger in the rut of results."[17] ("Ne t'attarde pas à l'ornière des résultats.")[18] One might keep on translating this line as: "Gum up the works of affairs of state! Dare to interfere! Commit the crime of *polupragmonein*!" With each act of translation, from political event to event glossary, from poetry to call to arms, the lexicon of historical riot joins the language of the poets in answer to the query about how to translate the Untranslatable at the very opening of the book: "What is happening to us in the early years of the century—something that would appear not to have any clear name in any accepted language?"[19] Badiou adopts a similar politics of renaming in *The Communist Hypothesis* as he distinguishes four typologies of May '68. Of particular urgency is the need to recall the word "Communism" from its corrupted usage in neoliberal circulation, thus returning it to its signification prime as a word equal to egalitarianism and coincident with the reauthorized right to words and expressions like "the people," "workers," and "the abolition of private property." The recourse to political Untranslatables in this instance is not (as it is with Cassin) a matter of creating political solidarity in and through philosophizing in languages, but a labor of rescuing radical political philology from the censors:

> We have to put an end to linguistic terrorism that delivers us into the hands of our enemies. Giving up on the language of the issue, and accepting the terror that subjectively forbids us to pronounce words that offend dominant sensibilities, is an intolerable form of oppression.[20]

---

16   Ibid., 81.

17   Ibid., 99.

18   Alain Badiou, *Le Réveil de l'histoire* (Paris: Lignes, 2011), 147.

19   Badiou, *The Rebirth of History*, 1.

20   Alain Badiou, *The Communist Hypothesis*, trans. David Macey and Steve Corcoran (London and New York: Verso, 2010), 65. Originally published as *L'Hypothèse communiste* (Paris: Lignes, 2009).

Language is crucial to Badiou's reformulation of the communist hypothesis, as when he translates Guizot's hortatory prescription at the dawning of French capitalism, "Get rich!," as "Live without an Idea!" And from thence, an active retranslation that inverts Guizot's injunction: "Have the courage to support the idea, and it can only be the communist idea in its generic sense."[21]

Ayman El-Desouky has similarly worked the political Untranslatable in his scansion of the early days of the Egyptian Revolution with reference to "the *amāra* on the Square." A term with a long history, *amāra* is recalled in the context of Tahrir as the name for the conflation of political connective agency with aesthetic praxis:

> The terms *amāra* and *amār* have their roots in classical Arabic, origi-
> nally denoting a pile of stones set up in a waterless desert to signal
> the right direction to those who may have lost their way (according
> to alFayrūzābādī's lexicon, *alQāmus almuḥīṭ* and Edward Lane's
> ArabicEnglish Lexicon). *Amāra* has also evolved into denoting signs,
> marks, signposts or elevated ground and has come to indicate an
> appointed time—lexical metaphors rather appropriate for the reso-
> nant revolutionary acts in Tahrir . . .
>
> The specific usages current in Egyptian Arabic have been noted
> by ElSaid Badawi and Martin Hinds in their *Dictionary of Egyptian
> Arabic,* defining it as sign or indication or as evidence of good faith,
> an example of which is given from everyday mundane practice: "give
> me an *amāra* so that your home helper will let me into your flat." This
> example of a social *amāra* captures the potential range of the forms
> of *amāra* as either particular signs or details and information only
> the participants are privy to, or a narrative of an incident known
> only to them. The visual forms of recognition are encapsulated in the
> stock phrase "on his face are the *amārāt* of . . ." (*"ala wishshu
> amārāt . . ."*) The narrative offered in the exchanges, emphasizing a
> shared identity or a common bond, usually begins with the stock
> phrase: "by the *amāra* of . . .," which traverses social boundaries . . .
> The import of this spoken phrase was transmuted into the lexical
> and syntactic patterns of the slogans and the visual iconicity of the

---

21   Ibid., 67.

signs, street art and performances on Tahrir Square, and beyond. Unspoken but extending into the dimensions of social reality, invisibly as in the suggested extension of a gesture, *amāra* constructions offered the forms in which the verbal as well as visual resonances that seemingly individual and disparate acts have struck with the collective Egyptian imaginary.[22]

Referring to Badiou, El-Desouky extends the auguring force of the expression "by the *amāra* of . . ." to something "hitherto untheorized" associated by Badiou with "movement communism" and by Žižek with a "new political reality" posed against "ideological objective reality." Unlike "movement communism" or "new political reality," however, *amāra* is not aporetic; its contents are substantiated by immanent aesthetic practices of connective agency accessed on the oblique of Arabic philology[23] *Amāra* joins a glossary of translational politics responsive to subversive pedagogy and forms of agency afforded by actions in the square; in short, a politics of interference, of *ingérance illicite*.

---

22   Ayman El-Desouky, *The Intellectual and the People in Egyptian Literature and Culture: Amāra and the 2011 Revolution*, (New York: Palgrave Macmillan, 2014), 81-82, 83, 84.

23   In a similar way, the artist Silvia Kolbowski repurposes the aesthetics of "virtuosity" for political work. It is cast as public action "clarified by means of an ancient, but by no means ineffective, category: *virtuosity*—defined as the special capabilities of a performing artist, the activity that finds its fulfillment in itself and exists only in the presence of an audience, without an end product or object which survives the performance." Though the objection could be raised that "virtuosity" fuels capitalist markets of the performing arts, Kolbowski is interfering with the word's semantic purpose, detourning it toward uncapitalized collective experience and connective agency. Silvia Kolbowski, "Do you see what I hear," *Silvia Kolbowski blog*, December 28, 2014, silviakolbowskiblog.com.

Obstinacy

Ostinato, the musical term for what continues, like a *basso continuo*, calls for an obstinate reading. In des Forêts's vocabulary, music is responsible for some of what he calls *les temps forts*—those stressed moments of intensity or exaltation that are often diminished, or lost altogether, upon reaching the paper as we try to inscribe or describe them. They are uncapturable. And yet the writer, reader, listener will persevere, stubbornly, *obstinately*. Like the aftercoming translator.

— Mary Ann Caws, translator's preface
to Louis-René des Forêts, *Ostinato*[1]

Then there is the purposeless obstinacy of the id, in its fixity and incorrigibility. It's hardwired to last. Structurally impervious to modification, indifferent to contradiction, the unconscious is the embodiment of motiveless intransigence in its pure form.

— Rebecca Comay, "Resistance and
Repetition: Freud and Hegel"[2]

The idea of lying flat before a tank, of "going limp" in the face of police power, involves a cultivated capacity to hold a certain position. The limp body may seem to have given up its agency, and yet, in becoming weight and obstruction, it persists in its pose. Aggression is not eradicated, but cultivated, and its cultivated form can be seen in the body as it stands, falls, gathers, stops, remains silent, takes on

---

1   Mary Ann Caws, Translator's Preface, to Louis-René des Forêts's *Ostinato* (Lincoln: University of Nebraska Press, 2002), vii.
2   Rebecca Comay, "Resistance and Repetition: Freud and Hegel," *Research in Phenomenology* 45, 2015, 253.

the support of other bodies that it itself supports. Supported and supporting, a certain notion of bodily interdependency is enacted that shows that nonviolent resistance should not be reduced to heroic individualism.

> — Judith Butler, *Notes Toward a Performative Theory of Assembly*[3]

During the first week of September 2015, Kentucky county clerk Kim Davis, after defying a Supreme Court order to issue marriage licenses to gay couples on the grounds that it violated her Apostolic religious beliefs, retreated to her office and drew the blinds, communicating through her lawyers (as the *New York Times* reported) that she would "*neither* resign *nor* relent." A gay couple, demanding that she confront them face to face, yelled through the closed door that they would continue the fight for their civil right to marry. Through an intermediary Davis replied, "I have *no animosity* toward anyone and harbor *no ill will*. To me this has *never* been a gay or lesbian issue." Casey Davis, her assistant, would also deploy the syntactic stonewall of the double negative: he had, he insisted, "'*not* tried to *prevent*' same-sex marriages but was only acting on his First Amendment rights."[4] Preterition, an affirmation secured through the subtractive logic of "not, not," as in "not resigning, not relenting," "no animosity, no ill-will," "not … preventing," recalls us to Bartleby's signature phrase "I would prefer not to."

Melville's canonical motto, invented in his novella *Bartleby, the Scrivener*, has played host to political resistance tactics ranging across civil disobedience: work stoppage, interference, suspension, and obstruction to obstruction, as in micro-aggressive contestations of micro-aggression in the workplace; lie-ins and die-ins that refute legal indifference to violations of social justice; delegitimations of the capitalist first principle of shareholder hegemony, itself predicated on the abrogated right to a living wage. "I would prefer not to" heralds notions

---

3 Judith Butler, *Notes Toward a Performative Theory of Assembly* (Cambridge, MA: Harvard University Press), 188.

4 Alan Blinder and Richard Pérez-Peña, "Kentucky Clerk Defies Justices on Marriages," *New York Times*, September 2, 2015, A15.

of inoperative, noninstrumental community that expose the limits of existential politics, from Sartrean *engagement* to post-'68 theories of being and event. An incursion into the sphere of ordinary politics— lobbying, scandal-mongering, impeded legislation—the incantatory "formula" poses an alternative micropolitics under the gathering term *ostinato*, borrowed from musical composition to underscore what is Bartlebyesque in forms of protest and mobilized postures of autoimmunity.

Negative articulations, offended meliorism; these are signal features of "Bartleby Politics" in Melville's tale. Bartleby first employs the famous phrase in an unassuming way, but his employer immediately takes it as an offense to his self-regard as a benevolent and indulgent manager:

"Bartleby! Quick, I am waiting."

I heard a slow scrape of his chair legs on the uncarpeted floor, and soon he appeared standing at the entrance of his hermitage.

"What is wanted?" said he mildly.

"The copies, the copies," said I hurriedly. "We are going to examine them. There"—and I held towards him the fourth quadruplicate.

"I would prefer not to," he said, and gently disappeared behind the screen.

For a few moments I was turned into a pillar of salt, standing at the head of my seated column of clerks. Recovering myself, I advanced towards the screen, and demanded the reason for such extraordinary conduct.

"Why do you refuse?"

"I would prefer not to."

With any other man I should have flown outright into a dreadful passion, scorned all further words, and thrust him ignominiously from my presence. But there was something about Bartleby that not only strangely disarmed me, but in a wonderful manner touched and disconcerted me.[5]

---

5   Herman Melville, *Bartleby, the Scrivener: A Story of Wall Street*, in *Benito Cereno, Bartleby, the Scrivener, and the Encantadas* (Stilwell, KS: Digireads, 2005), 60.

The reference to the Old Testament character of Lot's wife, turned into a pillar of salt because she refused to obey God's prophylactic command to resist looking back on the city of Sodom in flames, is especially significant. Unprepared for Bartleby's noncompliance with basic commands, the lawyer is flummoxed. How can he respond to Bartleby's *pharmakon* of weak resistance, which works like a leeched toxin of incapacitation to effectuate sovereign disempowerment? ("Indeed it was his wonderful mildness chiefly, which not only disarmed me, but unmanned me, as it were.")[6] Derrida would identify this syndrome with sovereign autoimmunity in relation to the condition of the United States post 9/11, characterizing as autoimmune America's "War on Terror," in which a state of exception is diffused into all-over, unexceptional war. Bartleby personifies this exceptionalist defeat of sovereign exceptionalism; his weapon of choice is the phatic element of "preference" anomalously introduced into the restricted field of calculated perlocutionary interchange. As Giorgio Agamben notes, "'I would prefer not to' . . . extinguishes the place of reason in the domain of will and potentiality."[7]

> "Bartleby," said I, "Ginger Nut is away; just step round the Post Office, won't you? (it was but a three minute walk,) and see if there is any thing for me."
> "I would prefer not to."
> "You will not?"
> "I prefer not"[8]

This is a speech act that, instead of misfiring is simply obstructed on its path by a change of channel. The language logic that produces meaningful communication is, as Deleuze famously argued, put out of action by another language logic:[9]

> The usual formula would instead be *I had rather not*. But the strangeness of the formula goes beyond the word itself. Certainly it is

---

6   Ibid., 64.
7   Giorgio Agamben, *Potentialities*, trans. Daniel Heller-Roazen (Stanford, CA: Stanford Univeresity Press, 1999), 258.
8   Melville, *Bartleby, the Scrivener*, 63.
9   Gilles Deleuze, *Critique et clinique* (Paris: Seuil, 1993), 95.

grammatically correct, syntactically correct, but its abrupt termina-
tion, *NOT TO*, which leaves what it rejects undetermined, confers
upon it the character of a radical, a kind of limit-function. Its repetition and its insistence render it all the more unusual, entirely so.
Murmured in a soft, flat, and patient voice, it attains to the irremis-
sible, by forming an inarticulate block, a single breath. In all these
respects, it has the same force, the same role as an *agrammatical*
formula.[10]

Bartleby Politics relies on an agrammaticality that singularizes
serial and limitless acts of resistance. It baffles the discursive struts
and logical infrastructures of sovereign force, foregrounding a
psychopolitics distinguished by gridlock, blockage and a host of
other symptoms associated with *stasis*. A key Greek term for both
peace and civil war, predicated on the equilibrating standoff
between equal factions, stasis, as Rebecca Comay has analyzed it,
retains its significance as the armature of theories of political
resistance:[11]

> Stasis forces us to reconsider the opposition of motion and rest. It
> puts the very antithesis of stasis and kinesis into question. Too
> much stability can be destabilizing, while excessive mobility
> produces deadlock. In a medical register, stasis refers to digestive
> sluggishness, circulatory constriction, gastric blockage, constipa-
> tion, the toxic coagulation or clogging of bodily humors, a stagna-
> tion that will eventually throw the whole organism into crisis. In a
> political register, stasis is a kind of hardening or rigidity that can
> precipitate upheaval precisely because in its obduracy, its one-
> sidedness, its refusal to adapt to circumstances, to go with the flow,
> it exposes the rigid armature sustaining the status quo, provoking
> violent counter-reactions and thus forcing latent antagonisms to

---

10   Gilles Deleuze, "Bartleby; or, The Formula," *Essays Critical and Clinical*,
trans. Daniel W. Smith and Michael A. Greco (Minneapolis: University of Minnesota
Press, 1997), 68.
11   See my discussion of "stasis" in relation to the concept of "peace" in *Against
World Literature: On the Politics of Untranslatability* (London and New York: Verso,
2013), 131–7.

the surface. We are *in a state* when our confinement, our stuckness, becomes explosive.[12]

Thus, "Bartleby Politics," broadly construed, names the stasis of stuckness, whether pointing to a defenestration of the Reason of State, a recalcitrant willing affirmed outside institutional frameworks of political agency and decision; or to what Oskar Negt and Alexander Kluge, in their seminal work *History and Obstinacy*, would imagine as a kind of civil war of the subject, riven between the drives of *Enteignung* (capitalized selfhood, the expropriated autonomy of the proletarianized laborer) and *Eigensinn* (willfulness, obstinacy); or to the vacuity of political speechifying, which normalizes self-sabotage, horror vacui, ruts of governance.[13]

In the heyday and aftermath of the Occupy Wall Street movement of 2011, the very name "Bartleby," drafted directly from the gaunt and ghostly Melvillean character, singularized, and made finite, limitless and indeterminate micro-events. We were left with questions: What did OWS actually stand for? Is it over or not? Where did it lead or purposefully "prefer not to" lead? Did it allude to micro-practices involving care, unowned or unbranded efforts to reverse exploitation and destitution? To a metaphysics of divested *Eigentum* (Max Stirner's term for the ego's "ownness")?[14] To a paradigm of "the Political" other than the aporia of the state of exception? To resignation to opaque and

---

12   Rebecca Comay, "Resistance and Repetition: Freud and Hegel," *Research in Phenomenology* 45, 2015, 240.

13   In his introduction to the English edition of *History and Obstinacy*, Devin Fore provides the essential background on Negt and Kluge's notion of *Eigensinn*: "Whenever something is repressed, it become autonomous and intractable, Negt and Kluge observe. Capital's violent expropriation is countered by the subject with obstinacy, *Ent-eignung* with *Eigen-sinn*. Like Marx's old mole, a favorite image of Negt and Kluge, marginalized traits vanish from sight, but, exiled to the hinterlands of the psyche, they do not die. Instead, they mutate and enter into unexpected alliances with other capacities ... The word *Eigensinn*—rendered variously into English as 'autonomy,' 'willfulness,' 'self-will,' and, here, 'obstinacy'—implies a degree of stubborn obtuseness, an imperviousness to directives from above." See Devin Fore, "Introduction," Alexander Kluge and Oskar Negt, *History and Obstinacy* (New York: Zone Books, 2014), 35–6.

14   See Max Stirner, *Der Einzige und sein Eigentum* (1844), in *The Ego and its Own*, trans. Steven Byington, ed. David Leopold (Cambridge, UK: Cambridge University Press, 1995).

pointless modes of political speech, including those that grant money the protected status of free speech? It has often been said that the very *disponibilité* of the name "Bartleby"—its amenability to being claimed by opposing factions on the political spectrum—accounts for its traction. It is hardly hyperbole to assert that Bartleby, the character, outlives all rivals in the long history of political literature (including Plato's Socrates, master of the annoying rejoinder), perhaps because Bartleby, the concept, is synonymous with the obstinacy that a concept performs at specific historical conjunctures.

Bartleby, the Scrivener: A Story of Wall Street originally appeared in 1853 in the November and December issues of *Putnam's* not long after *Moby Dick* (1851) and was immediately tagged as a narrative enigma in Melville's corpus as well as in world literature. Among the ever-proliferating interpretations of the tale, several stand out. Critics have argued that *Bartleby, the Scrivener* channels Melville's abolitionism and anti-slavery journalism; that it echoes Henry David Thoreau's 1849 broadside "On the Duty of Civil Disobedience"; that it recounts a messianic parable of survival and bare life; that it performs as a how-to primer on squatting; that it functions as a case study of autism and locked-in syndrome; that it affirms the liberal doctrine of possessive individualism (Wyn Kelley maintains that Bartleby's "self-possession asserts such a primary claim that it has the force of actual proprietorship");[15] and that it documents New York's early history of borough politics, finance capitalism in the Wall Street district, and monumental architecture of the law courts and debtor's prison (Bartleby is finally removed to the Tombs—an Egyptian-themed New York municipal jail located at Collect Pond and known as a debtor's prison).[16] It has been read as a document of the shift in the law from *equity* (based on "individual circumstances and peculiarities" and upheld in chancery court) to *equality* (based on "deciding like and

---

15   Wyn Kelley, *Melville's City: Literary and Urban Form in Nineteenth-Century New York* (Cambridge, UK: Cambridge University Press, 1996), 205–6. This reference came to my attention via Jane Desmarais's astute essay "Preferring not to: The Paradox of Passive Resistance in Herman Melville's 'Bartleby,'" *Journal of the Short Story in English* 36, 2001, 25–39.

16   Laurie Robertson-Lorant, *Melville: A Biography* (New York: Clarkson Potter, 1996), 335.

unlike cases by a single standard"), as well as a practical guide on how to survive in the cutthroat arena of politics and business (securing a "snug business among rich men's bonds and mortgages and title-deeds" by avoiding "juries and the public eye.")[17]

Dubbed "the patron saint of Occupy," Bartleby resurfaced mightily during the Zucotti Park protests in slogans, street signs and an outpouring of articles; one hailing him as "America's first slacktivist" (*New Yorker*), another as the hero of the movement against the 1 percent (*Atlantic*).[18] Several essays took pains to link OWS to Bartleby's affront to American capitalism as defined in Melville's time. Russ Castronovo adumbrated Bartleby's anticapitalism: "His lack of interest in capitalist productivity, and his steadfast refusal to assent to charita-ble proposals that attempt to put a kind face on hierarchical wage labor."[19] Jonathan Poore, in "Bartleby's Occupation: 'Passive Resistance' Then and Now," drew out the novel's prescient grasp of the collapse between the market and the state, and its anticipation of contempo-rary neoliberalism:

> One line of "Bartleby" criticism, beginning with a 1945 essay by Egbert Oliver and extending to contemporary critics like Michael Rogin and Brook Thomas, without claiming categorically that Melville had read Thoreau's "Resistance to Civil Government," none-theless regards the short story as an extension of or, alternatively, a parody of the anti-authoritarian argument of the essay. What these (otherwise very different) critical interpretations have in common is that they ultimately regard Bartleby and Thoreau as resisting a version of the same thing, described variously as "society," "social institutions" or "the social system." In my view, however, these terms collapse an important distinction between two kinds of social "insti-tution"—the market and the state—that is fundamental to

---

17   Naomi C. Reed, "The Specter of Wall Street: 'Bartleby, the Scrivener' and the Language of Commodities," *American Literature* 76:2, 2004, 261; Melville, *Bartleby, the Scrivener*, 55.

18   Jonathan D. Greenberg, "Occupy Wall Street's Debt to Melville," *The Atlantic*, April 30, 2012, theatlantic.com.

19   Russ Castronovo, "Occupy Bartleby," *Journal of Nineteenth-Century Americanists* 2:2, 2014, 253.

understanding the nature of Bartleby's resistance and its difference from Thoreau's.[20]

Bartleby Politics is consistently reduced to the idea of radical refusal, inclusive of and exceeding the gesture of dissent. Hester Blum, recounting an event on November 10, 2011, at which writers, booksellers and OWS participants performed a public reading of *Bartleby, the Scrivener*, stresses how they "invoked the long American history of refusal that informs and enlivens Occupy."[21] Bartleby, many note, endures as an icon of "refusal" because he channels the refusal of others, from the slights and insults directed at him by his cohort of clerks, to his "refused" status in the physical space of the office, where he is subject to quarantine and invisibilization. (As Leo Marx observed, "the walls are controlling symbols of the story, and in fact it may be said that this is a parable of walls, the walls which hem in the meditative artist and for that matter every reflective man").[22] Foregrounding the image of the protagonist's occupation of a corner hemmed in by folding doors, reinforced by a screen, "Bartleby Politics," in this scenario at least, is synonymous with small acts of defensive micro-aggression and *ressentiment*, inflated by the latent threat of what Michael Jonck calls "permanent riotocracy."

Poore's observation that "Bartleby has arguably become the avatar for leftist political resistance—to both market *and* state—in recent years," has been more recently echoed in discussions related to the "Grexit" referendum, many of which affirmed Bartleby's relevance to the conflictual relation between markets and national-popular sovereignty. Akis Gavriilidis and Sofia Lalopoulos, under the heading "Bartleby; A Story of Sophocleous Street," associate Bartleby's name with a street-space in Athens's Syntagma Square and the banner

---

20   Jonathan Poore, "Bartleby's Occupation: 'Passive Resistance' Then and Now," *Nonsite*, May 1, 2013, nonsite.org.

21   "Melville and Protest; Melville Occupies Wall Street," *Leviathan* 15:1, 2013, 109–15.

22   Leo Marx, "Melville's Parable of the Walls," in *Bartleby the Inscrutable: A Collection of Commentary on Herman Melville's Tale "Bartleby the Scrivener,"* ed. M. Thomas Inge (Hamden, CT: Archon, 1979), 84–106.

movement of the *Aganaktismenoi* (the Outraged).[23] They interpret it as a paradoxical space situated between "non-strategic strategy" and Rancière's notion of "non-entitled entitlement."[24] Such non-strategic strategies or manifestations of non-entitled entitlement acquire concreteness in acts of physical occupation, interruption, civil disobedience, passive resistance, conscientious objection (redolent of the Bartleby of the Vietnam War protest movement), and dismissal of "the system" in the name of "real" democracy. Slavoj Žižek, following his characteristic mode of "cutting off one's nose to spite another's face," would identify Bartleby Politics with the gesture of "pure subtraction" embodied in the offense to political correctness:

> We can imagine the varieties of such a gesture in today's public space: not only the obvious "There are great chances of a new career here! Join us!—I would prefer not to"; or "Are you aware how our environment is endangered? Do something for ecology!"—"I would prefer not to"; or "What about all the racial and sexual injustices that we witness all around us? Isn't it time to do more?"—"I would prefer not to." This is the gesture of subtraction at its purest, the reduction of all qualitative differences to a purely formal minimal difference.[25]

For Žižek, Bartleby's gesture of withdrawal is not merely a "no" of resistance as such, nor a simple distance-taking from the "what is" of politics, but a parallax shift, aporetically manifest as "what remains of the supplement to the Law when its place is emptied of all its obscene superego content."[26] It is an assertion of resistance to the

> *rumspringa* of resistance, all the forms of resisting which help the system to reproduce itself by ensuring our participation in it—today, "I would prefer not to" is not primarily "I would prefer not to participate in the market economy, in capitalist competition and profiteering," but—much more problematically for some—"I would prefer

---

23   Akis Gavriilidis and Sofia Lalopoulos, "Chaos: Our Own 'Gun on The(ir) Table," *Law and Critique* 23:3, 2012, 299–311.

24   Ibid.

25   Slavoj Žižek, *The Parallax View* (Cambridge, MA: MIT Press, 2006), 382.

26   Ibid., 382.

not to give to charity to support a Black orphan in Africa, engage in
the struggle to prevent oil-drilling in a wildlife swamp."[27]

The opt-out on bien-pensant liberalism, the adamant imperviousness
to any form of "hegemonic interpellation," is read by Žižek as proof of
the symbolic order's collapse; it has foundered on the "holophrastic"
signifier-turned-object (embodied in "I would prefer not to") and
thrives on the violence inhering in "immobile, inert, insistent,
impassive *being*."[28] Žižek's three principles of Bartleby Politics—
subtraction, the aporia of the legal supplement, and the formal gesture
of refusal as symptom of the demise of the symbolic order—claim the
empty formal gesture for a non-optimized, non-instrumentalized,
unaccounted-for ontology. Living passively and resistantly, abstaining
by withholding, and waiting into worklessness are all taken as strategies to undo neoliberal pieties and flush out the new hegemons lurk-
ing in the names for new activisms.

In the context of OWS, Bartleby's quixotic, uncooperative phrase
"I would prefer not to" became a rallying cry for groups practicing the
micropolitics of civil disobedience; groups that categorically rejected
neoliberal models of "democracy" grounded in homogenized opinion
and engineered consent, and that subscribed to forms of the Political
stipulating the "possibility of a rupture with what exists."[29] This rupture
was often formulated as *the impossible demand*, expressed in the bodily
assemblies of OWS, Antifa, Podemos, Maidan and Les Indigènes de la
République;[30] in Arab Spring's rallying slogan *ash-sha'b yurīd isqāṭ
an-niẓām* (people want to bring down the regime); and the anti-
austerity, anti-debt-slavery vote of "No" (Oxi) in the Greek referendum. The force of impossible demands resided in their being made

---

27   Ibid., 383.

28   Ibid., 385.

29   Alain Badiou, "Against 'Political Philosophy,'" in *Metapolitics*, trans. Jason
Barker (London and New York: Verso, 2005), 24.

30   "The Republic's Indigenous," a political party representing the
neighborhoods and mostly immigrant populations of the French banlieues, who
want to stress in their party name the relevance of French colonialism to a host of
government-sanctioned operations that involve military intervention in national
cities or communities on their outskirts. See Hacène Belmessous, *Opération
Banlieues* (Paris: La Découverte, 2010).

vocally, again and again; and in the assertion of "a right to . . .", as Judith Butler, speaking in the heat of the OWS movement would affirm:

> Perhaps to the skeptic the idea of making "impossible demands" is equivalent to vacating the field of the political itself. But that response should call our attention to the way that the field of the political has been constituted such that satisfiable demands become the hallmark of its intelligibility. In other words, why is it that we have come to accept that the only politics that makes sense is one in which a set of demands are made to existing authorities, and that the demands isolate instances of inequality and injustice from one another without seeing or drawing any links among them? . . . We might say the particular politics that defines practical and intelligible politics as the production and satisfaction of a list of discrete demands is committed in advance to the legitimacy of existing economic and political structures, and to a refusal of the systematic character of inequality.[31]

"Impossible demands" imply the rejection of the competition model of rival demands. They stake an activist claim on the act of claiming itself: the right to assembly; the right to a living wage; the right to education; the right to housing; the right to education; the right to health and safe harbor; the right to a life unthreatened by racism, misognyny and homophobia; and not least, the right to have rights, especially in the face of police brutality, compromised systems of legal punishment, carceral extradition and extraordinary rendition.

In each of these cases Bartleby prevails as an aporetic figure of the Political, of "inoperative power," compositing Jean-Luc Nancy's subject of "inoperative community," Roberto Esposito's *l'impolitico* (a construct of impossible political institution and self-annulling sovereignty), and Giorgio Agamben's "refugee"—a figure of temporary power who "would prefer not to" be repatriated, mirroring in reverse the inhospitable host nation, which would certainly "prefer not to"

---

31   Judith Butler, "So, What are the Demands? And Where Do They Go from Here?," *Tidal: Occupy Theory, Occupy Strategy* 2, 2012, 10.

grant asylum or safe harbor.[32] But Bartleby is just as easily invoked as the premier self-managing agent of biopolitics, dubbed by Wendy Brown, in this respect, as "the miniature sovereign." In Brown's terms, this Bartleby, recalled to his profession as a clerk, personifies the residues of *homo politicus* lingering "in the subject's relation to itself" in the era of the waning state—a state that is autoimmune, walled off from community, and "receding as a destination for our equality, freedom, and orientation toward public life."[33] This wasted Bartleby, symbol of a dying demos, would be the neoliberal pendant to Deleuze's metaphysical Bartleby, a creature of "being as being, and nothing more," and "original" subject of American democracy.[34] Both Bartlebys make sense within a larger structure of political allegory, the former as a Lear of post-democracy, the latter as the *Dasein* of American exceptionalism.

Yet another kind of Bartleby Politics emerges from Jean-Claude Milner's attempt to analyze the strange contentlessness of political speech; what he calls "le parler politique," (political talk, or "talk politics"). For Milner, political speech is the filler that provides the primary substance of politicking; it "fills silences by asserting force and setting the relation between governors and governed."[35] "Talk-politics" rests, he argues, on a "rhetoric of division that brandishes indifference to facts and collects the dirty run-off water."[36] Milner harks back to the discourses of praise and blame elevated to a high art during the French revolutionary assemblies. The rhetoric of speeches encases politics in a fog of language, blunting perception of the exchange of deadly force between opponents.

---

32   Arne de Boever, "Overhearing Bartleby: Agamben, Melville, and Inoperative Power," *Parrhesia* 1 (2006), 142.

33   Wendy Brown, *Undoing the Demos: Neoliberalism's Stealth Revolution* (New York: Zone Books, 2015), 97. As Michael Zakim observes, Bartleby, in his chosen profession, not only administered, but embodied the circulation of property. See Michael Zakim, "The Business Clerk as Social Revolutionary; or, a Labor History of the Nonproducing Classes," *Journal of the Early Republic* 26, 2006, 567; and also, Thomas Augst, *The Clerk's Tale: Young Men and Moral Life in Nineteenth-Century America* (Chicago, IL: University of Chicago Press, 2003).

34   Deleuze, "Bartleby; or, The Formula," *Essays Critical and Clinical*, 71.

35   Jean-Claude Milner, *Pour une politique des êtres parlants: Court traité politique 2* (Paris: Éditions Verdier, 2011).

36   Ibid., 7, 9.

"Talk politics" is rendered Bartlebyesque by its indifference to facts and its phatic dimension (typically associated with shaggy-dog stories). In testing the premise that politics is inseparable from "talk politics," Milner draws attention to the waste matter in political chatter. The banal, deadening, mimetic aspect of politics—heard in every canned speech and sound bite and reproduced by every blogger, on-air bloviator, shill or professional pol—points to a basic conundrum posed by political speech: Why, to be effective, do politicians rely on pleonasms and vacuous formulae? On phrases riddled with redundancy and equivocation? On gibberish? We are here reminded of Georges Sorel's denunciation in *Reflections on Violence* of the parliamentary socialists, whose influence over their working-class, bourgeois and rich constituents "is founded upon gibberish" and their skill at spreading "confusion among the ideas of their readers."[37])

In a 1988 episode of the British sitcom *Yes, Prime Minister* entitled "The Tangled Web," the specter of political vacuity looms large in the guise of absurdist circular locutions and didactic humbuggery. In this example, Prime Minister Hacker interrogates his aides on whether they have actually bugged the telephone of MP Hugh Halifax:

Hacker: You mean we are bugging Hugh Halifax's telephones?

Sir Humphrey: We were.

Hacker: We *were*? When did we stop?

Sir Humphrey: *[checks his watch]* Seventeen minutes ago.

Bernard: The fact that you needed to know was not known at the time that the now known need to know was known, and therefore those that needed to advise and inform the Home Secretary perhaps felt that the information that he needed as to whether to inform the highest authority of the known information was not yet known, and therefore there was no authority for the authority to be informed because the need to know was not, at that time, known or needed.[38]

---

37   Georges Sorel, *Reflections on Violence*, trans. T. E. Hulme, ed. Jeremy Jennings (Cambridge, UK: Cambridge University Press, 1999), 110.

38   "The Tangled Web," *Yes, Prime Minister*, series 2, episode 8, dir. Sydney Lotterby (London: BBC, 1988).

This is "talk politics" at its most obstructionist: a way of speaking that indexes mental cul-de-sacs, performs epistemic failure, and satirizes political failure.

Written and produced by members of the clubby world of public school–trained civil servants, BBC writers and PR coaches, the show's portrayal of public choice politics (associated with James Buchanan's self-interest-based theory of public choice economics, which dismisses as romantic and illusory any theory of politics predicated on concern for others) has been denounced as a smoke screen for Thatcherism. The documentary filmmaker Adam Curtis deemed it "ideological propaganda for a political movement," citing, in his film *The Trap*, one of the show's writers, Sir Antony Jay:

> In *Yes, Minister*, we showed that almost everything that the government has to decide is a conflict between two lots of private interest— that of the politicians and that of the civil servants trying to advance their own careers and improve their own lives. And that's why public choice economics, which explains why all this was going on, was at the root of almost every episode of *Yes, Minister* and *Yes, Prime Minister*.[39]

Curtis rightly calls out a political philosophy powered exclusively by private interest and the cynical conviction that government—an engine of failure—is better off doing nothing than anything at all. The self-defeating prophecy of this philosophy was encapsulated by the famous "politician's syllogism" for which *Yes, Minister* was credited as the source. This is a non-following argument from a true premise that "commits the fallacy of the undistributed middle": "(1) We must do something; (2) This is something; (3) Therefore, we must do this."[40]

---

39   "F*ck You Buddy," *The Trap: What Happened To Our Dreams of Freedom*, episode 1, dir. Adam Curtis (London: BBC, 2007).

40   "The politician's fallacy was identified in a 1988 episode of the BBC political sitcom Yes, Prime Minister titled "Power to the People", and has taken added life on the Internet. The syllogism, invented by fictional British civil servants, has been quoted in the real British Parliament. The syllogism has also been quoted in American political discussion." "Politican's syllogism," *Wikipedia*, en.wikipedia.org. Entry citations include George Howard Joyce, *Principles of Logic* (London: Longmans, 1908), 205; and Raymond Chen, "The politician's fallacy and the politician's apology,"

What Curtis and fellow critics fail to really appreciate, however, is the syllogism's reworking of "the formula"—for it brings to light the logic of sovereign autoimmunity, with the excluded middle acting pharmacologically to hasten the defeat of individual interest. Bartleby in this case would not be identified as the mouthpiece of public choice politics but as an inhibitor of all "choice-ism"—a demotivator or disabling device of privatized willing and possessive individualism. To push further on this point, Bartleby is the individual subject dispossessed; he figures forth heteronomy of action possessable by no one. Under such conditions, notions of free choice, consent, and self-determination give way to "inadequate causation," a state of subordination to material alterity. As Frédéric Lordon elaborates, drawing on Spinozist ethics, "All things are in the grip of inadequate causation; namely, they are partially determined to act by other, external things."[41]

Bartleby embodies the strange figure of deactivated self-sovereignty coupled with active stasis. We see how this works in Melville's tale when the lawyer describes Bartleby's reaction after being arrested as a vagrant and sent to prison: "As I afterwards learned, the poor scrivener, when told that he must be conducted to the Tombs, offered *not the slightest obstacle*, but in his pale *unmoving way*, silently *acquiesced*."[42] This acquiescence without compliance arguably converts "the formula" into "the position"—a position which, according to the lawyer, is "unaccountably eccentric" and "yet greatly to be compassionated"; which is to say, it is the position of being *in* position to "front the dead-wall" of the Halls of Justice.[43] Bartleby baffles justice, not by directly obstructing it, but by foregrounding an attitude—*obstination*—that poses the very question of what justice is. As Judith Butler observes, when justice dissolves into the question of itself, politics tilts into philosophy:

> To demand justice is, of course, a strong thing to do—it also immediately involves every activist in a philosophical problem: What is

---

The Old New Thing blog, 2011, blogs.msdn.microsoft.com/oldnewthing.

41   Frédéric Lordon, *Willing Slaves of Capital*, 37.
42   Melville, *Bartleby, the Scrivener*, 75 (emphasis mine).
43   Ibid., 75, 76.

justice, and what are the means through which the demand for justice can be made, understood, taken up? The reason it is sometimes said that there are "no demands" when bodies assemble in this way and for this purpose is that the list of demands would not exhaust the meaning of justice that is being demanded.[44]

To Žižek's Bartleby (a walking aporia or node of epistemological opacity), Agamben's Bartleby (avatar of inoperative politics), Brown's Bartleby (neoliberal champion of an eviscerated demos), Milner's Bartleby (the star of "talk politics"), and Butler's Bartleby (baffler of justice), we add Bartleby the obstinator, an ontologist of the curiously impactful effects of mutism, obduracy and stubbornness.

Still more Bartleby . . .

The French writer Louis-René des Forêts, a founder in 1955 with Robert Antelme, Dionys Mascolo and Edgar Morin of the "Action Committee of Intellectuals against the Algerian War," embarked on a path of traumatic literary withdrawal after his daughter died in an accident in 1965. Mutism became his refuge, untranslatable expressivity an abiding resource for living on. John T. Naughton contends that his

> entire oeuvre is concerned with the untranslatable dimension of our experience and with the inadequacy of human language to transmit the true nature of what we have lived and felt . . . his work records the failure of writing, and given that his is so often a writing about not being able to write, his undertaking has been viewed by some as one of the truly exemplary projects of the postwar era.[45]

He also notes that "Raymond Queneau once compared Des Forêts to Melville's Bartleby—the scrivener who 'would prefer not to.'"[46] Des Forêts's Bartleby, one could say, resembles Agamben's Bartleby, that "last, exhausted figure of what Avicenna refers to as complete or

44 Butler, *Notes Toward a Performative Theory of Assembly*, 25–6.

45 John T. Naughton, "Louis-René des Forêts' *Ostinato*," in *Contemporary French Poetics*, eds. Michael Bishop and Christopher Elson (Amsterdam: Rodopi, 2002), 1.

46 Ibid.

perfect potentiality that belongs to the scribe who is in full possession of the art of writing in the moment in which he does not write."[47]

Well before his vow of silence, in May '68, amid the clamor of joyful protest and demonstration, Des Forêts discovered the political force of silence:

> Our mutism—which has the meaning of a pathos-filled vigil—is the only form in our possession that will allow us to make present the arrival of a new force, one that is stormily hostile to anything that might come along and capture or enslave it, subordinate it to the sovereign movement that might carry it off . . . it's the dream of rupture without return with the world of calculation.[48]

Though he would in fact continue with sporadic worldly contact and professional assignments (as editor, journalist, actor, and translator), in 1975 he began experimenting with a recessive form of autobiographical prose narrative, published in 1997 under the title *Ostinato*. An unfinished and "unfinishable" work, the author insisted when he was interviewed in 1995 in *Le Nouvel Observateur* that while the work could be established as a manuscript, it could never be a book.[49] This book which was not a book adds something distinctive to the definition of Bartleby Politics: it highlights obstinacy as the site of reserves of resistance. This is conveyed in Des Forêts's writing through peculiar grammar—a language at once awkward, gnomic, limpid and abstruse. In one instance, there is a remarkable rendering of the obstination of "without destination." The syntax deters the paths of thought in sentences that double back on themselves, and which toss and turn like a sailboat on waves. In this example, the sentence tacks to oblivion, jibs to abandon, and gets beached on the shoals of stymied decision and strangely empowered forcelessness:

---

47 Giorgio Agamben, "Bartleby, or On Contingency," in *Potentialities: Collected Essays in Philosophy*, trans. Daniel Heller-Roazen (Stanford, CA: Stanford University Press, 2000), as cited in de Boever, "Overhearing Bartleby," 143.

48 Louis-René des Forêts, *L'Ephémère* 6, 1968, in *Oeuvres complètes*, ed. Dominique Rabaté (Paris: Gallimard, 2015), 79. Translation my own.

49 Interview with Jean-Louis Ezine, Louis-René des Forêts, *Le Nouvel Observateur*, February 16, 1995, in *Oeuvres complètes*, 133.

Without destination, not wandering or distraught, not even avid to return to the heart of childhood to take back from oblivion [l'oubli] what was lost or to find again outside his own face and meaning [par le dehors de sa propre figure et son propre sens], nor to make himself anything other than what he was, but summoned, beckoned, seized, carried off by a movement having the force of an injunction to which he cedes in an ingenuous abandon [un abandon ingénu], like a legendary hero, his whole vigor of innocence letting him triumph over the obstacles set on his path by the evil angels of doubt powerless to turn him from it [impuissants à l'en détourner]. Too intimately linked to what he contests to be forced to any decisive test of confrontation and perhaps drawing from this very impossibility itself the power to traverse in all candor these base and shadowy depths to the extreme end of the path, even having to skip a few steps or to fall from very high in a descent so terrifying that the furious appetite of destruction dwelling in him would not quench itself therein.[50]

In another instance, we are asked to parse the narrator's "astonishment" at his "state of being in life" ("un si grand étonnement d'être en état de vie"), which opens onto a memory, occluded by a "thickness" that cannot be perforated:

So astonished at living that he tries as far back as his memory reaches for the obscure traces of his first death, but no thread leads back to the knot of the web. So many chimerical efforts to perforate the thickness of this indestructibly hard metal preventing any access to the enigma-less desert of immemorial night.[51]

Sentences like this one make impossible demands, posing the question of what something could "impossibly" mean as they take the reader through a welter of stoic abstractions and labored negations. Fronting the dead wall of obtuseness, the reader is taught—through a

50   Louis-René des Forêts, *Ostinato* (Lincoln, NE: University of Nebraska Press, 2002), 18; original French in *Oeuvres complètes*, 1055.,

51   des Forêts, *Ostinato*, 22; original French in *Oeuvres complètes*, 1060. "*Autant* d'efforts chimériques pour perforer l'épaisseur de ce très dur minéral qui ne se laisse pas détruire et interdit tout accès au désert sans énigme de la nuit immémoriale."

rhythm of ostinato at the level of syntactic phrasing—to persevere in the face of recessionary aesthetics.[52] When Deleuze observed that Bartleby does not outright refuse, but rather rejects both the preferred and the not-preferred, he opened a space for a something else that begs to be identified with *ostinato*. Though commonly used as a technical term for the repetition of a musical phrase that anchors a movement or an entire composition, as well as the fancy name for a hook or jazz riff played at the lower register and usually understood as the background to a main melody in the foreground (improvised or otherwise),[53] Des Forêt's *ostinato* is marked as a term of stylistic, philosophical abstention, with affinity for the styles of his better-known cohort: Bataille, Blanchot, Beckett, Duras.[54] Des Forêts's syntax explores the perimeter of incommunicability, affirming the remoteness of a narrator who addresses himself by the third-person pronoun "he."

If Raymond Queneau nicknamed Des Forêts "Bartleby the Scrivener," it was not just because his muteness approached him to Melville's clerk or that his narrator, in *Ostinato*, demonstrates a similar inclination to demur (as a captive member of the French Resistance, the narrator rehearses in his mind how he *will not* ask himself how he will remain silent when it is his turn to submit to torture), but also because he may have sensed a common psychic ground in explorations of the relation between obstination and humiliation.[55] Many fragments offer a window into the ways of a subject who discovers

---

52   For a study in recessionary aesthetics linked to ecological quietism within Romantic lyric, see Anne-Lise François, *Open Secrets: The Literature of Uncounted Experience* (Stanford, CA: Stanford University Press, 2008).

53   This accent on musical improvisation obviously points us to the work of Fred Moten, Alexander Weheliye and Brent Hayes Edwards on jazz and black politics, the "sounding" of black citizenship and black vernacular poetics. See, Stefano Harney and Fred Moten, eds. *The Undercommons: Fugitive Planning & Black Study* (New York: Minor Compositions, 2013), Alexander Weheliye, *Phonographies: Grooves in Sonic Afro-Modernity*, (Durham, NC: Duke University Press, 2005) and Brent Hayes Edwards, *Epistrophes: Jazz and the Literary Imagination* (Cambridge, Mass: Harvard University Press, 2017).

54   Little wonder that Derrida saw something philosophical in *ostinato*, a point raised when he interviewed Ornette Coleman on jazz. See Jacques Derrida and Ornette Coleman, "The other's language: Jacques Derrida interviews Ornette Coleman, 23 June 1997," trans. Timothy S. Murphy, *Genre: Forms of Discourse and Culture* 37:2, 2004, 319–28.

55   Des Forêts, *Ostinato* [French edition], in *Oeuvres complètes*, 1093.

ostinato while quickening to the ordeals of domination, as in this instance of sexual hazing:

> The resolve to remain silent frustrates the satisfaction of the boy tormentor and outplays the equally sadistic hand of the school administrators who want to blame the victim not just for refusing to deliver the perpetrators, but for allowing himself to be punished:
>
> *The obstinate refusal* of any denunciation required by the rules of honor answers still more powerfully the repugnance of having to hear these masters garbed as inquisitors deflower, vilify what was a revelation of a stupefying intensity, although linked to fright and a feeling of extreme shame.[56]

The references are to Christ's calvary of torture and humiliation, but the images throughout this section function less like compositional elements of an allegorical tableau and more as a set of hooks that, like the *ostinato* musical riff, score the attitudes of obstination; they become aesthetic exercises in willpower, training the reader in the art of winning by losing through small acts of perseverant obstruction that bespeak indifference to the why and how:[57]

---

56   Des Forêts, *Ostinato* [English edition], 22 (emphasis mine).

57   *Ostinato* is possibly worthy of inclusion in the chain of terms for negation that Jane Bennett associates with the "*comprehending* materiality" or "thing-power" obliquely accessed in human being: "Because the human too is a materiality, it possesses a thing-power of its own. This thing-power sometimes makes itself known as an uneasy feeling of internal resistance, as an alien presence that is uncannily familiar. Perhaps this is what Socrates referred to as his *daemon* or nay-saying gadfly. Recent work in cultural theory has highlighted this force that is experience as in but not quite of oneself. This indeterminate and never fully determinable dimension of things has been called *difference* (Jacques Derrida), *the virtual* (Gilles Deleuze), *the invisible* (Maurice Merleau-Ponty), *the semiotic* (Julia Kristeva), and *nonidentity* (Theodor Adorno). Jean-François Lyotard describes this obstinate remainder, which hovers between the ontological and the epistemological registers, as 'that which exceeds every putting into form or object without being anywhere else but within them.' These various terms of art mark the fact that thing-power often first reveals itself as a negativity, a confounding or fouling up of an intention, desire schema, or concept. But, as many of the thinkers named above have noted, such negativity is also the same stuff out of which positive things emerge. It is a negativity that is profoundly productive: the materiality that resists us is also the protean source of being, the essentially vague matrix of things." Jane Bennett, "The Force of Things: Steps Towards an Ecology of Matter," *Political Theory* 32:3, 2004, 361.

To persevere requires maintaining a sort of ingenuity exempt from intention, indifferent to the why and the how . . .

Every wish of nothingness has limits that cannot be over-stepped . . . A position all the less tenable in that it is incompatible with the use of language maintained toward and against everything —that is in fact the obstacle. Remain right there without saying anything and your wish will be in large part answered . . .

Where is this sudden firmness coming from?

From fear. A fear like abulia, like that of a man who, knowing himself in mortal peril, would invoke the heavens without even moving his little finger.[58]

Obstination is distinguished not as a moral value earned through survival in adverse circumstances, but as an interval of experience (of subject dissolution and recomposition) that mobilizes the obsta-cle within existence and as well as resistance, as Kluge and Negt have underscored to "primitive expropriation."[59] Historically speak-ing, such intervals connect in a chronotope leading from existen-tialist inoperativity (Beckett, Blanchot, des Forêts), to the *ostinato* of '60s jazz (where the politics of black empowerment was arguably aligned with the move to modal or free jazz), to the phrasings and musings on micro-aggression in Claudia Rankine's *Citizen: An American Lyric*, to scenes drawn from the visual archive of Black Lives Matter.

"He can no longer hold out his hand toward the others but some-times contemplates the hand of his neighbor as a support."[60] This ambivalent image in des Forêts's *Ostinato* of the neighbor's hand as proxy unit of obstinate force has special resonance in the era of the Black Lives Matter movement, in which hands—raised up in surren-der or self-defense, curled into fists and defiant power grips ("grip-ping" for Kluge and Negt signifies essential labor powers and human

58   Des Forêts, *Ostinato* [English edition], 143, 145.

59   Kluge and Negt write in their "Obstinacy" entry in the "Atlas of Concepts," an appendix of *History and Obstinacy*, "A fundamental current observable throughout human history. It develops out of a resistance to primitive expropriation." *History and Obstinacy*, 390.

60   Ibid., 21.

capacities), folded across locked arms on protest days, clasped in prayer for peace or open in outreach— belong to a language of gesture attesting to the persistence, renewal and ongoing relevance of Bartleby politics.[61]

---

61   Kluge and Negt, *History and Obstinacy*, 88–9.

III. POLITICAL SCIENCE

III. POLITICAL FICTIONS

Political Fiction

Political fiction, as distinct from the historical novel or Hegelian epic, captures the random motion of backstories, conspiracy and calculation.[1] It records the transference of magnetic properties, animal touch, meteorological elements, pollution, microbic contagion, affective disorders of the ambient surround, nuances of what Anahid Nersessian calls "worldfeel" (incipient in Hippolyte Taine's concept of *milieu*). Bruno Latour ascribes these image networks to the "atmosphere" of a new *Dingpolitik* or "object-oriented democracy." Latour considers *Realpolitik*, cast historically as a "positive, materialist, no-nonsense, interest-only, matter-of-fact way of dealing with naked power relations" to be "deeply *unrealistic*." Summoning the neologism *Dingpolitik*, he wants to extend how we think of political procedure—indebted, from Hobbes to Rawls, or Rousseau to Habermas, to notions of contract, representation, and ideal speech conditions—into what he calls "*matters* that matter," focusing on the "*what* which is at issue," the

---

1   On the contradiction in Hegel's notion of the "novel as bourgeois epic" (from which all dominant accounts of the novel as *the* literary form of bourgeois individualism derive), and Lukács's attempt to resolve them, David Cunningham notes, "Hegel's assertion that the novel is the modern bourgeois *epic* contains, from the outset, a self-conscious contradiction – in so far as the very nature of bourgeois sociality does not, on this account, admit of epic form—one which Lukács precisely sought to *overcome* via his theorization of the historical novel. For, by re-reading Hegel's definition of the novel as the modern bourgeois epic in terms effectively antithetical to Hegel's own—that is, precisely as an epic *of* the bourgeoisie—Lukács locates in the historical novel, the representation and narration of the bourgeois class as themselves a collective *subject of history*. It is this collective dimension that will, for Lukács, later find itself dissolved in modernism and naturalism." See David Cunningham, "The Historical Novel of Contemporary Capitalism," *Raison publique*, May 4, 2014, raison-publique.fr.

res in *res publica*.[2] Latour points toward a thorough redefinition of the nature of a "thing" in politics, notionally reconceiving it as a mix of material and immaterial, human and object, act and ceremonial locus. The vocabulary of archaic parliaments underscores this thingness within acts of the Political; he notes the Saxon fixation on Stonehenge, as well as numerous Nordic names for gathering-places: the Norwegian *Storting*, the Icelandic *Althing*, the German *Thingstätten*.[3] This expanded field of *Dingpolitik* highlights the minerality of infrastructure constitutive of political ideas and ideologies.

Political fiction is no singular genre but is defined by the glossary brought to bear on it, which exceeds but also dips into the conventional language of *institutions* (parliamentarianism, monarchy, ministries, trade unions, parties, municipal government, legislating bodies, state government, foreign relations councils, embassies); the "isms" of *ideologies* (despotism, monarchism, absolutism, constitutionalism, federalism, liberalism, republicanism, anarchism, communism, capitalism, possessive individualism); the lexicon of *political theory* (citizenship, polis, governmentality, polity, slavery, usurpation, franchise, national assembly, state apparatus, social welfare, state of exception, emancipation, biopolitics, social antagonism, deterritorialization); the technical language of *policy* (nationalization, privatization, income distribution, laissez-faire, trickle-down economics, free trade, environmental protection, entitlement program); the vocabulary of *political process* (diplomacy, elections, polls, campaign, redistricting, protest, courts of appeal, grass roots, single-issue, referendum); and the catalogue of *political theory* (Plato, Aristotle, Machiavelli, Hobbes, Spinoza, Locke, Rousseau, Jefferson, Bentham, Marx, Gramsci, Lenin, Schmitt, Mao, MacPherson, Arendt, Althusser, Rawls, Balibar, Habermas, Unger, Negri, Rancière, Laclau, Mouffe).

I am loathe to narrow the definition of political fiction, as *Wikipedia* does, as a subgenre "that deals with political affairs" on the order of More's *Utopia, Candide, Gulliver's Travels, Uncle Tom's Cabin, War and*

---

2   Bruno Latour, "From Realipolitik to Dingpolitik—or How to Make Things Public" in *Making Things Public: Atmospheres of Democracy*, eds Bruno Latour and Peter Weibel (Cambridge, MA: MIT Press, 2005), 14, 15, 16 (original emphasis).
3   Ibid., 23.

Peace, Fahrenheit 451, Animal Farm, or *Ragtime.*[4] In my own view, political fiction stands apart from the national *roman d'énergie* (Maurice Barrès's *The Uprooted*), and from biographical novels (Gore Vidal's *Burr,* Giles Foden's *The Last King of Scotland*) or historical panoramas dealing with world-historical topics: slavery, dictatorship, the gulag, genocide, apartheid. Rather, it connotes the weak, downgraded, or ironically deflationary version of the historical novel; it is a form found wanting in focalization, or in the epic gravitas necessary to communicating a world-transformative, singular event. Whereas in the bildungsroman, protagonist and historical turn tend to be aligned, in political fiction the hero is upstaged and edged out by a welter of minor characters. Distinct plotlines of war and nation-building are lost to diversionary accounts of political intrigue. In lieu of the ideological didacticism of the *roman à thèse* or the totalizing retrospect of the historical novel (indebted to Lukács), political fiction is distinguished by chart lines of the psychic life of political calculation. What comes to the fore is a realism that hews to interest-driven political thinking and a view of sovereignty (to borrow Stephen Krasner's phrase) as "organized hypocrisy": a state of affairs in which the relatively open violation of norms and rules becomes accepted practice, as the price of placating constituents and consolidating power.[5]

"Organized hypocrisy" is one of many names that can be imputed to a Machiavellian narrative form honed by Stendhal in *Le Rouge et le noir, La Chartreuse de Parme* and *Lucien Leuwen,* and reworked by a number of his nineteenth-century successors, most notably Flaubert, Zola, and Maupassant. In Britain, Disraeli, Thackery, Dickens and Trollope top the list of authors examining the social life of political and financial microcultures. The resurgent popularity of Trollope's *The Duke's Children,* recently brought out in an unabridged edition, attests to the contemporary interest in this kind of political fiction, whose ongoing attraction is felt in John Lancaster's best-selling satire of the London real estate market, *Capital.* North American counterparts include David Foster Wallace's *The Pale King,* a journey into the

---

4   "Political Fiction," *Wikipedia,* en.wikipedia.org.
5   Stephen Krasner, *Sovereignty: Organized Hypocrisy* (Princeton: Princeton University Press, 1999), 66.

byways of the American insurance industry, and Thomas Pynchon's *Bleeding Edge*, which walks the reader through the securities industry and the finer points of Ponzi schemes.[6]

Political fiction finds its generic footing in infill dialogue, manifest, for instance, in the legions of arguments over which party or minister should be in power. It takes shape as a virtually unintelligible skein of references to half-forgotten political actors. In Flaubert's *Sentimental Education*, readers are left to ponder, who was Pritchard? (Answer: an English Protestant missionary in Tahiti bought off by Guizot.) Who was Changarnier? (Answer: a monarchist anti-Bonapartist who had fallen out of favor by 1851.) Can we discern whether *La Mode* was a real or fictitious journal, or pick up that it had Legitimist tendencies? Who were the Carbonari of the nineteenth century, whose name, meaning "charcoal-burners," referred to revolutionary, anti-clerical secret societies? What was, in fact, the political fallout of "l'affaire Praslin" in which the duke, suspected of murdering his wife, used his peerage to trump the justice system? Subtending this blurry threshold of historical information lies the even more impenetrable groundswell of yammering and rabbiting on, as when, in another passage in *Sentimental Education*, "the conversation descended into current events: Spanish marriages, Rochfort's market speculations, the new chapel in Saint-Denis."[7] Scenes in which characters gossip, talk politics, or evoke temporal worlds made up of tiny, evanescent incidents that don't quite make it into history demonstrate how impulses are neutralized by the forces of inertia, inaction and nonproductivity. They provide an x-ray of the ways governmentality translates into what Roberto Mangabeira Unger, as we have already seen, called frameworks of "habitual social life," which guarantee immunity to disturbance and ensure resistance to transformative will.

---

6   See Adam Gopnik, "Trollope Trending," *New Yorker*, May 4, 2015. Gopnik insists that it is Trollope's preoccupation in the Palliser series with "small things" that gives his text appeal: "Trollope's people are all doing things that are small: getting on committees, making sermons, writing to newspapers, finding misplaced checks. Even Prime Ministers end up obsessed with trivial actions and tiny disputes. (Trollope's Prime Ministerial hero is obsessed with decimal coinage). Yet these acts are highly important to them, and become so to us" (28).

7   Gustave Flaubert, *Sentimental Education: A Young Man's History* (London: H. S. Nichols, 1898), 160, 342, 405.

Political fiction, then, is the medium that affords the most subtle scenography, the most sophisticated cognitive and social mapping, of political machinations that condition the thrum and habitude of this "small p" politics—politics, that is, condemned to the reproduction of will-lessness.

Psychopolitics

In our times, alas, politics has stolen literature, which is now a make-shift stand-in.
— Stendhal, letter published in *Le Globe* (1825)[1]

Politics in a literary work is a pistol shot in the middle of a concert—a vulgarity—but impossible to ignore.
— Stendhal, *La Chartreuse de Parme* (1839)[2]

In *Beyond Good and Evil* Friedrich Nietzsche described a special kind of philosophical politics which "Europe owes the Jews." He argued that, for better or worse, "the artists among the spectators and philosophers" are grateful to the Jews for "the grand style in morality, the terribleness and majesty of infinite demands, of infinite meanings, the whole romanticism and sublimity of moral questionabilities—and hence precisely the most attractive, captious, and choicest part of those plays of color and seductions to life in whose afterglow the sky of our European culture, its evening sky, is burning now—perhaps burning itself out."[3] A bit further on, dilating on the superiority of French to German culture, Nietzsche singles out Stendhal as the premier "man of interrogation" and "the last great psychologist of

---

1   "De nos jours hélas, la politique vole la littérature qui n'est qu'un pis-aller." Stendhal, letter published in *Le Globe*, March 31, 1825, in *Correspondence*, (Paris: Gallimard, 1967), 59.
2   "La politique dans une œuvre littéraire c'est un coup de pistolet au milieu d'un concert–quelque chose de grossier et auquel pourtant il n'est pas possible de refuser son attention." Stendhal, *La Chartreuse de Parme*, Chapter xxiii (1839), in *Romans et nouvelles*, vol. 2, trans. S. H. (Paris: Gallimard, 1968), 405.
3   Friedrich Nietzsche, *Beyond Good and Evil*, trans. Walter Kaufman, (New York: Random House, 1989), 185.

France," setting him up indirectly as a kind of "Jewish" theorist of psychopolitics:

> By way of contrast to the German inexperience and innocence *in voluptate psychologica*, which is none too distantly related to the tediousness of German company, and as the most consummate expression of a typically French curiosity and inventiveness for this realm of delicate thrills, Henri Beyle, that remarkable anticipatory and precursory human being, who ran with a Napoleonic tempo through *his* Europe, through several centuries of the European soul, as an explorer and discoverer of this soul: it has required two generations to *catch up* with him in any way, to figure out again a few of the riddles that tormented and enchanted him, this odd epicurean and question mark of a man who was France's last great psychologist.[4]

This Nietzschean Stendhal invites being read not so much as a stereotypical Napoleonic man of action, imperial ambition and imagination, but more as a modern theorist of the passions, who, as Deleuze was acutely aware, understood how "the Jew" converted *ressentiment* into political nihilism. For Nietzsche it is the "the priest in his Judaic form" who is the master of dialectics, conceiving "love, a new love that the Christians take up, as the conclusion, the crowning glory, the venomous flower of an unbelievable hatred." Deleuze stresses that it is the Jewish power of dialectic, working over the negative until it becomes something that enables the slave to sublate *ressentiment*, that explains how Nietzsche could single out Jews as the people capable of saving a decadent, spiritually enervated Europe from itself.[5]

Stendhal wrote an unfinished novella in 1831 titled *Le Juif* that resonates surprisingly well with Nietzsche's Jewish avatar of Stendhalian psychopolitics. The text makes use of stock clichés about Jews: the protagonist, a handsome Italian merchant named Filippo, is

---

4   Ibid. 193–4.
5   Gilles Deleuze, *Nietzsche and Philosophy* Trans. Hugh Tomlinson, (New York: Columbia University Press, 1983), 126–7. Nietzsche's discussion of "the Jewish priest" occurs in *The Genealogy of Morals*.

distinguished by his preternatural knack for calculating profit margins and for his shrewd opportunism in establishing himself as the supplier for a Croatian brigade in Napoleon's army. But lest we assume this is just another exercise in ethnic stereotyping, Stendhal treats his subject as a case study in psychopolitics much like he had with Julien Sorel in *Le rouge et le noir: chronique du XIXe siècle* (1830) or would later with Fabrice del Dongo in *La Chartreuse de Parme* (1839). Filippo's particular psychological interest lies in his ability to turn adversity into the material of survival. As he says to an unidentified interlocutor at the story's outset: "j'étais juif, méprisé de vous autres chrétiens, et même des juifs, car j'avais été longtemps excessivement pauvre." [I was the Jew, despised by you Christians, and even by other Jews, because I was for many years extremely poor"] When the listener replies with a show of Enlightened conscience, "On avait le plus grand tort de mépriser. . ." [How wrong we were to treat you with contempt] he is brushed off with: "Ne vous mettez pas en frais de phrases polies."[6] [Don't bother compensating with polite phrases]. Filippo's strength comes through in his acceptance of anti-Semitism as a condition of Jewish existence, but instead of being consumed by *ressentiment* or defeat in the face of his *malédiction*, he extracts profit from setbacks. Stripped of his meager heritage by his mother; beaten and robbed by soldiers, denuded of his capital, Filippo surmounts each hardship and builds up discipline from adherence to self-prescribed moral law (the latter an important tenet of Beylism).

Stendhal's Jewish protagonist, true to Nietzchean type, follows the arc of what Simon Critchley, echoing Nietzsche, calls the "infinitely demanding," by which he refers to an "ethics of commitment," a "politics of resistance" that marshals the resources of philosophical nihilism. There are two kinds of nihilism in Critchley's view: "active nihilism" (characteristic of "those who seek a violent destruction of the purportedly meaningless world of capitalism and liberal democracy"), and "passive nihilism" (for instance, in "forms of 'European or American Buddhism', contemplative withdrawal, where one faces the meaningless chaos of the world with eyes wide shut"). Critchley rejects

---

6 Stendhal, "Le Juif" in *Oeuvres romanesques complètes* ed. Philippe Berthier, Vol. 2 (Paris: Gallimard, 2007), 5.

both forms, but argues that each expresses a deep truth: "namely, their identification of a motivational deficit at the heart of liberal democracy, a sort of drift, disbelief and slackening that is both institutional and moral. In the drift of this deficit, we experience the moral claims of our societies as externally compulsory, but not internally compelling."[7] In this scheme, it would be Nietzsche's Jew, or Stendhal's, who moves us along, from "an infinitely demanding ethics of commitment" that "'dividuates' us from ourselves humorously and humanly, showing the eccentricity of the human being with respect to itself," to a politics of remotivated democracy nourished by the arousal of responsibility in the face of injustice, anarchist militance, and the nomination of a new political subject ready to surrender naked self-interest and committed to "politics conceived at a *distance* from the state."[8] Critchley's call to responsibility, his focus on "demand"—as something between a drive and an injunction, an appetite and an idea, a self-consuming rage and a strategy for action—reaffirms the psychic dimension of the political. It inspires an analysis of Stendhal's *Lucien Leuwen* (his never-completed masterwork of political fiction published in 1894 some fifty-two years after his death), focusing on his invention of a "hero" of psychopower; a subject riven by the conflicting poles of the "infinitely demanding" (metaphysical politics, aligned with the psychic life of the suffering subject), and the profane, expedient politics of rogues.

Lucien is enraptured by the call of the politico-theological ideal yet obedient to the instincts of the political realist. He distinguishes himself as a star member of the cast of *coquins* who, unlike ordinary party hacks and ministers, acquires grandeur in performing the political dumbshow. Though Lucien never takes possession of his demand the way Filippo does, he remains a figure of the Spinozist *conatus*, which is to say, a figure whose unlearning of political conscience requires effort, endeavor, impulse, striving—in short, a force of character up to the task of living a dastardly intention and cultivating intelligence to the full capacities of psychopower.

---

7   Simon Critchley, *Infinitely Demanding: Ethics of Commitment, Politics of Resistance* (New York: Verso, 2007), 39.

8   Ibid. 89, 93, 103,112

This drama of the *conatus* unfurls through Lucien's training as a government fixer, a narrative which dominates the part of the novel titled "Le Télégraphe" in reference to the semaphore system that was revolutionizing communications in Stendhal's time. Returning to Paris after a heartbreak in Nancy, ejected from the École Polytechnique as well as the army, Lucien resolves to transform himself from loser son (*raté*) into successful rogue (*coquin*). Lucien distinguishes himself as a star in the cast of *coquins*, acquiring grandeur, unlike ordinary party hacks and ministers, through performing acts of scurrilous underhandedness. His apprenticeship in political nihilism occurs under the tutelage of his father, a banking magnate modeled on Pillet-Will, regent of the Banque de France and a founder of the Caisse d'Epargne. The year is 1834, a low point in the government of Louis-Philippe, as it put in place enhanced censorship legislation and police surveillance systems that came to be associated with "les lois liberti-cides" of 1835. Leuwen *père* issues an imperative to his son: "Be free!" ("Soyez libre!")—exhorting him not only to act without regard for political ideals (be they Napoleonic or Republican), but to submit himself to the exigencies of going rogue: "Will you be rogue enough for the job?" ("Serez-vous assez coquin pour cet emploi?").[9] After reading a novel about a character like himself—*Edgar, ou le Parisien de vingt ans*, whose protagonist is depicted as a fatuous philosopher with pretensions to aloofness from the juste-milieu—Lucien takes the leap, pronouncing to himself the words of the new faith: "I will be a rogue!"[10] Going rogue will entail seducing women he does not love, chasing the money, and above all, mastering the art of political decep-tion in a playbook taken from Machiavelli's *The Prince*. An avid reader of Machiavelli between 1804 and 1806, especially chapter 18, "How Princes Should Keep Their Word," Stendhal hailed him as the premier philosopher of non-hypocrisy in his *Mémoires d'un touriste*.

As a how-to manual for rigging election results or ejecting a sitting minister, and as an aesthetic appreciation of the craft of political deception, *Lucien Leuwen* surpasses *The Red and the Black* and *The*

---

9   Stendhal, *Lucien Leuwen* (New Directions, [1894] 1950), 364.
10 Ibid., 370.

Charterhouse of Parma.[11] For Maurice Bardèche, *The Charterhouse of Parma* is the definitive work on "how one governs," whereas *Lucien Leuwen* exposed the mechanics of "how one administers." This is a useful distinction because it draws attention to the level of detail brought to bear on politics as métier We watch Lucien observing every move by the deputy minister, as he engages in insider trading with help from Lucien's father, a banker with a seat on the stock exchange. Leuwen *père* advises his son to harness his mathematical intelligence to psychopolitical ends; to game the system not by wasting time on petty speculators but by manipulating the insecurities and vanities of his superiors. As master of petitions, Lucien lays traps for his rivals; intercepting and doctoring secret missives. This is how he fells the feckless Monsieur des Ramiers, dubbed the "modern Fénélon," who is eventually publicly humiliated by the Russian ambassador in the salons of high diplomacy. He also excels at the art of spinmeistering. In the Kortis affair, based on the real-life "affaire Corteys," Lucien is deputized when an agent provocateur, hired by the king's secret police to sow dissension between soldiers and disenfranchised civilians, botches his operation and is wounded by the soldier whom he has attacked. When a surgeon refuses a general's bribe to finish off Kortis with a draught of opium—which recalls the scandal of Jaffa in which Napoleon poisoned Turkish prisoners of war—there is a huge risk of government embarrassment. Lucien fulfills his damage control mission by buying the wounded man's silence and then staging a great public show of concern over his condition. Over and over he is shown devising schemes involving payoffs, cover-ups, blackmail, spying, and information traffiicking. He must arrest the flow of compromising information leaked to the liberal press, while spreading viral rumors through government back channels. Such machinations are helped along by the telegraph, the ancestor of high-tech financial instruments and social media.

If there is one lesson, packaged in advice given to Madame Grandet (Lucien's match in social climbing and political ambition), it is that the banks control the political classes. Ministers make the fortunes of

---

11   Jacques Rancière, *Aisthesis: Scènes du régime esthétique de l'art* (Paris: Galilée, 2011), 63.

anyone they please, but it is the banks, owned by families like the Rothschilds and Leuwens who make the ministers.[12] Stendhal's anti-banking sentiments were already clear in his early writings as a pamphleteer. In his proto-Keynesian 1825 tract *D'un nouveau complot contre les industriels,* he derided *les industriels*—a loose term for bankers, investors, or venture capitalists—for using their money-lending capabilities to dictate policy. Here he followed the liberal economist Jean-Baptiste Say in criticizing the appropriation of Saint-Simonian rhetoric by financial elites such that economic opportunism and worker exploitation were passed off as providential social welfare and the enjoyment of productivity.[13]

Though Stendhal himself had contradictory, mercurial political convictions—anti–ancien régime, yet captivated by the aristocratic way of life; anti-Empire, yet aggrandizing of Napoleon in his *Mémoires sur Napoléon*; opposed to universal suffrage, yet sympathetic to the multitude—critics have cast Lucien Leuwen as a closet Jacobin. A Jacobin gone astray, for he strives for a political future that he has lost the ability to discern, thus remaining doomed to obtuseness in the face of July Monarchy corruption, and of his own status as a paramount agent in the mounting of corrupt schemes.

Michel Guérin reads *Lucien Leuwen* as the portrait of a society that prefigures the capitalo-parliamentarianism of the Mitterrand era. His *La Politique de Stendhal,* published in 1982 with a preface by Régis Debray, features aptly enough in a book series titled "Politics Exploded" (La politique éclatée). Guérin credits Stendhal with being the first psychopolitical scientist of Europe, the one who grasped most fully how politics explodes out of the subjective arenas of happiness, love and death.[14] For Guérin, *Lucien Leuwen* also blows up each model of politics that seemed possible or plausible in the post-revolutionary period: legitimist monarchy (the Bourbons), the July Monarchy

---

12   Stendhal, *Lucien Leuwen,* 107.

13   Gareth Stedman-Jones, "Saint Simon and the Liberal Origins of the Socialist Political Economy," in *La France et l'Angleterre au XIX siècle: Échanges, représentations,* comparaisons, eds Silvie Aprile, Fabrice Bensimon (Grane: Créaphis, 2006), 21–47.

14   Michel Guérin, *La Politique de Stendhal* (Paris: Presses Universitaires de France, 1982), 11–12.

(bourgeois, juste-milieu), the Republic, or American-style democracy (dismissed as a republic driven entirely by money). The novel is read, then, as a demonstration that reason has turned into the art of governing without belief, passion has become another name for truths that have no impact, and facts have become little more than thinly disguised errors. In their place are irony, cynical reason, an active nihilism suited to the political operative, hyper-individualism, and sovereign egotism laced with residual sentimentalism (think here of the Rousseauistic *clinamen sentimental* embraced by Stendhal in his *Souvenirs d'égotisme*). It is this inclination, a weak force, but one to be reckoned with in its distribution of affect and interest across the political spectrum, that in Guérin's reading distinguishes *Lucien Leuwen* as a masterwork for political science.

In a 1958 essay comparing political science and sociology ("Science politique et sociologie: réflexions d'un Sociologue"), François Bourricaud singles out the novel as a canonical work of political science. In his view, only Spinoza's *Tractatus Theologico-Politicus* comes close to *Lucien Leuwen* as a political anthropology of the governing caste focused on the mutual dependency of the monarch and his ministers, generals, counselors and friends. For Spinoza, the transmutation of the governing body from the one to the ruling few creates a secretive aristocracy of power that evades the rule of law even as it is vested as its guarantor. Where Bourricaud emphasizes the analogy between *Lucien Leuwen* and the *Tractatus Theologico-Politicus* as monographs of the political class and the threat this class poses to democracy, I would underscore how the *Tractatus Theologico-Politicus* anticipates Stendhal's novel in articulating that which eludes philosophical formalization in political theory. "Statesmen have written about politics far more happily than philosophers," Spinoza wrote;

> In applying my mind to politics, I have resolved to demonstrate by a certain and undoubted course of argument, or to deduce from the very condition of human nature, not what is new and unheard of, but only such things as agree best with practice . . . I have laboured carefully, not to mock, lament, or execrate, but to understand human actions; and to this end I have looked upon passions, such as love, hatred, anger, envy, ambition, pity, and the other perturbations of

the mind, not in the light of vices of human nature, but as properties, just as pertinent to it, as are heat, cold, storm, thunder, and the like to the nature of the atmosphere.[15]

Spinoza's practical guide to the rules of monarchical dominion covers the importance of preserving the firmness of law, encouraging transparency in government, selecting counselors through non-nepotistic procedures, ensuring that judges not be easily bribed, properly timing ambassadorial missions, and maintaining the separation of church and state. But, most of all, he dissects, as Stendhal would later, the way individual passions and demands—the stuff of psychopolitics— complicate paradigms of enlightened rationalism and its contemporary variant, the political science of rational choice. As Steven Smith observes in *Spinoza, Liberalism, and the Question of Jewish Identity*, Spinoza

> was deeply attuned to the realities of political power and in the idiom of his time sought to reach an understanding of the human condition as it really was, not as it was imagined or wished for. Spinoza was passionately political, and he made the theological-political predicament the wellspring of his thought.[16]

He also had, according to Smith, "greater respect for the power of the prophetic imagination and more acceptance of the fragility of human rationality [than is often thought to be the case]."[17] For Antonio Negri, coming at Spinoza from the position of an affirmative communism in *The Savage Anomaly* (1982), the *Tractatus Theologico-Politicus* traces the conditions of political emergence.[18] Politics ("small p"), or the chronicling of "les jeux de prince," gives way in Negri's account, as Balibar has observed, to "a materialism of surfaces and singularities

15   Benedictus de Spinoza, *Tractatus Theologico-Politicus*, Gephardt Edition, trans. Samuel Shirley (Leiden: Brill, [1670] 1991), 289.

16   Steven Smith, *Spinoza, Liberalism, and the Question of Jewish Identity* (New Haven: Yale University Press, 1997), xv.

17   Ibid.

18   Antonio Negri, *The Savage Anomaly: The Power of Spinoza's Metaphysics*, trans. Michael Hardt (Minneapolis: University of Minnesota press, [1982] 1991).

without mediation or transcendence and a political theory of the constitutive power of the multitude."[19] Negri gives us Spinoza becoming Stendhal; the avatar of political life-forms that both inhabit and exceed classic models of liberalism, republicanism and democratic institutionalism. But what Negri edits out—psychopolitics, psychopower, the yearning for metaphysical absolutes and new existential modes of being—is what Sartre may have gestured toward when he enigmatically pronounced his desire in *Situations* I, 1947 "to be Stendhal and Spinoza at one and the same time" [*Être à la fois Stendhal et Spinoza*].[20]

---

19   Étienne Balibar, *Spinoza and Politics*, trans. Peter Snowdon (London and New York: Verso, 1998), xiv.

20   "Être à la fois Stendhal et Spinoza." Jean-Paul Sartre, *Situations I* (Paris: Gallimard [1947] 1964).

Collateral Damage

In focusing on "political annihilation"—in the sense of taking out an enemy, plotting to derail a rival, advancing political ambition by means of a calculus of collateral damage—one traces a cartography of kill zones shaping the plotlines of nineteenth-century political fiction. These narratives are distinct from those associated with epics of catastrophism, as in the explosive arcs of the "last man" genre, popular after the French Revolution, and arguably linked to the violent restructuring of social class and the succession of public executions during the Terror. "Last man" novels were built on the chassis of Biblical apocalypse, featuring shipwrecks, pandemics, natural disasters, eco-catastrophe, human devolution, and cosmological extinction. Secular, yet rife with theodicy, these works took hold during the French Restoration.[1] They complemented sagas of national decline, military defeat, and depression over the loss of political idealism.

In political fiction, by contrast, historical events are no longer identifiable with a national cataclysm, epistemic break, world-historical turn or tragic attack even if they appear as the backdrop (as in Flaubert's *L'Education sentimentale*). History is recessive, played out in cramped arenas in which "what happens" is difficult to localize or temporalize. The battlefield is a social space crowded with major and

---

1 The canon included Jean-Baptiste Cousin de Grainville's *Le Dernier homme*, Mary Shelley's *The Last Man*, H. G. Wells's *The War of the Worlds*, Jules Verne's "L'Éternel Adam" (in which a tsunami wipes out human civilization), Jack London's *The Scarlet Plague* (a pandemic leading to a culture of tribal survivalism), and J. -H. Rosny's *La Mort de la terre* (an eco-horror story of water shortage). Darwin's *On the Origin of the Species* (1859) and Herbert Spencer's eugenics of selectionism, *Principles of Biology* (1864), lent further impetus to the rise of the warlocks, and to a decadent fin-de-sièclism bracketed by Max Nordau's *Entartung* (Degeneration [1892]) and Freud's *Civilization and its Discontents* (1930).

minor characters moving from the deputy chambers to the gaming table, from the ballroom to the bedroom, from Paris to the redoubts of rural constituents and impoverished family members. In this picture, the sovereign state may loom as an impersonal power from which force emanates, but its institutional structures of governmentality dissolve within distributed networks of sociality. Loosely associated agents arrange themselves into coalitions or enemy factions around the void of community, their ambitions muddied by short-term ends and compromise formations. In place of tragic allegories of revolutionary social change, we have sideshows of Realpolitik. Political fiction, in this sense, documents the foreclosure of a progressive, revolutionary program, wherein party infighting is substituted for collective solidarity, and the "Quai"—with its culture of diplomatic formalities—is elevated over and above the legislation of equality and justice. It provides a virtual instruction manual on how to survive "in the thick of it," with lessons in information trafficking, publicity-mongering, hamstringing the opposition, political hostage-taking and the use of proxies to bring down enemies. As Balzac wrote of Restoration society in *La Duchesse de Langeais*, "The Faubourg Saint-Germain played with batons, believing that they were power itself."[2] Balzac is recording how political operatives think: doubtful of their own real authority, they rely on the prosthetics of sovereignty. Similarly, in Balzac's novella *Another Study of Womankind*, the ability to take the pulse, to perform the social read, is the deadliest weapon of all. When Prime Minister de Marsy is asked how he learned to be a skilled politician, he notes his special knack for "observing as if from without all the movements of our life."[3] The wide-view lens trained on an open field of social relationality brings to mind a drone's remote surveillance camera or shooter.

The comparison of the political field to a war zone is a well-worn trope, but drone theory brings something specific to the comparison. It lends weight to political forensics, to the calculated ratios of return

---

2   Honoré de Balzac, *The Duchess of Langeais*, trans. Carol Cosman, in *The Human Comedy: Selected Stories* (New York: New York Review of Books, 2014), 306.

3   Honoré de Balzac, *Another Study of Womankind*, trans. Jordan Stump, in *The Human Comedy*, 21.

on damages that transform the routine pursuit of power into a deadly business. The drone model of warfare provides a specific way of thinking—albeit anachronistically—about the technics of statecraft consolidated by the two Napoleons, both of whom refined techniques of spying, censorship, and domestic policing within a democratized culture of micropolitical management. In this picture, the sovereign comes to resemble a drone operator, a remote-controller of the political field, itself mediated by "society." The political social climber, in order to succeed, must learn to mimic the sovereign controller by becoming predatory towards others, and by de-collateralizing him or herself from the damage wrought by others. Consider, in this regard, Lucien de Rubempré in *Illusions perdues*, honing the skills required to undo his own social annihilation:

> So that is society! Lucien thought to himself as he went down to l'Houmeau . . . Far from discouraging him, Lucien's rage and the repulse to his ambition, served only to give him new strength . . . As he walked, he drew out one by one the poisoned darts that had wounded him, and demolished in his own mind the fools with whom he had had to deal; he thought of witty repartees to the stupid questions that they had asked him, and was in despair to think that these brilliant replies had only occurred to him after the event.[4]

In their work on drone theory, the philosopher Grégoire Chamayou and the architectural theorist Léopold Lambert characterize drone targets as force fields of vulnerability, inclusive of and surpassing their discrete bodies. Around the epidermal envelope is an apocalyptic halo, a "perimeter of destruction," a zone of potential harm where collateral damage happens. Chamayou considers this halo of potential annihilation to be a key component of the forensics of drone warfare. I would extend the concept to "small p" political warfare. The drone effect becomes perceptible when the target is eliminated, and those falling under the nimbus of its halo are collaterally destroyed. In this case the apocalypse is invisible, or only remotely apparent in the aura

---

4 Honoré de Balzac, *Lost Illusions*, trans. Kathleen Raine (New York: Modern Library, 1997), 101.

projecting off of the bodies of political actors. This is especially apparent in Zola's *Son Excellence Eugène Rougon*, in which Napoleon III is first encountered in the form of a giant, public shadow whose silhouette merges with a figure on a billboard advertisement. The aureole of danger coming off of the political strongman transfers to the perimeter of smoke that hangs over the scene of a bomb attack. When the Orsini plot to assassinate the emperor (involving Risorgimento militants placing a bomb beneath his carriage) is recounted in the novel, we see the emperor emerge unscathed out from under "the crude glare of the gas" and the "wreathing smoke." Meanwhile, the hapless bystanders who entered the radius of the kill zone are reduced to mere statistics of collateral damage:

> More than fifty people were struck. A woman in a blue silk dress was killed on the spot and stretched stark in the gutter. Two soldiers lay dying on the road. An aide-de-camp, wounded in the neck, left drops of blood behind him.[5]

The themes of human targeting and calculated damage will be repeated over and over throughout the work, often through the motif of the minor accident.

When Rougon plots to take out his political rival Count de Marsy, for example, there are numerous little "accidents" noted that seem to be unmotivated narrative surplus, but which prove crucial to the goals of political connivance and successful attack because they limn the radius of danger and vulnerability that encircles unsuspecting victims. Madame de Combelot, cozying up to the emperor, mentions an accident she suffered getting into a cab where a flounce of her dress was torn away. This anecdote sets in motion a whole *machine de guerre* that leads another member of the entourage to recount the tale of "a woman, a well-known dealer in perfumery, who had fallen from her horse during the previous week and broken her arm."[6] The social scene then shifts to a hunting party where de Marsy's blowsy, jealous mistress

---

5   Emile Zola, *Son Excellence Eugène Rougon*, in *Oeuvres complètes*, vol. 3, ed. Henri Mitterand (Paris: Fasquelle, Cercle du Livre Précieux, 1967), 194.

6   Ibid., 142.

Madame de Llorentz happens to overhear a story about a stag that ran into a farmyard "and charged the hounds so suddenly that a lady had her leg broken amid the confusion."[7] This anonymous lady—yet another victim of collateral damage—leads by association to Clorinde de Balbi. Within earshot of Madame Llorentz, Clorinde describes an accident she had when out horseback riding with de Marsy. Having "almost broken her leg," she repairs somewhere with him to recover. Tongues start to wag:

> They had perhaps, both dismounted for a few minutes' rest; there were a large number of shelter places, huts and sheds and pavilions, in the forest. However, it seemed to Madame de Llorentz that this suggestion prompted more smiling, and that the others were stealthily eyeing her jealous anger. As for Rougon, he kept silent, but beat a feverish tattoo on his knees with his fingertips.[8]

Psychopower is applied like a military technology to attack the target's brain, filling him or her with paranoia. Madame de Llorentz, much like the autobiographical narrator in Rousseau's *Rêveries du promeneur solitaire*, becomes increasingly caught in its grip. Everything— the hint of a smile on the faces of the other guests, the tapping of a knee by Rougon—becomes evidence of romantic betrayal, bringing her closer to seeking revenge by releasing a cache of letters that will destroy de Marsy's career and allow his archrival Rougon to return to power. Sensing the heightened vulnerability of their prey, Rougon's ground troops move in on their target:

> They availed themselves of everything, they drew whatever advantage they could from the most trivial incidents, and worked and worked from the first thing in the morning until the last thing at night. They enlisted their friends as accomplices, and their friends enlisted others. All Paris seemed to share in the intrigue.[9]

---

7   Ibid., 161.
8   Ibid.
9   Ibid., 167.

Like drones launched from remote sites, the minions take out obstacles to Rougon's power, almost like automatons or robots: "In the most out-of-the-way districts people began to yearn for Rougon's triumph without being able to say why."[10]

As Rougon triumphs in his new position as minister of the interior, he becomes the sovereign's body double—a caricature of imperial statecraft and authoritarian muscle: "'No moderation, mind! They must be made to fear you.'" The Emperor "had just armed him, too, with that terrible Law of General Safety, which authorized confinement in Algeria or the expulsion from the empire of anyone who might be convicted of a political offence."[11] Enemies of the state must be systematically routed out and crushed; we see this happen in the case of Martineau, a minor character with Republican political sympathies. He is denounced as an accomplice in the Orsini assassination plot by his sister-in-law Madame Correur, who stands to inherit his property. Rougon dispatches an unscrupulous henchman to bring Martineau in for questioning, despite his being gravely ill, and of course, the Republican martyr dies.

The Martineau episode of spying, betrayal and ideological repression conforms to the generic outlines of what D. A. Miller dubbed "the novel of the police." Miller argues that the police function of surveillance and regulation bleeds into "a pervasive culture of social discipline," yielding distinct subgenres of literature, including detective fiction. Luc Boltanski makes a similar argument when he casts the police procedural and the spy novel as responses—like the nation-state itself—to post-revolutionary class volatility and unstable financial markets. In his discussion of his book *Enigmes et complots: une enquête à propos d'enquêtes* (Mysteries and Conspiracies: Detective Stories, Spy Novels and the Making of Modern Societies), Luc Boltanski conjectures that

> if a link exists between the Nation-State and the birth of the police procedural, we should be able to see that different forms of literature are linked to different types of State organization . . . In the case of

---

10 Ibid.
11 Ibid., 197.

the spy novel, it is the State itself, and not just a local reality, or a village, which is destabilized. Movements and flows of unknown origin imperil the integrity of the whole territory. In the global space of a country, not one single thing can be above suspicion, even at the highest level of the State, where moles can now be found.[12]

For Boltanski, the spy novel, and before that, detective fiction, capture not only the citizen's fear of targeting by the state, but also the state's fear of being penetrated by moles and rogue agents. The ante is raised as the century proceeds: the state in its oppressive reactivity becomes not only a model of "discipline and punish," but one of "survey and annihilate" (Chamayou's "surveiller et anéantir").

Both Miller and Boltanski fix on the state as the Leviathan, a totalitarian allegoreme in which the control society burrows into the citizen's psyche and destroys free will. The specter of hyper-sovereignty haunts the fiction of "énigmes et complots" (mysteries and conspiracies, invisible plots, shadowy agents, bankers, anarchists, secret societies) and points it in the direction of Orwellian dystopias of dictatorship and mind control. While my own view of top-down, supranational drone operations is not incompatible with Miller and Boltanski's tentacular projections of the paranoid security state and its policing apparatus, my focus is not on the personification of sovereign power, but on its narrative forensics, which project a topography of remote responsibility composed of political targets and collateralized indirect objects. These direct and indirect objects, when annihilated or wounded, allow for the advancement of political agendas (they clear an obstacle out of a pathway to power), or impede the achievement of premeditated goals by producing damage that stiffens the resolve of the opponent or adds recruits to the enemy camp. Either way, collateral effects add complexity to the art of calculation. They are manifest in the novel as body counts that often barely register or accidents that are enumerated only in passing. They appear as intrigues that do not obviously sway the plot, nor rise to the level of a cataclysm, and yet prove to be tipping points that make an attack backfire or render the

---

12   Sylvain Bourmeau, Luc Boltanski, "Luc Boltanski interroge Holmes et Maigret," *Libération*, February 16, 2012, next.liberation.fr.

protagonist vulnerable to retributive justice. Characters, sometimes so minor they do not warrant names, stray into the harm's way of story-telling, just as they might meander into a kill zone marked out by a drone operated from afar. They are part of the statistics used to calculate cost/benefit ratios in political campaigns. They are the spent fuel of manipulative politicians seeking expedient byways for advancing their careers. The lady who breaks her arm or falls off a horse; the mistress who is shamed in order to motivate her to destroy the career of the man who supports her; the cuckolded husband shelved to a minor post in order to provide cover for his wife, herself the important political operative; the fatally ill widow of a left-wing attorney denounced by his venal sister, soon to inherit the couple's home; the druggist, arrested by a thuggish commissary incentivized to meet his quota of political arrests; all these miniature, virtually anonymous catastrophes add up to no singular event, no sublime assertion of Reason of State or political theodicy. If the nation-state is a force majeure, it makes itself intelligible not as a force of history or formative condition of political ontology or superstructure of ideology, but rather as a delocalized network of potential kill zones in the social field. The outlines of the bodies of the minor characters who have been disappeared or rendered inoperative exert a virtually imperceptible pressure on the visible plotlines, but they can be traced in negative relief. They provide forensic evidence of political annihilation as a virtual geography of micropolitics.

This spectacle of low-grade micropolitical disaster is hardly the stuff of apocalypse, but it describes the damages and fatalities embedded in what passes for "just politics," that is, politicking, blocking or eliminating your political rivals. This form of unexceptional politics ultimately leads to a question posed by Chamayou: "What is the state made of?"[13] To which one answers: no longer the king's body, the corporate body of legislators, a collectively shared idea of national governance, or that which remains anathema to political community. The state, rather, is invested in a cynegetic power, manifest, as in the case of drone warfare, in a cartography of manhunts, kill zones and calculated halos of collateral damage.

---

13   Grégoire Chamayou, *Théorie du drone* (Paris: La fabrique, 2013), 305.

Thermocracy

According to Leo Strauss, "Machiavelli is the only philosopher who has lent the weight of his name to any way of political thinking and political acting which is as old as political society itself."[1] In *Machiavelli in the Making*, Claude Lefort takes this observation yet further by itemizing the myriad and often contradictory associations attached to the philosopher's proper name:

> Before reading Machiavelli, we have a certain idea of Machiavellianism. Although we may know nothing about the man and his work, we use the term without hesitation. It designates a character, a mode of behavior, or an action as surely as the word doorknob designates a certain object; embedded in the language, its derivation matters little: it serves. What Guiradet wrote at the end of the eighteenth century, it seems we can still repeat: "The name Machiavelli seems consecrated in all languages to recall or even to express the detours and heinous acts of the shrewdest, most criminal politics" . . .
>
> What is a Machiavellian personage? A Machiavellian undertaking or destiny? . . . Machiavellianism implies first of all the idea of a mastery of one's conduct. To be Machiavellian is to do evil intentionally, to put one's knowledge at the service of a design that is essentially detrimental to someone else. Hence one cannot be Machiavellian in the way one just is crafty or devious, by nature. If it includes ruse, it is a methodical ruse, if a crime, then one that bears the mark of an operation rigorously adjusted to the intention of the agent, or fully aware of what it is about . . .

1   Leo Strauss, *Thoughts on Machiavelli* (Chicago, IL: University of Chicago Press, 1978), 10.

[The Machiavellian] allows himself to be distracted by neither hatred nor resentment, nor by any prompting that would risk putting him in another's power, This last trait is essential: he is sovereign . . .

Malefic logic, trick after trick, serene perversity, the voluptuous enjoyment of crime—such are no doubt the components of a term to which we have grown accustomed through literature, the press, and everyday linguistic usage.[2]

Balzac famously wrote of *The Charterhouse of Parma* that Stendhal "had written the modern version of *The Prince* that Machiavelli himself would have written if he were living in exile from Italy during the nineteenth century."[3] Eminent critics would challenge this reduction of the novel to its political content, but Balzac's reading is persuasive and worth recuperating when one takes stock of how Machiavellianism—a popularized synonym for political realism—came to define a whole subgenre of nineteenth-century political fiction.

It is Zola's 1876 novel of parliamentary life, *Son Excellence Eugène Rougon*, that best exemplifies Machiavellianism in the guise of a Second Empire political fiction. It was one of the least successful novels in the Rougon-Macquart series, as well as one of the most difficult for Zola to write given his distaste, as Robert Lethbridge has observed, for the kind of overcomplicated plots exacted by political fiction.[4] For background, Zola drew on his experience as a political journalist (for *La Tribune*, *Rappel*, and *La Cloche* among others), and in particular, on his coverage of trips by the National Assembly to Bordeaux and Versailles in 1871 and 1872. During this early period of the Third Republic, in which Parliament was adrift in the wake of *la défaite*, politics was marked by "sterile discussions, mediocre

---

2   Claude Lefort, *Machiavelli in the Making*, trans. Michael B. Smith (Evanston, IL: Northwestern University Press, 2012), 62–4.

3   Honoré de Balzac, "Études sur M. Beyle," *La Revue parisienne*, September 25, 1840, in *Oeuvres complètes* (Paris: Cercle du Bibliophile, 1967), 452. Translation my own.

4   Robert Lethbridge, "Zola et la fiction du pouvoir: Son Excellence Eugène Rougon," *Cahiers naturalistes* 44, 1998, 294.

bureaucratic initiatives, [and] the distribution of favors and legal end-runs."[5] Zola worked this prevailing mood of political enervation into his depiction of the Napoleonic oligarchy, a regime notorious for its illegitimate origin in a coup d'état, rule by plebiscite, absence of democratic procedure, skill at playing parties and classes off against each other, predilection for corruption as the reigning modus operandi, and sophistication in the production of propaganda and state pageantry. What is most interesting for my purposes, however, is the way Zola translates the "malefic logic" of Machiavellianism into a total political environment.

In chronicling the career of Eugène Rougon, the fictive minister and lieutenant of Napoleon III—a composite of real-life politicians Eugène Rouher, General Espinasse, the Duc de Persigny, and Guizot (Napoleon's Karl Rove, or conservative "brain")—Zola added special biographical depth in the prequel *The Fortune of the Rougons* (1871, the very first work in the Rougon-Macquart series). Here, Zola recounts Rougon's upbringing by lower-middle-class parents in the fictional town of Plassans. An early, fervent supporter of Louis-Napoleon, attested to in letters to his father that are secretly perused by his mother Félicité, Rougon exhibits a preternatural flair for divining the political future. This talent endows his own fortunes with the same aura of predestination as the one he accords to the emperor.

> He had believed in him prior even to his return to France, at a time when Bonapartism was treated as a ridiculous chimera. Félicité understood that her son had been a very active secret agent since 1848. Although he did not clearly explain his position in Paris, it was evident that he was working for the Empire, under the orders of personages whose names he mentioned with a sort of familiarity.[6]

The fact that Rougon is identified as a professional spy—and as a seer who anticipates which way the political winds will blow by catching,

---

5   Georges Bafaro, "Quelques aspects du pouvoir dans *Son Excellence Eugène Rougon*," *Cahiers naturalistes* 44, 1998, 305. Translation my own.

6   Emile Zola, *The Fortune of the Rougons*, trans. Alfred Vizetelly (Charleston, SC: Bibliobazaar, 2006), 103.

quite literally, what is in the air—approaches him to Zola himself, whose aggrandized mastery of the elements comes through in his preface to *The Fortune of the Rougons*, where he congratulates himself for "resolving the duplex question of temperament and environment":

> And when I have posessession of every thread, and hold a complete social group in my hands, I shall show this group at work, participating in an historical period; I shall depict it in action, with all its varied energies, and I shall analyse both the will power of each member and the general tendency of the whole.[7]

Son Excellence Eugène Rougon opens with a striking evocation of the atmosphere permeating the legislative chamber. If the intangibles of politics could actually be traced to a sensorium, they would appear in the rapid-fire babble ("balbutiement rapide") listened to by none of the deputies, and the "brouhaha" filling the chamber; we hear the subterranean rumble of "small p" politics.[8] This hum lulls the senses, as does the damp of the May weather that emanates directly from the boredom of somnolent legislators:

> Some were reclining in their red velvet-covered seats, with listless eyes, already half-asleep. Others, leaning over their desks, as though wearied by the compulsory labour of a public sitting, were beating a gentle tattoo on the mahogany with their finger-tips. Through the ceiling-window, which revealed a crescent of grey sky, the light of a rainy May afternoon streamed down perpendicularly upon the pompous severity of the Chamber.[9]

Zola depicts politics as contagious affect, a layer of pollution that courses through social spaces, often in the form of gossip:

---

7   Ibid., 15.

8   Emile Zola, *Son Excellence Eugène Rougon*, in *Oeuvres complètes*, vol. 3, ed. Henri Mitterand (Paris: Fasquelle, Cercle du Livre Précieux, 1967). Translated by Ernest Alfred Vizetelly as *His Excellency* (New York: Mondial, 2006).

9   Zola, *Son Excellence Eugène Rougon*, 289.

They repeated the stories which were told about those two Italian women—mother and daughter—who were semi-adventuresses and semi-grand ladies, and were to be met everywhere, at all the parties and gatherings, at the houses of state ministers, in the stage-boxes of minor theatres, on the sands at fashionable watering-places, and even in out-of-the-way hostelries.[10]

It animates whispering campaigns, as when Rougon's supporters mobilize to get him back into power through press leaks and partisan attacks:

Each of them took some special *rôle*; and whispered councils were held in the corners of Rougon's own drawing room on Sunday and Thursday evenings. They portioned out the various difficult matters, and every day they scattered through Paris, invincibly determined upon gaining some influence or other to their cause. No assistance was too insignificant for their acceptance; the most trifling help might be useful. They availed themselves of everything, the drew whatever advantage they could from the most trivial incidents, and worked and worked from the first thing in the morning until the last thing at night. They enlisted their friends as accomplices, and their friends enlisted others. All Paris seemed to share in the intrigue.[11]

And it is tracked like a miasma that filters into private rooms, transforming them into spaces of entropy and reliquaries of dirty little secrets. When Rougon peers into the boudoir of Clorinde Balbi—the political adventuress modeled after the Comtesse de Castiglione—he catches sight of an unmade bed and soiled clothes:

Upon a screen standing in front of the bed and half concealing the tumbled coverlets, some splashed petticoats which the girl had worn the previous day had been hung to dry, while a wash-basin, full of soapy water, stood on the floor in front of the window, and the cat of

---

10   Zola, *His Excellency*, 9.
11   Ibid., 167.

the house, a grey one, slept, comfortably curled, in the midst of a heap of garments.[12]

The bedroom prepares the way for a scene in which Clorinde, costumed as a semi-naked Diana, cavorts with a posse of spies, artists, and refugees, all of whom jockey for position in a suffocating gallery where hothouse plants expire, sculptor's clay lies in a heap of excremental waste, and a crush of furniture creates labyrinthine passages that obstruct foot traffic.

In a meteorological evocation of Parisian streets in the wake of a failed terrorist bomb attack on the emperor (the "attentat d'Orsini" of January 14, 1858), Zola distills the essence of anti-Imperial violence as an airborne malevolence that converts into authoritarian weather and enables environments to message human agents. Feeling stultified, Rougon leaves his apartment and experiences the weight of the sky as revenge for that brilliant, clear day when the emperor—at great tax cost to the state—staged his son's baptism before a roaring crowd:

> The sky was black and moonless; the city was terror-stricken and dumb; the quays were deserted and swept by a shudder which seemed to scare the very gaslights . . . Rougon drew in long breaths of air, and felt that he loved that cut-throat Paris, in whose terror-stricken gloom he was regaining supreme power.[13]

Sleaze, fear, and criminality come together as the elements that will forge Rougon's aggrandized power. As he breathes in the fatal atmosphere he gathers resolve for a more ruthless mode of governance. "Jules, give me a synonym for authority," Rougon says to his secretary, as he prepares a series of repressive decrees. "'Well, there's power, government, empire,' the young man answer[s] with a smile."[14]

Walter Benjamin's gnomic assertion, in *Paris, Capital of the Nineteenth Century*, that "Empire is the style of revolutionary terrorism, for which the state is an end in itself" refers to the empire of

---

12 Ibid., 48–9.
13 Ibid., 194–5.
14 Ibid., 196.

Napoleon I, but finds equal exemplification in the Second Empire of Napoloeon III.[15] For, as Benjamin implies, Napoleon III's success lay precisely in crafting a Second Empire style—repressive governance infused into the materials of technological, aesthetic modernity—that sublated revolution and subsumed bourgeois domination and state functionalism. In *Son Excellence*, one could say, the "Empire Style" is immanent not only in the pompier décor of the Assembly, the salon, and the public square, festooned with pompous emblems of state power (let us recall the ridiculous statue that Napoleon III commissioned of himself in the likeness of Vercingétorix, which graces the excavation site at Alésia), but also in authoritarian weather; a stultifying atmosphere of corrupted democracy, approximating what Gilles Châtelet dubbed "thermocracy," a term applying broadly to "*hydraulic despotisms*" and to "*social chemistry* that operates *internally*, through dissolutions, catalyses and fermentations that implcably inundate the bulkheads that supposedly divided oft the spheres of politics, economics, and the social."[16]

Second Empire politics is an abiding subject of the entire Rougon-Macquart series, most notably of *La curée* (The Quarry), where government collusion in schemes for kickbacks from windfall profits in the area of real estate speculation are lifted from the playbook of Baron Haussmann's memoirs. But there is no novel in Zola's corpus, nor for that matter, any literary work of, or about, the Second Empire, in which politics is so exclusively the focus. What comes into view—and reinforces the thermocratic or environmental structure of the political novel—is the narrative armature of countless subplots, built up from backstories that involve illicit or illegal transactions: patronage, nepotism, scandal-mongering, earmarking, sexual affairs. Sorting through these episodes one cannot but be

15   Walter Benjamin, "Paris, the Capital of the Nineteenth Century," trans. Howard Eiland, in *Walter Benjamin: Selected Writings*, vol. 3 (1935–38), eds Howard Eiland and Michael W. Jennings (Cambridge, MA: Harvard University Press, 2002), 33.

16   Gilles Châtelet, *To Live and Think Like Pigs: The Incitement of Envy and Boredom in Market Democracies*, trans. Robin Mackay (New York: Sequence Press, 2014), 67 and 77. For Châtelet, thermocracy "shatters politics into 'microdecisions' and relies on a thermometer that calibrates and neutralizes the market-chaos of opinion," 60.

struck by historical parallels with events that occurred during the administration of George W. Bush.

Most notable is an episode involving earmarking that resembles the "Bridge to Nowhere" scam spearheaded in 2005 by Alaska Senator Ted Stevens (he proposed financing the Gravina Island Bridge, which would be longer than the Golden Gate and would serve only a small airport and fifty residents). In this case, Kahn, a Jewish deputy, joins forces with du Poizat, a sub-prefect who represents Bressuire, to divert a new rail line projected to run from Niort to Angers. Bressuire happens to be the town where Kahn owns a blast furnace operation that will fail to prosper without a transportation link. Kahn had been close to sealing the deal, but he was suddenly blocked by Rougon's rival, de Marsy, who was furious at being excluded from the deal. Marsy then becomes the target of "Rovian" tactics: namely, political smears and guilt by association.

> They spoke of Marsy with all the rageful hostility which politicians show for an adversary. They revelled in the strongest language, bringing all kinds of abominable accusations against him, and so grossly exaggerating those stories which had a foundation of truth that they became mere lies. Du Poizat, who had known Marsy in former days, before the Empire, declared that he was kept at that time by a baroness whose diamonds he had exhausted in three months.[17]

Marsy is accused of taking bribes, of forking over huge sums to an actress at the Opéra bouffes, and of defrauding shareholders through a shell company investment in Egyptian canals: "The shareholders discover[ed] that not a single shovelful of earth had been turned, although they had been paying out money for a couple of years or so."[18] Here, Zola puts on full view the familiar tactic of accusing the political opponent of graft and corruption so as to distract attention from it in the home district.

Another episode calls to mind the Hurricane Katrina scandal in

---

17   Zola, *His Excellency*, 32.
18   Ibid., 33.

New Orleans. In 1856 there was devastating flood damage in the Rhone and Loire valleys, which the emperor was not above exploiting for publicity. Lithographs capture him astride his horse, a prostrate woman on a mattress holding up her hand on the left, and a posse of decorated soldiers on the right, as if anticipating the staging of the modern photo op. David Baguley notes key examples in two paintings—Lazergues's and Janet-Lange's *Napoléon III distribuant des secours aux inondés de Lyon*, and Antigna's *Napoléon III visitant les ouvriers des ardoisières d'Angers*—in which, he remarks,

> the emperor stands surrounded by a host of respectful workers and their families arriving in boats by the banks of the swollen river. Both paintings were shown in the 1857 Salon, as was the most studied and impressive of such compositions, Bourgereau's *Napoléon III visitant les inondés de Tarascon* (1856).[19]

Zola's prose description is clearly indebted to these iconic scenes:

> Thousands of families had been rendered homeless. The subscriptions which had been opened on all sides were insufficient for the relief of such great distress. However, they asserted that the Emperor had exhibited most admirable courage and generosity. At Lyons he had been seen fording the low parts of the inundated city, and at Tours he had spent three hours rowing in a boat through the submerged streets; and everywhere he had lavishly distributed alms.[20]

David Baguley contends that Napoleon's image-mongering on the occasion of the floods exemplifies the crucial shift from the martial-heroic register into the humanitarian-religious one:

> The military features of the scene are totally overwhelmed by the religiosity of the composition, as the Savior brings succor to his

---

19 David Baguley, *Napoleon III and His Regime: An Extravaganza* (Baton Rouge: Louisiana State University Press, 2000), 157.

20 Zola, *His Excellency*, 87–8.

people, with one hand dipping into the money bag and the other reaching out in a benign gesture to the beautiful young supplicant girl on her knees, shown in remarkable relief in the full light.[21]

Noting that there is "at times something absurdly incongruous about such scenes where the stiff and thoroughly conventionalized military presence seems out of place," Baguley places special emphasis on the political impact of Napoleon's shrewd use of conventionalized images. Emptied of any real content, they signify "Second Empireness," or "Napoleonicity."[22]

In addition to recording how the Second Empire used new media to project a political "extravaganza," Zola tracked the workings of low-level politicking, revealing the likelihood of drag on politicians' careers by relatives or people from their hometowns. Rougon finds himself compromised by members of the Charbonnel family, who hail from his native Plassans; at regular intervals throughout the novel, they petition him to intervene on their behalf to break a family will that has legated 500,000 francs of inheritance to the Sisters of the Holy Family.

Against this backdrop of petty special interests, Zola presents Clorinde de Balbi, the consummate Second Empire *intrigante*. Nicknamed Mademoiselle Machiavel, Clorinde is a courtesan-spy whose origins and ambitions are murky. Is she the daughter of a count? Or was she born after he died? Her marriage situation is equally unclear; she is rumored to have a complicated ménage that blurs open marriage, a French divorce, and concubinage. She is thought to have exercised power in the Italian court of King Victor-Emmanuel through a lover who was high in government, but a scandal has forced her to leave Turin and move with her mother to Paris. Rougon investigates their police files and discovers that they live in luxury, with no clear source of income. Throughout the novel Clorinde is engaged in mysterious and elaborate operations. She nurtures "dreams of turning Europe topsy-turvy, and would go twice a day to Chevalier Rusconi's to meet his diplomatic acquaintances."[23] She goes out "superbly

---

21 Baguley, *Napoleon III and His Regime*, 157.
22 Ibid., 158.
23 Zola, *Son Excellence Eugène Rougon*, 327.

arrayed," using her beauty as a weapon, first to seduce Rougon, who decides she is too dangerous to marry himself, and second, to work for Rougon as a go-between, securing favors from the Emperor and information from Rougon's rivals.

Clorinde is modeled directly on the real-life Countess de Castiglione (better known as La Castiglione), a notorious Second Empire character immortalized as an occult figure in one of the Arsène Lupin novels, and the subject of several major exhibitions after an essay by Abigail Solomon-Godeau brought attention to the bizarre poses and anatomical close-ups that La Castiglione staged in the famous photographic studio of Mayer and Pierson in the 1850s. The mistress of Napoleon III from 1856–57, La Castiglione was pushed into Napoleon's orbit as the envoy of her distant cousin Camillo di Cavour, King Victor Emmanuel's minister and a fervent supporter of the Risorgimento hero Giuseppe Mazzini. After infiltrating the court, she lobbied for the cause of Italian unification. And though she came under a cloud of suspicion after the Orsini attack on Napoleon by a band of Mazzini-inspired patriots, it eventually dissipated. After the defeat of 1870, she was even entrusted by the French government with a mission—ultimately successful—to dissuade Otto von Bismark from ordering the Prussian occupation of Paris.

La Castiglione belonged to a large cast of courtesans and consorts who manipulated the ennobled and politically powerful during the Second Empire. The star lineup included Céline Montaland, an actress who, much like La Castiglione, installed herself with her mother in Paris and became a mistress of Napoleon III; Anna Deslion, a favorite of prince Napoleon and the Comte de Rouget; Suzanne Lagier, *la tribade* famous for performing sex acts with women for gentlemen voyeurs; Hortense Schneider, a lover of the Duc de Gramont-Caderousse who reportedly lavished such huge sums on her that he was brought to ruin; and Cora Pearl, an opera star who used her lovers to indulge an extravagant appetite for luxury homes, stables and race-horses. Though many of these mistresses exerted political influence and trafficked in compromising information, none surpassed "la divine comtesse" (Robert de Montesquieu's sobriquet) in the art of mixing sex and political ambition.

Zola's Clorinde incarnates La Castiglione as an indispensable yet unstable fixture of Second Empire Machivellianism—a form of politics that remains ever-present yet mysterious to the beholder. Through Rougon's eyes Clorinde appears as "a fixed point of the unknown;" a magnet of vicious gossip, a woman of dubious virtue, and an embodiment of sovereign surveillance and networks of espionage. Like the spy-heroines in a classic thriller, Clorinde demonstrates skill at mixing seduction with fact-finding. She manipulates Rougon into bragging about his important roles in the security council and the senate, and only after he has leaked information about the new government that is being formed does he realize he has been played: "You are very curious, aren't you mademoiselle Machiavel."[24] Rattled by Clorinde's smoke rings and irritating smile, which blur his perception of reality and truth, Rougon struggles with the suspicion that she is the one in charge of his political destiny. "Here you are on the pinnacle which you were so anxious to reach,' Clorinde says tauntingly;

> "Everyone has helped to lift you to it, and events themselves have worked for you" ... As she spoke these words in slow deliberate tones he glanced at Clorinde, lowering his heavy eyelids so as to conceal the fact that he was trying to penetrate her meaning. Why had she spoken of his luck? he wondered. What did she know of the favorable events to which she had referred?[25]

Clorinde functions as an agent of what Ian Hacking calls "tamed chance," revealing how patterns of random motion or contingent occurrences (Machiavellian *fortuna*) appear in historical retrospect as grand schemes. Clorinde's hectic back-channeling and intimate encounters, described as "disordered," "full of holes," and "illogical," will thus be revisioned as designed influence. That this is the source of her strength, her will, betrays an essential indifference to the effects of destruction that her actions wreak on political outcomes. Like a zombie warrior of "small p" politics, operating in a somnambulant state, she throws out small bombs of information that land where they may.

---

24   Zola, *His Excellency*, 100.
25   Zola, *Son Excellence Eugène Rougon*, 213.

The nickname "Mademoiselle Machiavel" feeds into shop-worn clichés around sex and politics, but Zola nuances these clichés, focusing on the transfer of bodily fluids and flows of information that turn sex and politics into mediums of vital materialism or (to borrow Jane Bennett's term) "vibrant matter." Clorinde is a kind of vibrating portal lined with receptors that pick up and transmit political influence. When Rougon asks directly what she did to advance his return to power, she admits to trafficking in influence: "You will never know all that was done for you ... I won over to your side several men who were strongly opposed to you. And I destroyed the influence of others."[26] Clorinde's influence over Rougon is carried on rings of cigarette smoke that cloud his reason. When Rougon abases himself, showering Clorinde with grateful kisses, she brands his forehead with the cigarette. Their contact becomes an exchange of electromagnetic current registered in physical tremors: his shakes migrate to her fidgety hands, and back to him as he squeezes her fingers tight. The pressure of body against body describes politics at its most micrological; at the level of its transference of bacteria, pathogens, affect, pulse, libidinal force, telepathic eros. It is here that the reader registers most palpably the claustrophobic ether of thermocracy, identified not just with an imperial state bureaucracy propped up by apparatuses of spying, policing, and censorship, but more importantly, with the substances and currents that circulate by air—political atmospheres that bear aloft the confluence of influence.

---

26 Zola, *His Excellency*, 216.

Milieu

In the concluding pages of his 2005 broadside *Hatred of Democracy* (La haine de la démocratie), written during Chirac's presidency and Sarkozy's short stint as minister of finance in the lead-up to the global financial crisis, Jacques Rancière would draw a parallel between "intellectuals today" and the authoritarian elites in Second Empire France who wage all-out war against "the democratic torrent":[1]

> To understand what democracy means is to hear the struggle that is at stake in the word: not simply the tones of anger and scorn with which it can be imbued but, more profoundly, the slippages and reversals of meaning that it authorizes, or that one authorizes oneself to make with regard to it. When, in the middle of the manifestations of heightening inequality, our intellectuals become indignant about the havoc wreaked by equality, they exploit a trick that is not new. Already in the nineteenth century, whether under the *monarchie*

---

1 The expression "torrent démocratique" appears in quotes without a specific reference in Rancière's footnote. In Taine's *Graindorge* we find an allusion to "cette prodigieuse multitude mouvante" (that prodigious multitude in motion) which seems roughly approximative. It appears in a chapter of Taine's novel titled "Society" that links democratization not only to certain pastimes but also to the exploding demographics of cultural access, the rise in the numbers of those taking the entrance exams to the *grandes écoles*, the increase in artists presenting at the salons, the surfeit of musicians playing all over town, and so forth. This spread of mediocre talent, in Graindorge's vision, is accompanied by the enhanced commercialization of daily life, including self-advertising. Hippolyte Taine, *Vie et opinions de Monsieur Frédéric-Thomas Graindorge* (Paris: Hachette, 1959), 300. In addition to the explicit reference to Taine as a source for political attitudes towards democracy in Second Empire France, Rancière also cites Armand de Pontmartin's musings on "democracy in literature," a critique of *Madame Bovary* published in the *Nouvelles Causeries du samedi* in 1860.

censitaire or under the authoritarian Empire, the elites of official France—of France reduced to two hundred thousand men, or subject to laws and decrees restricting individual and public liberties—were alarmed at the "democratic torrent" that prevailed in society. Banned in public life, they saw democracy triumphing in cheap fabrics, public transport, boating, open-air painting, the new behavior of young women, and the new turns of phrase of writers. However, they were not innovative in this regard either. The pairing of democracy viewed both as a rigid form of government and as a permissive form of society is the original mode in which the hatred of democracy was rationalized by Plato himself.[2]

Rancière identifies democracy with "a paradoxical condition of politics" associated with the "egalitarian contingency that underpins the inegalitarian contingency itself."[3] One can take this formula literally as a reference to the suspicion and contempt of elites toward the leveling effects of mass culture and the widening of the franchise, but it really may have to do with the supposition that democracy ungrounds itself by spreading democratization. For Rancière, political practices in the domains of art, leisure and work furnish conditions for redistributing power even as they engender new forms of policing and censorship. Thus a process of making-equal is inseparable from inegalitarianism and vice versa: such paradoxes hold as the essence of "politics."

Hatred of Democracy makes scant reference to literature and, unlike other works by Rancière, it offers no concerted politics of the aesthetic.[4] But there is one figure who surfaces as a literary point of

---

2   Jacques Rancière, *Hatred of Democracy*, trans. Steven Corcoran (London and New York: Verso, 2006), 93–4.

3   Ibid., 94.

4   See Rancière, *La parole muette: essai sur les contradictions de la littérature* (Paris: Pluriel, 1998) [*Mute Speech: Literature, Critical Theory, and Politics*, trans. James Swenson (New York: Columbia University Press, 2011)]; *Le partage du sensible: esthétique et politique* (Paris: La fabrique, 2000) [*The Politics of Aesthetics*, trans. Gabriel Rockhill (London: A&C Black, 2013)]; *Politique de la littérature* (Paris: Editions Galilée, 2007) [*Politics of Literature*, trans. Julie Rose (Cambridge, UK: Polity, 2011)]; *Aisthesis: scènes du régime esthétique de l'art* (Paris: Editions Galilée, 2011) [*Aisthesis: Scenes from the Aesthetic Regime of Art*, trans. Zakir Paul (London and New York: Verso, 2013)]; and *Le fil perdu* (Paris: La fabrique, 2014) [*The Lost Thread: The Democracy of Modern Fiction*, trans. Steven Corcoran (London:

reference in Rancière's suggestive parallels between Second Empire society and neoliberal Europe in the early 2000s, and that is Hippolyte Taine. Those popular pastimes, leisure pursuits and objects of consumption—those fleeting figures of a mass society that both offend and energize the conservative state alluded to by Rancière—are tallied on the basis of an anthology of Second Empire attitudes and mores in Taine's 1867 novel *Frédéric Graindorge* (originally published in French as *Notes sur Paris: vie et opinions de Frédéric-Thomas Graindorge*).[5] Rancière footnotes this obscure text in a perfunctory way, but the reference bears further unpacking, pointing to the novel's portrait of a "democratic torrent" that brings out paradoxes of egalitarianism, and illuminates the difficulty of defining what politics is or is not, outside the discourses of political institutions or theories of democracy. (And for Rancière, as we know, *democracy* is the name for a presumptive legal equality valid only for those parts of the people who are counted.)[6]

Taine, in Rancière's reading, elucidates the messy, hateful contents of democracy—which, in embodying a reckless adherence to "limitless growth," induces the contraction of political space. As Rancière underscores in *Hatred of Democracy*,

> The "government of anybody and everybody" is bound to attract the hatred of all those who are entitled to govern men by their birth, wealth, or science. Today it is bound to attract this hatred more radically than ever, since the social power of wealth no longer tolerates any restrictions on its limitless growth, and each day its mechanisms become more closely articulated to those of State action . . . State power and the power of wealth tendentially unite in a sole expert management of monetary and population flows. Together they combine their efforts to reduce the spaces of politics.[7]

Rancière never delivers the hypothetical piece he might have written on Taine's Graindorge, one which might have approached the text as a

---

Bloomsbury, 2016)].

5   Jacques Rancière, *La haine de la démocratie* (Paris: La fabrique, 2005), 102.

6   Jacques Rancière, *Disagreement: Politics and Philosophy* trans. Julie Rose (Minneapolis: University of Minnesota Press, 1999), 61–2.

7   Rancière, *Hatred of Democracy*, 94–5.

sociology of obstructions to a politics worthy of the name; as a study in the evacuated foundation of democracy; or as an exemplary document of the capitalization of existence and the curtailment of political space.[8] But I will argue that Graindorge links the "democratic torrent" to Rancière's aesthetics of milieu, in ways that activate Taine's own theory of milieu in its full philological development. Picking up the threads of Rancière's disparate, occasional allusions to Taine, there are clues to the materialities of his politics.

Graindorge is a document of the "democratic torrent" that by and large failed to endear him to his readers. This comes through in a written exchange with Charles Augustin Sainte-Beuve, in which Taine anxiously acknowledged his influence on this experiment in "moral physiology," requesting the literary critic's frank assessment when the work came out in book form (it was originally published as a series of articles with illustrations by Isidore Planat in *La vie Parisienne*).[9] Sainte-Beuve responded with fair warning that the book would not be well received, because it was too judgmental and harsh in its depictions of social types. "Why," he asks, "are you in such a hurry to translate your impressions into written notes, and these notes into laws?"[10]

Graindorge answers that question in its probe into the laws of the market at the dawn of a new era of finance capital. Perhaps even more than Balzac, Flaubert or Marx, Taine devised a language for describing distribution networks of material artifacts and determinations of the market value of goods and social advantage. According to Jonathan Dewald, from Graindorge's "sharp interest in contemporary material life" we learn

---

8   Rancière holds to the belief that the figment of "democratic man," going back to Plato, "is the product of an operation . . . that aims to ward off an impropriety pertaining to the very principle of politics. The entertaining sociology of a people comprised of carefree consumers, obstructed streets and inverted social roles wards off the presentiment of a more profound evil: that the unnameable democracy is not a form of society refractory to good government and adapted to the lowest common denominator, but the very principle of politics, the principle that institutes politics in founding 'good' government on its own absence of foundation" (*Hatred of Democracy*, 37).

9   Hippolyte Taine to Sainte-Beuve, June 15, 1867, in *Hippolyte Taine: sa Vie et sa Corrrespondance* (Paris: Hachette, 1904), 339.

10   Sainte-Beuve to Taine, July 16, 1867, ibid., 341.

the cost of women's dresses, their fabrics and colors, how marriage proposals were made and what went through the minds of the parties to them, how much income the different levels of Paris society required ... Graindorge's opinions (in addition to appreciation for material comfort) also display a radical detachment from conventional moralities and a readiness to acknowledge the harsh realities of modern life. *Notes sur Paris* can be read as exemplifying the mode of intellectual life that the Magny group represented; one that combined engagement with contemporary social life, philosophical materialism, and freedom from institutional and pious moralizing.[11]

Taine, one could say, prefigured the present theoretical moment: one of philosophical materialism attuned to the financialization of everything. His urban picaresque (anticipating the acidulous "socio-philosophical croquis" of Gilles Châtelet's 1998 *To Live and Think Like Pigs: Envy and Boredom in Market-Economy Democracies*) records how new forms of finance capital generate a milieu that permeates all modes of existence.[12]

Graindorge is an uprooted Frenchman, educated in Britain and Germany, and enriched in America, where he made a fortune by investing in pork and oil and profiting from slave labor. His character is a mystery, and must be painstakingly reconstructed after his death through techniques of forensic autopsy.[13] In this task, "Taine," his

---

11   Jonathan Dewald, *Lost Worlds: The Emergence of French Social History, 1815–1970* (University Park, PA: Penn State University Press), 25. See also, Anne Green, *Changing France: Literature and Material Culture in the Second Empire* (London: Anthem Press, 2011); and Sudhir Hazareesingh, *From Subject to Citizen: The Second Empire and the Emergence of Modern French Democracy* (Princeton: Princeton University Press, 1998).

12   Gilles Châtelet, *To Live and Think Like Pigs: Envy and Boredom in Market-Economy Democracies*, trans. Robin Mackay (New York: Urbanomic, 2014), 2.

13   The final chapter offers more insight into Graindorge's character. Its conceit is a letter addressed to Mssr Marcelin by Graindorge's "private secretary and chiropodist." After outlining the indignities he endured while in Graindorge's employ, and criticizing "the unfortunate traces which a grossly commercial life had left on his mind," he churlishly registers the meager estate left to him upon Graindorge's death. Hippolyte Taine, *Notes on Paris: The Life and Opinions of M. Frédéric Graindorge*, trans. John Austin Stevens (New York: Henry Holt and Co.,

eponymous executor, relies on one Mssr Marcelin (director of *La vie Parisienne*), who had "several views taken of the apartment of the deceased by a photographer in repute. By the aid of several portraits he had obtained the principal traits of the person and costume of M. Graindorge."[14] The photographic evidence turns up strange artifacts—a stuffed crocodile in the boudoir, a portrait of his black servant Sam—but they are mere trace elements of eccentricities belied by the character's bland self-presentation: "His phrases in themselves were mere statements of facts, dull, and very precise."[15] Graindorge applies this fact-based orientation to his Paris venture, a principal aim of which is the creation of a matchmaking service modeled on the Bourse.

> Is not marriage an affair? Is anything else considered in it but proper proportions? Are not these proportions values, capable of rise and fall, of valuation and tariff? Do we not say, a young girl of one hundred thousand francs? Are not life-situations, a handsome figure, a chance of promotion, articles of merchandise quoted at five, then, twenty, fifty thousand francs, deliverable only against equal value?[16]

The business plan for a "universal matrimonial agency" (a kind of Match.com, Facebook, or Grindr avant la lettre) is outlined in chapter 14, titled "A Proposition, New, and Suited to the Tendencies of Modern Civilization, Designed to Assure the Happiness of Households and to Establish on a Sound Basis a First-Class Institution Hitherto Left to Arbitrary Direction and to Chance."[17] Graindorge's business angle is to fine-tune the marriage market by applying the financial instruments of data and risk management: "Each offer inscribed at the agency shall be accompanied by a demand, specifying approximately the amount of fortune, and the kind of position demanded in exchange."[18] A photographic record that includes close-ups of teeth,

---

1875), 351.

14   Ibid., v.
15   Ibid., vii.
16   Ibid., 174.
17   Ibid., 176, 169.
18   Ibid., 176.

feet and hands will accompany a complete dossier of "medical certifi-cates, mortgage clearances, title-deeds, evidences of income and of property, legal attestations as to correct life and habits."[19] Marriage prospects will be put up as investment opportunities, and buyers will be insured against the risk of shoddy goods by religious, educational and legal authorities. Graindorge thus shifts the patrician model of intermarriage and fortune consolidation into the speculative economy of stock trading and hedging. A prospect's value will be adjusted for inflation and deflation according to political fluctuations:

> A threat of war will send down the value of officers. The news of peace in America will raise the value of merchants. Each one, on opening his newspaper in the morning, will have the pleasure of finding his value inscribed, and quoted.[20]

Graindorge sees his proposal as the natural outgrowth of the positive sciences "extending everywhere unceasingly; everybody is now occu-pied with statistics, political economy, publicity, industrial, commer-cial and practical customs."[21] What project, he reasons,

> gives more guarantee to private interests, more publicity to commerce ... which creates at once more commercial men and more functionaries; which renders life at once more convenient and more mechanical; which brings man nearer to those stamped and quoted values, duly registered and circulating, to which he is striving to assimilate himself?[22]

So certain is he of the venture that he declares himself willing to stake his own capital, which, he wagers, will earn 10 percent more in inter-est than his salt pork or oil shares. To ensure the success of his agency, Graindorge must learn the social networks of Paris, and here is where Tainian milieu theory capitalizes its inventory of Second Empire

---

19   Ibid., 177.
20   Ibid., 179.
21   Ibid., 180.
22   Ibid.

mores and social hierarchies. Spaces of the "democratic torrent" are registered in every detail: shabby recycled couches, jostling bodies, dirty dancing, smells of gas and tobacco, heat and steam, cast-offs and clothing for hire.

Graindorge consistently charts the inegalitarian effects of egalitarian contingencies, as democratization comes to be identified with acts of appraisal. Graindorge relies on a ledger to keep track of profit in everyday existence. He devises a math sheet for his opera experience by dividing agreeable and disagreeable sensations into credit and debit columns, calculating the cost of the enjoyment. ("A pretty pastoral rondo, credit 1 franc, an 'Incomparable stupidity of the figurants dressed as lords,' debit 1 franc.")[23] Thoughts and impressions are similarly computed: "I only know how to jot down my thoughts when they come and as they come, to describe the furniture of a drawing-room after the manner of an appraiser, in broken sentences and with all sorts of absurd remarks."[24] It is this appraising consciousness, the necessity of calculating the price of everything, that transforms the "democratic torrent" into a total environment of financialization. Fabrics produce a music and a poetry of valuation: "I hear a hum of words; moire antique, spangled velvet, tarlatan, poplin, guipure, flounces and the like."[25] "Temperature" is gauged in the quality of an evening; the "Voltaire," for example, is an atmosphere that comes off the sparkle of a supper table and the champagne "effervescing in the brain."[26] These barely perceptible material and immaterial elements are the site of politics because they afford a way of seeing the organization of the senses, of apprehending the unaccountable in what is manically accounted for. When Graindorge takes note of vulgarity and cheapness as characteristics of mass culture, he inadvertently names the happiness derived from freeloading or acquiring free stuff. This uncounted stuff pushes back against the price of everything, constituting a micropolitical environment of what "anyone" desires.

---

23   Ibid., 145.
24   Ibid., 23.
25   Ibid., 9.
26   Ibi., 10.

Taine is a reference point for Rancière as a sociologist of democratic contradictions under conditions of burgeoning finance capitalism, but it must not be forgotten that Rancière's theory of the demos is informed by an anti-sociological imperative. Sociology, in his view, harbors strains of miserabilism and moral judgment carried over from philosophy. Social reproduction, as underscored by Pierre Bourdieu's ordering of class distinctions, social attitudes, and distributed symbolic capital, is explicitly targeted, most pointedly in the 2006 preface to *The Philosopher and His Poor* (Le philosophe et ses pauvres [1983]), where Rancière insists that suffering begins by being treated as one who suffers.[27] As a reader of literature, Rancière, in contrast to Bourdieu, refuses to place an author like Flaubert within a "literary field" gridded by the socio-logic of *doxa, habitus,* and class conformation. Instead, he gives us a Flaubert who democratizes literature by accessing the "what is" of metaphysical substance; the elements of ousia, primary substance, the singular or essential property in which the particular inheres. In *Le fil perdu* (2014) (The Lost Thread [2017]) Rancière's approach to Flaubertian realism dispenses with the Barthesian "reality effect"—which treated supernumerary detail as the symptom of reification—in favor of what might be called an "equality effect," whereby things, worlds, and characters are equally important or unimportant.[28]

This "equality effect" of sensible effects is given full sway in *Aisthesis: Scenes from the Aesthetic Regime of Art* (2013), an account of Euro-American modernism that builds on his thesis that "anything whatsoever can belong to art."[29] The book intends to interpolate

how a regime of perception, sensation and interpretation of art is constituted and transformed by welcoming images, objects and performances that seemed most opposed to the idea of fine art: vulgar figures of genre painting, the exaltation of the most prosaic activities in verse freed from meter, music-hall stunts and gags,

---

27 Jacques Rancière, *Le philosophe et ses pauvres* (Paris: Flammarion, 2007), xii.
28 Rancière, *Le fil perdu,* 23.
29 Rancière, *Aisthesis,* x.

industrial buildings and machine rhythms, smoke from trains and ships reproduced mechanically, extravagant inventories of accessories from the lives of the poor.[30]

In fourteen "episodes," many taken from "poets who have fallen into the purgatory of literary anthologies, talks by thinkers or critics who have fallen from grace, sketchbooks for stagings rarely performed," Rancière restitutes "the genealogy of forms and perceptions of thought that were able to make them events in the first place."[31] It is the "scene"—"the little optical machine"—that redistricts art. By no longer permitting art to be walled into the precinct of aesthetic autonomy, a re-spacing of political sociality becomes possible, manifest in the very small event. Stendhal's *The Red and the Black* will provide a typology consisting of

> small causes that produce large effects, like refilling a mattress or a dropped pair of scissors, that makes Madame de Rénal Julien's accomplice, despite her best intentions. Others are not linked in any chain of causes or effects, means or ends. On the contrary, they suspend these links in favor of the sole happiness of feeling, the sentiment of existence alone: a day in the country, a butterfly hunt, or the pleasure of a summer evening spent in the shade of a linden tree with the soft noise of the wind blowing. In the heterogeneous weaving of small events, the grand schemes find themselves torn between two kinds of logic: there is Julien's duty that orders him to take revenge on those who humiliate him, by mastering his master's wife; and there is the pure happiness of a shared sensible moment: a hand that surrenders to another in the mildness of the evening under a tall linden tree.[32]

If there is one aspect of Rancière's political aesthetic that seems consistent—if not easily graspable—it is its micrological scale, its virtual ineffability. Whether we are dealing with "small causes" that escalate into whirligigs of psychopolitical calculation or exquisite,

---

30   Ibid., xii.
31   Ibid.
32   Ibid., 44.

fleeting moments of the "shared sensible," Rancière expounds a radical ecumenicalism according to which

> everything can be interesting, it can all happen to anyone, and it can all be copied by the penman. To be sure, this law of new literature depends upon the other novelty: anyone can grab a pen, taste any kind of pleasure, or nourish any ambition whatsoever.[33]

Rancière reads fiction politically, countering the historical novel, which he considers to be too indebted to Aristotelian principles of dramatic action and character, and of structural and historical causality. He seeks out in literature evidence of the least visible forms of sociality: the finest of fine-grain politics. Whereas Sartre, as Badiou points out in an exchange with Rancière, took as his philosophical project the advent of subjective freedom in the materiality of existence, Rancière relinquishes the whole idea of a philosophical project, opting instead for immersion in an inchoate mix of gestures, material practices, and environmental interactions that form something like an atmosphere, an ambiance, a milieu:

> "Transition of sonorities to fabrics." This phrase of Mallarmé does not imply that the flowing veils of Loïe Fuller are transposed into music of some kind. Commentators on the serpentine dance apparently pay little attention to music. They occasionally evoke the flower-girls of Parsifal or the flame surrounding Brunehilde, but these Wagnerian references are aesthetic ideas, not musical themes. The movement of the veil transposes no musical motif, but the very idea of music. This idea is that of an art that serves as a material instrument to produce a sensed immaterial milieu.[34]

Rancière will refer to the idea of milieu in two apparently contrasting ways. On the one hand, in *Hatred of Democracy* milieu is the subterfuge and scaffolding of the formation of elites, as in Jules Ferry's tracking of citizens into the ranks of the republican professional and

---

33 Ibid., 51.
34 Ibid., 151.

political classes. This subterfuge distracts the people from seeing that a collectivity inclusive of "anyone" has been foreclosed [35] On the other hand, milieu carries a democratizing force.

What René Wellek criticized as "Taine's astonishingly uncritical use of evidence"—referring to his indiscriminate habit of "drawing on all sources: fiction, history, documents, anecdotes, etc."—is precisely that which makes it sympathetic to Rancière's way of working, where "indiscrimination" is a first principle of emancipatory procedure.[36]

Taine's milieu theory is laid out in the preface to his 1858 *Essais de critique et d'histoire*, and in the introduction to the 1864 *Histoire de la littérature anglaise* (History of English Literature). Influenced by Herder's analysis of collective dispositions of the nation; by Comte's historical positivism and extension of the French term *milieu* to encompass not only the physical medium that surrounds an organism, but the general scope of external conditions that are necessary to support the organism's existence; by Darwin's adaptive environment; and by Guizot's recourse to fact-based, quantitative history ("only circumstantial, naked facts express quantity"), Taine cemented the trilogy "race, milieu, moment." Roughly translatable as "nation/Volk/cultural heritage," "environment/situation," and "time/Zeitgeist/acquired speed/impulsion of historical process", *milieu* resembles a thick description of context bridging fact and literature, science and history, situation and environment—all posed against romantic ideals of national genius, of sui generis creation sprung from the singular personality of a people.[37] It is easy to see how Taine's use of milieu became vulnerable to caricature, with its recourse to clunky, overdetermined constructs of heredity, climate, digestion, topography and psychological laws. Italian civilization, for example, is divided in two—with one side outward-looking, bellicose and imperial; the other, inward-looking,

---

35   Rancière, *Hatred of Democracy*, 67–8.

36   René Wellek, "Hippolyte Taine's Literary Theory and Criticism," in *Criticism* 1:1, 1959, 15.

37   See Taine's essay, "M. Guizot," in *Essais de critique et d'histoire*, as cited by Patrizia Lombardo, "Hippolyte Taine between Art and Science," *Yale French Studies* 77, 1990, 129.

passive, reliant on papal directives, influenced by neighboring territories. This kind of simplistic cultural projection is what renders
Taine's thought irredeemably outmoded. But when one delves into
the actual descriptions of how a person "lives" in space, one gleans
a unique *aisthesis*, an infra-world of perceptible phenomena, a sociology of seeing. This is certainly the gist of Taine's exhortation, in
the preface to the *History of English Literature,* to sharpen observation by focusing on

> a man in motion, corporeal and visible, who eats, who walks, who
> fights, who works . . . try to see people in their studios, in their
> offices, in their clothing, at their meals, as you would, on disembark-
> ing in England or Italy, scrutinize the faces and gestures, the side-
> walks and taverns, the strolling city-dweller and the workingman
> having a drink.[38]

History of English Literature undresses the social "type" to reveal a
body produced by the physics of animation. Racine is brought back to
life through his comportment. Taine imagines him at the court of
Versailles, elegant and bewigged, cuing his body language to the
"policed" protocols of a sociality that emanates from the palace décor.[39]
In another instance, the figure of a "poet" is portrayed not as a freestanding genius, but as a social agent whose swollen ego issues forth
from the atmosphere of corrupted democracy,

> decked out in a black suit and gloves, worthy of a woman's approv-
> ing gaze, dispensing twenty bons mots a night to society, reading
> the morning newspapers, often lodged on the second floor, not too
> gay because of his nerves. Because, in this heavy democracy in
> which we suffocate, the discredit he endures from official dignitar-
> ies has puffed up his pretentions, given him an exaggerated sense of

---

38 Hippolyte Taine, *History of English Literature*, trans. Henri Van Laun
(London: FB&C Limited, [1873] 2016), viii.
39 This kind of milieu reading retains its currency, as evinced by Pierre
Bergounioux's channeling of *grand siècle* literature in and through architecture,
décor and forms of sociality. See, *Exister par deux fois* (Paris: Fayard, 2014),
239–40.

importance and inclined his fine-tuned sensibilities towards a desire for God.[40]

Taine attends to the minutest inflections of voice and shifting posture; no alteration of mood, energy, or inhibition should go unregistered.[41] For Zakir Paul, this attentiveness is crucial to Taine's semiotic theory of intelligence (published in 1874 as the monumental *De l'Intelligence*), which effects "the shift of intelligence from a faculty to a sign."[42] As Paul argues, no innate ideas ground the thinking being (Descartes); no "faculties of the soul" inscribe the metaphysical subject (Maine de Biran); what Taine will imagine as a "self" is a collection of psycho-physiological signs indexing the individual's status and vocation, and more profoundly still, their cognitive and performative animating traits. A language of biosemiosis, or "inner-micro-kinesis"[43] is mobilized, describing how each visible action serves as a direct line into a subliminal matrix—a window into infinitesimal worlds of rationalization, emotion, sensation, and proprioceptive hallucination. In *History of English Literature*, this theory of intelligence is not yet worked out, but already in evidence is a sensorimotorial approach to the analysis of the person within the social type, with emphasis on thinking patterns as they interact with minute shifts in attitude and expulsions of energy.

---

40   Taine, *History of English Literature,* vol. 1, vi.

41   Taine could be said to anticipate the social theorist Erving Goffman, who (drawing on Georg Simmel, Durkheim and theories of theatrical performance) would categorize his 1956 landmark *The Presentation of Self in Everyday Life,* as "a sort of handbook detailing one sociological perspective from which social life can be studied, especially the kind of social life that is organized within the physical confines of a building or plant." It is the notion of physical confines that is significant here: Goffman's work builds up a vast inventory of everyday sociality, from body language in the business world, to social protocols in the workplace, and they are shown as responsive to their physical environment. From the relays of power bouncing off gazes we move to the relays of power glancing off rooms, walls and furniture. The workspace or domestic habitat is an ambient surround rife with micropolitical anecdote and performative interactivity.

42   Zakir Paul, "Disarming Intelligence: On a Modern French Faculty," PhD Thesis, Princeton University, 2015. See chapter, "Gathering Intelligence: From Taine to Bergson."

43   The terms are borrowed from François Dagognet, *Faces, Surfaces, Interfaces* (Paris: Vrin, 1982).

Milieu *is* intelligence insofar as physical data form part of a continuum coextensive with moods, memories and sensory impressions
stored by the "brain-eye."[44] The body becomes a sensating interface of
social space and cognitive plasticity. This plasticity is glossed by
Rancière in *Aisthesis* when he draws on Taine (and Taine's reading of
Hegel in his *Philosophy of Art*) to parse Rodin's transcription of movement. Taine's diagnosis of "nervousness," a symptomatic condition of
modern life, generates a micro-milieu in which mass spectacle, calis-
thenics (new ways of moving and throwing), and volitional dissipa-
tion coalesce in Rodin's sculptural praxis:

> Taine wanted to determine what separates modern life from the old
> ideal of it in the plastic arts: it was no longer just a question of the
> dark and fitted clothing in which the bourgeois century draped the
> athletic Olympian body. It was the physiological character typical of
> modern man: its "nervosity" ("le nervosisme"), the disordered agita-
> tion of individuals dragged into the tumult of urban life, bombarded
> by a multitude of ideas and spectacles, overwhelmed by a thousand
> little preoccupations that made it impossible to focus on definite
> goals or tailor gestures towards precise ends—the hurling of a discus,
> an army to thrown into battle—which had animated the classical
> statues. In transcribing new ways of holding and throwing, of tight-
> ening up or gesturing; in exploring the infinity of transitions between
> action and inaction, Rodin expedited entire theses to the storehouse
> of antiquity, theses on modern nervosity . . . Plasticity would no
> longer be the conservator of ideal forms . . . it would march to the
> same rhythm as modern life . . . colored surface and sculptural
> volume henceforth would find their common principle in
> movement.[45]

Rodin's sculpture becomes an ambient milieu branded as "nervosity,"
a medium of the reorientated sensorium, of matter and spirit allocated

---

44   See Eric Alliez, *L'Oeil-cerveau: nouvelles histoires de la peinture moderne*
(Paris: Vrin, 2007). Translated by Robin Mackay as *The Brain-Eye: New Histories of
Modern Painting* (London: Rowman and Littlefield, 2015).

45   Rancière, *Aisthesis*, 200–1.

otherwise (*partes extra partes*).[46]

In *Le fil perdu*, ambient milieu is present in allusions to atmosphere, halo, mood, substance. In a chapter on *Madame Bovary*, Rancière draws on Aristotelian substance theory, specifically the notion of *kath' hekaston*, or "facts as they happen," to refine the notion of milieu still further. Emma Bovary's love is a little happening-fact situated at the moment when she and Rodolphe meet at the agricultural fair. Rancière lingers over the details of this "sensible" micro-event:

> the heat of a summer afternoon, the voices of the fair which resonate in the air, the braying of the oxen, the bleats of the goats, the golden flecks of light around black irises, an odor of vanilla and lemon, the plume of dust trailing in the wake of a passing carriage, the memory of a waltz and old desires stirring like grains of sand in the wind – of which had for its consequence the action of a hand—hers—slipping into another hand—that of her seducer. It is thus that her love is born as the effect of a multiplicity of sensible micro-events, which swept along in a single wave, swept up words read in books, images from plate-illustrations colorful vignettes embossed on prayer-books and keepsakes, the smell of the altar, and refrains from sentimental ballads.[47]

Woolf and Conrad, similarly, will mark out instances of *kath' hekaston* as they evoke an atmospheric halo that, instead of foregrounding the individual it surrounds, becomes the evidence of a parallel, semi-visible world existing alongside the subject. Woolf's phrase, "life is a

---

46 There is an interesting parallel between Rancière and Spitzer on Rodin and the choreographer Rudolf von Laban. Both use these artists to extend the idea of milieu to micro-worlds of embodied plasticity. As Leo Spitzer notes, in his treatise *Die Welt des Tänzers* (1920), von Laban conceptualized the receptacle of gesture as a *Raumkörper*, a "three-dimensional space in which the ballet dancer cuts his figures . . . What surrounds him is an indifferent environment not a plastic partner" (as cited by Spitzer, 315). Spitzer ends the notes to part 1 of his essay with the arresting image of the modern dancer Mary Wigman, a pupil of von Laban's, whose movements bring the outlines of the *Raumkörper* into visibility; they are described by Spitzer, in very Rancièrian language, as "the determinant tensions and crystallization in the choric medium." Leo Spitzer, "Milieu and Ambiance: An Essay in Historical Semantics," *Journal of Phenomenological Research* 3:2, 1942, 316.

47 Rancière, *The Lost Thread*, 21–2.

luminous halo, a semi-transparent envelope surrounding us from the beginning of consciousness to the end," is traced to the "luminous halo" of Conrad's *Heart of Darkness*, describing Marlow's way of wrapping the stories he tells in a special narrative envelope: "the flame is in the service of the mist, the light is there to reveal the atmosphere." The acting in concert of the elements, each of which continues to exist in its discrete capacity as a substance, blurs the line between being and becoming, between an action and its preparation. The indistinct "halo" in Flaubert, Conrad and Woolf is no mere plot device—a mood-enhancer on the order of smoke and shadow in film noir—but a parliament of substances of equal parts.

Taine, one could argue, gave Rancière a way of seeing the ubiquity and contingency of the "part of no part," on which democracy rides and falls; a particle physics of micropolitics. Here Rancière stands in contrast to Badiou, for whom

> "the part of no part" is "aristocratic" because it lives in the breach, apart from the regime . . . The space of the *polis*, the virtual city of the collectivity of equals, separates itself suddenly, while at the same time remaining in contact with the "police" . . . This body . . . is not immediately democratic in nature because its heterogeneity affects the multiplicity—the demos—at the heart of which it is constituted, in an immanent but separating manner. What makes possible the existence, or at least the propagation, of the egalitarian hypothesis is not itself an immediately equal regime.[48]

Where for Badiou the separation of true democracy, or how one "counts" equality, may be located in the absolute terms of mathematical equation, for Rancière equality is situated within diffusive ambiance, historical conditions, material and aesthetic experience. Both thinkers separate politics from the state, and both set out to articulate emancipatory moments of rupture; but where Badiou militates for a mathematical equality outside the state's accounting system, Rancière (at least according to Badiou) projects a political body that adds to

---

48   Alain Badiou, "Jacques Rancière's Lessons," in *The Adventure of Philosophy*, trans. Bruno Bosteels (London and New York: Verso, 2012), 108–9.

what can be counted, while not changing the terms by which the count is performed.[49]

Rancière's "politics," finally, is "politics" that falls, as he stipulates in *La mésentente* (Disagreement), neither into the category of the prepolitical ("archipolitics," ascribed to the Platonic elimination of politics as an activity on account of its total assimilation into the nomos); nor into the category of the absented or withdrawn political ("parapolitics," associated with the peasant demos whose constituents have been evacuated to distant fields and thus kept apart from each other); nor into the category of the "beyond political" ("metapolitics," associated with the exposure of democracy's empty set, its stake in false names or distance from the shores of realities that it purports to represent). Rancière's alternative "politics" is closer to an ambient milieu insofar as atmosphere and aureole, the intelligible in the material, the sensible and the aleatory, carry the possibility of equality.

In a chapter on Stendhal in *Aisthesis* devoted to "the plebian sky," it is the country air discovered by Julien Sorel during an interlude with Madame de Rénal that provides a new sensation of *otium*, of time outside the calculation of labor time, or the luxury of awaiting the unforeseen. For Fabrice del Dongo, imprisoned in a cell, the patch of sky becomes a space of "reverie." As matter (*matière*), the sky nurtures revolutionary aspiration; a limitless horizon, it suspends obedience to worldly dictates of court intrigue and fiscally organized romance.[50] In short, the sky is portrayed as an ambient milieu in which the repartition of hierarchized modes of existence can occur—in which politics can happen.[51] As Rancière wrote in the prologue of *Le fil perdu* in sentences that seem to distantly echo the philosophical project of Taine:

I will localize the politics of fiction not in the zone of representation,

---

49 This comparison between Rancière and Badiou is resumed by Adriel M. Trott, "The Truth of Politics in Alain Badiou: 'There is only One World,'" *Parrhesia* 12, 2011, 82–93.

50 Rancière, *Aisthesis*, 63–8.

51 On the question of air as a semantic mileu and as a problematic for philology, see Margareta Ingrid Christian, "*Aer, Aurae, Venti*: Philology and Physiology in Aby Warburg's Dissertation on Botticelli," *PMLA* 129:3, 2014.

but in how it operates, the situations it constructs, the populations it convenes, the relations of inclusion or exclusion that it institutes, the borders it traces or effaces between perception and action, between states of things and movements of thought; all those relations which it establishes among situations and significations, coexistences, temporal successions, and chains of causality.[52]

---

52   Rancière, *Le fil perdu*, 12–13.

IV. ECONOMIES
OF EXISTENCE

Schadenfreude

In notes for a seminar announced as "Proust and Photography: Examination of a Little-Known Photographic Archive," never delivered because of his fatal accident outside the Collège de France on February 25, 1980, Roland Barthes gave full sway to "the Social" (*la mondanité*) and "social desire" as political concepts. He was responding to Anne-Marie Bernard's catalogue *The World of Proust, as Seen by Paul Nadar* (Le Monde de Proust), which accompanied a 1978 photographic exhibition. Barthes wrote,

> Even before turning it into the precious metal of an unforgettable work, Proust transformed social desire into something serious (you'll see the trace of this in the photographs): an intense life (so-called life of a socialite) transformed by an ennobling power: madness, mad desire → Don't forget that—before he shut himself away to write *In Search*—Proust's social life was *exhausting*, like a veritable profession. More than a professional, a virtuoso of high society: a militant. Putting as much hard work, as much "attendance" into society's get-togethers as a political or trade-union militant at committee or branch meetings → In both cases, it's a phenomenon that would be worth analyzing (as a neurosis): the "meeting-ite" ["*réunionnite*"].[1]

The construct of a "trade-unionist of the party scene," or "militant socialite," or "militant of the Social" offers the rewards of a good

---

1   Roland Barthes, *The Preparation of the Novel: Lecture Courses and Seminars at the Collège de France (1978–1979 and 1979–1980)*, trans. Kate Briggs (New York: Columbia University Press, 2011), 312. Originally published as *La préparation du roman: notes de cours et de séminaires au Collège de France 1978–1970 and 1979–1980*, ed. Eric Marty (Paris: Seuil, 2003), 394.

oxymoron on the order of Baudelaire's figure of the stoical dandy. It throws into question what sociability actually refers to, especially with respect to the period frame—fin-de-siècle/Belle Epoque/new century—of Proust's *À la recherché du temps perdu*, particularly as it is filtered through the lens of Barthes's post–May '68 political era. "Militant of the Social" covers a wide range: First, it reflects the snob-bism, social connections, class coalitions, friendships, petty jealousies, and habits of conviviality and snideness animating Proust's social imaginary.[2] Second, it portrays a class construct on the order of Franco Moretti's "bourgeois," which focuses not so much on "actual relations between specific social groups—bankers and high civil servants, industrialists and doctors," but on "the 'fit' between cultural forms and the new class realities: how a word like 'comfort' outlines the contours of legitimate bourgeois consumption . . . how the tempo of storytell-ing adjusts itself to the new regularity of existence."[3] Third, it refer-ences social dimensions of a politics of *aisthesis* associated by Rancière, as we have seen, with "aesthetic acts that configure experience, creat-ing new modes of sense perception and novel forms of political subjectivity."[4] Fourth, it describes something specific to Barthes's own critical era, namely, the heuristic shift in the 1960s from the sociology of class consciousness to a micropolitical ontology of individuating presences (a shift effectuated in Proust studies by Deleuze's 1964 land-mark *Proust et les signes* [Proust and Signs]).[5] The term's valence is

---

2   Julia Kristeva, *Le temps sensible: Proust et l'expérience littéraire* (Paris: Gallimard, 1993), 326 (my translation); *Time and Sense: Proust and the Experience of Literature*, trans. Ross Guberman (New York: Columbia University Press, 1996).

3   Franco Moretti, *The Bourgeois: Between History and Literature* (London and New York: Verso, 2013), 4.

4   Jacques Rancière, *Aisthesis: Scenes from the Aesthetic Regime of Art*, trans. Zakir Paul (London and New York: Verso, 2013).

5   Gilles Deleuze, "Les boîtes et les vases," in *Proust et les signes* (Paris: Presses Universitaires de France, 1964). Deleuze speaks of two fundamental figures in *La Recherche*, the first associated with the image of the "open box," the second with the "closed vessel." The first figure is exemplified by proper names, treated as "half-open cases that project their qualities upon the beings they designate: 'The name Guermantes is also like one of those tiny balloons in which oxygen or some other gas has been stored' or else like one of those 'little tubes' from which we 'squeeze' the right color" (116). The second figure, is exemplified by the "whirl of a lottery wheel that shifts and even mixes the fixed prizes" (117).

further inflected by notions of the perdurability of aristocratic mores, and of the reproduction of hierarchical class structures in every new iteration of "society." Arno Mayer characterized this phenomenon in the post–World War I historical context, calling it "the persistence of the Old Regime" in his 1981 book of that title.[6]

Barthes was clearly fascinated by the vestiges of aristocratic society life in Proust's real and fictive worlds, some of which survived into his own in the form of dinner parties, fashionable openings, and globe-trotting. He scrutinized Nadar's photographs of the highly pedigreed society fixtures serving as Proust's real-life templates, analyzing their clothing and demeanor according to a sociology of distinction (borrowed from Pierre Bourdieu, whose *Distinction: A Social Critique of the Judgement of Taste* had been published in 1979). Though he provides commentary on the full gallery of chauffeurs, artists, musicians, courtesans, journalists, legal and medical professionals, and hangers-on who populate Proust's social worlds, Barthes seems especially sympathetic to the rarefied social set. The Marquis Boni de Castellane (an inspiration for Saint-Loup) is described as a "remarkable young socialite" (as well as "royalist" and "anti-Semite") possessed of an "elegant silhouette, dazzling pink complexion, cold lapis-lazuli eyes, pale skin, golden hair and a monocle flying about."[7] Robert de Montesquiou (the perfect "type" of the aristocratic dandy-aesthete on whom Charlus was grafted) is celebrated for the traits Proust ascribed to him: "legendary eccentricities, rude behavior, and little black teeth that he'd hide with a quick movement of his hand whenever he laughed."[8] General Marquis Gaston de Galliffet (a model for Froberville) is glossed by Barthes so familiarly one would think he were an actual acquaintance: "Vain and opportunistic . . . successful with society ladies because of a silver plate in his abdomen . . . Really very uptight. Peculiar uniform of the time: slim, austere, tight, maschio in its austerity: a baton, a stick)."[9] And the Comtesse Henri Greffulhe, née Elizabeth de Caraman-Chimay (a prototype for la Duchesse de

---

6 Arno Mayer, *The Persistence of the Old Regime: Europe to the Great War* (New York: Pantheon Books, 1981) 43–4.
7 Barthes, *The Preparation of the Novel*, 331.
8 Ibid., 359.
9 Ibid., 341.

Guermantes), is captioned a "supreme social beauty of her time," notable most particularly for her kinship to Montesquieu (she was his cousin) and social taste for an all-male coterie. Barthes could not resist drawing out his own connection to these subjects. "How did she age? How did she die?" he wonders with respect to la Comtesse Greffulhe; "1952. That's not long ago. I was writing *Degree Zero!*"[10] he writes of a family tie to Professor Édouard Brissaud (a model for the doctor who treats the Narrator's grandmother). Brissaud, it turns out, was the father of a certain "Dr. B who treated me—Rue Garancière, eau de Cologne: severing of adhesions."[11] (A version of his reaction to seeing the photograph of Napoleon III's youngest brother Jérôme appears in *Camera Lucida*: "I am looking at the eyes which looked at the Emperor!") This marveling at how one can belong to a chronotope that outgrows generational life span also comes through in Barthes's tongue-in-cheek lament for those "happy days when such things as right-wing intellectuals and writers existed," as he contemplates a line-up of anti-Dreyfusards in Nadar's portrait album.[12] In each of these cases, Barthes becomes the contemporary and fellow traveler of the inhabitants of Proust's milieu.

Barthes's self-insertion into this high society—even if something of a wink or inside joke—captures his fixation on the affective dimension of class relations as a locus of political encounter and as site for theorizing the politics of the Social. In the kind of coverage that mass media outlets depend on, with their endlessly recycled features of Kennedys and Radizwells, the Onassis dynasty, the British royals, Barthes discovered an anthropological archive allowing access to "a population, a 'social ethnic group' composed of 'the monarchical aristocracy,' the 'imperial aristocracy'"—the latter described as "losing money; many 'mixed' marriages, Jewish (Rothschild) and American money"—"and the upper middle classes, who mingle in the salons, often with a mediating element: artists (musical evenings)."[13] Almost all the characters, he observes, are Right Bank, their preferred quartiers

---

10 Ibid., 345.
11 Ibid., 328.
12 Ibid., 347.
13 Ibid., 311.

and streets—Malesherbes, Courcelles, Miromesnil, Monceau—marked as "areas linked to Orleanist France, that's where the real-estate money was." The so-called tribal aspect of socialite Paris—for which aristocratic exclusiveness is the sine qua non—radiates out from Proust's text to encompass the clan of "Marcellians" to whom Barthes's seminar will be addressed.

We glimpse overlapping networks of Proust's semi-extinct *mondains* (the circle of Left Bank intellectuals and aesthetes to which Barthes himself belonged) and the audiences for his courses, who enveloped him in an atmosphere of reverence that took different forms according to their size and venue. As the writer Claude Arnaud would recall in his memoir,

> I attended one or two sessions of the seminar that he gave at the École pratique des hautes études on the rue de Tournon, but the Ancien Régime feel of it left me cold, as did the protective barrier erected by his special favorites. At the Collège de France Barthes belonged to his public, he gave himself over to each one of us: his commentary formed an integral part of him, a substitute for life itself.[14]

The sociality of Barthes's seminar often became part of what was studied in a seminar. As Tiphaine Samoyault observes, all through his teaching and his writings, Barthes focused on "unexceptional modes of sociability, small acts of resistance to intimidation by society, organizations, and languages."[15] One class, on the topic "Tenir un discours," dissected the micropolitics of conversation. Samoyault also traces how the sociability of a seminar on the lover's discourse spilled over into the published best-seller *A Lover's Discourse*:

> Taking the lover's discourse as a subject of the course was an obvious way of engaging the state of play, of giving birth to new configurations . . . Barthes could push the limits of intimacy, where the subject was no longer diffuse, dispersed, or ungraspable, but there as pure

---

14   Claude Arnaud, *Qu'as-tu fait de tes frères?* (Paris: Grasset, 2012), 303. Translation my own.

15   Tiphaine Samoyault, *Roland Barthes* (Paris: Seuil, 2015), 617.

passion. A troubled space emerged, mixing the pedagogical relation with literary experiment and actual love-lives. A space of autofiction if ever there was one, it was Barthes' true invention and totally in step with the communitarian temptation and spirit of sexual liberation so prevalent at the time.[16]

Despite his "resistance to the group, the band, the social smorgasboard" avowed in *Roland Barthes par Roland Barthes*, and despite his deep preference for the one-on-one encounter (at least according to Arnaud), Barthes seems to have been wedded to the conviction that life is ennobled by adherence to the exigencies of the Social. In a vignette of a dinner party published in *Soirées de Paris* (Incidences), for example, he lauds a guest for simply being there:

> I felt comfortable with friends: A.C., Philippe Roger, Patricia, and a young woman, Frédérique, who was wearing a rather formal gown, its unusual shade of blue soothing; she didn't say much, but she was there, and I thought that such attentive and marginal presences were necessary to the good economy of a party. They talked about what they called "shaggy-dog stories" ("At Victoria Station, in England, I met a Spanish girl who spoke French"), arguing excitedly over the definition of the concept; and about Khomeini[17]

Barthes's "economy of the party" depends not just on the sheer joy of conversational banter, but more importantly on a non-negotiable, contractually sacrosanct commitment to showing up, bringing us back to the approval he accorded Proust's militant "réunionnite."

Barthes used the word "militant" advisedly. It was a post-'68 moment in which the fallout of the sixties was still far from clear as François Mitterrand's Socialist government came in to power. In 1980 the survival of activism remained palpable in feminist theory, experimental cinema, and militant gay movements. But the great cultural swerve rightward was fully underway. As watersheds, remember that

---

16   Ibid., 618–19.
17   Roland Barthes, *Incidents*, trans. Richard Howard (Berkeley and Los Angeles: University of California Press, 1992), 53.

in 1975 André Glucksmann published *La cuisinière et le mangeur d'hommes, réflexions sur l'État, le marxisme et les camps de concentration* [The Cook and the Cannibal: Reflections on the State, Marxism and the Concentration Camp] while Bernard-Henri Lévy would come out with *La barbarie à visage humain* [Barbarism with a Human Face] in 1977. These and other texts by the *nouveaux philosophes* sounded the death knell for the radical Left, repudiating its axiomatics of structural revolution: Maoist *doxa*, sympathy for the autonomists, and theories of anti-oedipal, anticapitalist, anarcho-schizo subjective modes. One could say then, that in historical context Barthes's use of the word "militant," yoked to the Social rather than to the Political, was a comment on the depoliticization of the Political, a version of Philippe Lacoue-Labarthe and Jean-Luc Nancy's "retreated" Political. In *Monogrammes X*, an epistolary exchange published after the failed Maastricht Treaty in Europe, and in an essay collection titled *Le retrait de la politique* (Retreating the Political [1997]), Lacoue-Labarthe and Nancy associated retreat with "the recognition of the closure of the political, and political deprivation of philosophy as regards itself and its own authority."[18] To retreat or militantly withdraw in these terms was to reject politics, political science and "politology" in their conventional forms, along with the transitory political movements that stand in for post-revolutionary politics (Gramscianism, Althusserianism, Maoism), and the "beyond-politics" stance of a Heidegger or Bataille— each of whom, they believed, provides the terms of a non-dialectical opposition to mastery or domination.[19] To retreat the political in a positive way was to return to the grounds of originary sociality and subjective relation, even if this required circumspection towards "the total immanentisation of the political in the social." Lacoue-Labarthe and Nancy proposed studying the impact of "micro-powers" (linked to discourse and the unconscious) as solvents of monolithic concepts of power—class, the state, or monopoly capitalism—even if it goes without saying that such monoliths would continue to have traction as "givens of the epoch of the domination of the political and technology

---

18   Philippe Lacoue-Labarthe and Jean-Luc Nancy, *Retreating the Political*, trans. Simon Sparks (1997). 117.

19   Ibid., 108, 115.

or the domination of political economy."[20] It was thus in the name of a project of "questioning the multiple and powerful motifs of sociality, of alterity, of relation as such" that, in 1980, Lacoue-Labarthe, Nancy and Derrida founded the Centre for Philosophical Research on the Political at the rue d'Ulm, conceived as a place of refuge and engagement that was withdrawn in relation to the sanctioned spaces of dialogue between politics and philosophy.[21]

The sociality conceived by Lacoue-Labarthe and Nancy is strategic: a way of carving out a new space for rethinking philosophy with politics far from the madding crowd of "small p" politics. It possesses similarities to Barthes's dream of a new Mount Athos, with its vow of poverty and acedia and its dedication to experimental modes of *vivre-ensemble* and a life tempo set by a collective yet individualized "idiorhythmy." Ultimately though, Barthes's Proustian Social is at odds with Lacoue-Labarthe and Nancy's prescriptions for a philosophical politics. It serves not as the basis for a critique of the foreclosure of the Political in a neoliberal New Europe, but as a means of apprehending micropolitical force fields constitutive of the particular version of the epic genre found in Proust's *Recherche*. "There is something epic," wrote Barthes, "about the Proustian monument: the 'evenings' (or afternoons, or receptions), are like the battles in an epic work: an in-itself that works independently of the whole."[22] In this respect, Barthes's Proust sits more comfortably in a continuum with Foucault's theory of *micropouvoirs* and Deleuze and Guattari's cartographies of *micropolitiques*. The militant partygoer in this continuum is not a tongue-in-cheek trope (as in: "you have to work hard to really succeed at being frivolous"), nor is it simply a throwaway line relevant to the death of the militant Left at the moment Barthes was preparing the seminar, but a reference to the intelligence and discipline required to engage in the social encounter, something more on the order of the rigors associated with what Deleuze called an "apprenticeship in signs," which entailed relinquishing the illusion of objectivism and ceding to the infinite play of subjective representations.

For Kristeva, Proust's Social is construed within a bounded

20   Ibid., 117.
21   Ibid., 118, 105.
22   Barthes, *The Preparation of the Novel*, 262.

discursive socius shaped by opinion. Proust's characters, she argues, were

> shaped less by *action*, for which they appear to have little talent . . .
> than by the *opinion* they create, manipulate, fear, or endure . . .
> Whether they are roguish or disreputable, silly, severe or vicious, the
> "Proustians" are salon types because they are creatures of gossip,
> conversation, and classical judgments cloaked in a secret language
> and a rhetorical style.[23]

Malcolm Bowie extends this discursive Social to the ripple effect of political aftershocks in the salon:

> It would be unwise to think of *A la recherche du temps perdu* as a
> documentary record of the Third Republic, or as the fictional
> recreation of a characteristically French political process. Thiers,
> Gambetta, Clemenceau and Jaurès flit through the pages of the
> novel as wraiths thrown up by salon conversation or by the narra-
> tor's reverie. They have no policies worth specifying; and their grip
> upon the crisis- and scandal-laden texture of current affairs is no
> tighter than that of Louis XIV, Napoleon or Talleyrand, whose
> ghosts are also astir in Proust's book. Political parties and factions
> are named but not described. Upheavals within the Church, the
> army or the judiciary are notable only for the shock waves and the
> ripples of curiosity they send through dinners and receptions. And
> the First World War, which provides the backcloth to the closing
> stages of the narrative, is as inscrutable as the Fronde or the
> Congress of Vienna. On learning that Swann has been invited to
> lunch at the Elysée, Mme Verdurin begins to regard Jules Grévy,
> the president of the Republic, as a particularly menacing bore.
> Politics, one might wish to say, fascinates Proust only in extreme
> dilution. It matters to him when it adds a new spice to social rela-
> tionships or to his narrator's self-analysis, but is otherwise lacking

---

23   Kristeva, *Time and Sense*, 134. On the workings of secret language, see
Daniel Heller-Roazen, *Dark Tongues: The Art of Rogues and Riddlers* (Cambridge,
MA: MIT Press/Zone Books, 2013).

in character and complexity.[24]

Big political stories of the day—the Dreyfus affair, the Vienna Congress—are "diluted," while, as Bowie argues, the "competing claims of republicanism and monarchism, or of the new and old aristocracies" are shown to consolidate formally "what were originally personal dispositions and the spasmodic upheavals of individual desire."[25] This double action of dissolution and solidification takes place in the inchoate space of social existence, where sociality potentially thickens into historicity and where history dissipates into the most trivial incidents, slights and flatteries. The vicissitudes of the political are thus revealed as contingent on seasonal, punctual "rhythms and intensities of individual experience."

Bowie's reading of Proust's *Recherche* may be keyed to Georg Lukács's take on Stendhal's *Charterhouse of Parma* as a novel of "court life within the framework of an Italian petty state."[26] For Lukács, Stendhal elevates the social novel of court intrigue and Machiavellian maneuver to the level of a world-historical form. He insists that Walter Scott's *Waverly* and *Rob Roy* usher in class consciousness by introducing "middling" characters: non-exceptional people, in place of classically abstracted, larger-than-life epic heroes. Characters with low counts of protagonicity allow the real star of the novel to come into focus, which in the case of Stendhal and Proust, is often the relatively minor character who gets ahead by dint of their psychopolitical intelligence.

As an example of how Proust produces psychopolitics in narrative forms of the Social, consider this finely pixilated rendering of Swann's perverse experiments in social engineering at the micro scale:

The pleasure Swann derived from his social contacts was not just the straightforward kind enjoyed by the cultivated man with an artistic bent who restricts himself to society as it is constituted, and enjoys

---

24   Malcolm Bowie, *Proust Among the Stars* (London: HarperCollins, 1998), 126–7.

25   Ibid., 132.

26   Georg Lukács, *The Historical Novel*, trans. Stanley and Hannah Mitchell (Lincoln: University of Nebraska Press, 1983), 42.

his familiarity with the names engraved in it by the past and still legible now. He also took a rather vulgar enjoyment in making as it were composite posies out of disparate elements, bringing together people from very different backgrounds. These experiments in the sociology of entertainment, which is how he saw them, did not have exactly the same effect—or, rather, did not have a constant effect—on all the ladies who visited his wife. He would say with a laugh to Mme Bontemps, "I'm thinking of having the Cottards to dinner with the Duchesse de Vendôme," looking like a gourmet whose mouth waters at the novel undertaking of adding cayenne pepper to a particular sauce instead of the usual cloves. But this design of Swann's, though it would certainly strike the Cottards as entertaining, was calculated to appear quite outrageous to Mme Bontemps. She, having herself only recently been introduced by the Swanns to the Duchesse de Vendôme, and having deemed this occurrence to be as pleasing as it was natural, had found that impressing the Cottards by telling them all about it had been not the least of the pleasures it afforded her. But, like those who, as soon as their own names figure in the latest Honors List, would like to see the supply of such decorations run dry, Mme Bontemps would have been better pleased if, after she had been presented to the Duchesse de Vendôme, nobody else from her circle could be. She secretly cursed Swann for the warped taste with which, merely to satisfy a misplaced aesthetic curiosity, he had wantonly squandered all the kudos she had seen reflected in the eyes of the Cottards as she told them about the Duchesse de Vendôme.[27]

Proust unearthes here the importance of *Schadenfreude* for any theory of politics. We peer into the political brain, observe how choices are motivated by the pleasure of subtracting pleasure from the other. *Schadenfreude* yields a host of political tactics of ambush from behind, of techniques for harvesting the resources of deceptive plays or the rewards of second-guessing how the enemy or rival sees and thinks. We learn how people act out petty despotism in order to shore up

---

27 Marcel Proust, *In the Shadow of Young Girls in Flower*, trans. James Grieve (New York: Penguin Books), 95.

narcissistic gratification. Swann gives us a "recipe" for how to win at the great game of the Social: the moves involve depriving others of satisfaction (giving your opponent cause for heartburn), selling a social asset high (in this case Swann's access to Duchesse de Vendôme), and then shorting the market (as when he gives non-exclusive exposure of the Duchesse to the Cottards). Important too is the exploitation to social ends of apparently useless, "bizarre" aesthetic enjoyments ("la bizarrerie esthétique," unsatisfactorily translated in English by James Grieve as "a misplaced aesthetic curiosity"). Proust, through Swann, affords insight into what it is to think politically within the matrix of social positioning.

In *Proust, Class and Nation*, Edward Hughes lends support to such a reading through his astute political parsing of Mme de Villeparisis' rankings of nineteenth-century French authors with respect to their class insecurities and rivalries. Balzac ranks low because he could hardly describe the society from which he was socially excluded; Hugo ranks not much higher since he owed his status to his sympathy with socialists; the fact that Alfred de Vigny was a count mattered little, and in any case he, like Alfred de Musset, was only a "mere Parisian." Hughes suggests that Mme de Villeparisis' "obsession with social assessments" render her, like the narrator, a master at measuring volatility: "For rather than opting for typecasting, Proust appears to show Mme de Villeparisis as a skilled operator working fluidly across different social fields."[28] One could extrapolate here and say that, for Barthes, to succeed at the party as well as Mme de Villeparisis does one must become a highly skilled master of social technologies, talented not only at code-switching among social fields, but also gifted in the art of reading the psychic shadows cast by *Schadenfreude*, or in divining the differences in social class or political position that escape notice by lesser *salonistes*.

In *The Bourgeois* Franco Moretti distinguishes himself as a latter-day Mme de Villeparisis in his ability to break down a social category into a taxonomy of subtle character traits and keywords, including probity, seriousness, utility, efficiency, assiduity, comfort, and

---

28   Edward Hughes, *Proust, Class and Nation* (Oxford, UK: Oxford University Press, 2011[online edition 2012]), n.p.

enterprise. Moretti rescues "bourgeois" from the more encompassing term "middle class" by arguing that the latter obscures the complexity of a group formation which does not fit neatly into lower, middle and upper stratifications. He notes, for example, that in the period preceding and following the 1832 Reform Bill in England, "middle class" provided a cover for "bourgeois." Deflecting attention from "the bourgeois"'s sociological investment in a delimitable set of attitudes and norms, "middle class" shielded the term (and by extension the class) of "the bourgeois" "from direct criticism, promoting a euphemistic version of social hierarchy."

Moretti's "bourgeois" is complicated historically and politically as a subject of fiction by a kind of propertied subjectivity, what he refers to as *Bildungsbürgertum*. It comes through in narrative "filler"—those places in the narrative where characters "talk, and hear, and think about each other" in a way that is not easy to quantify or explain since "they don't really do much."[29] They do not do much, and yet it is precisely this filler that weaves together bourgeois existence and conservative belief. It acts as adhesive material layering intelligibility over abstract, ideological values such as honesty, comfort, and seriousness. Filler is crucial to understanding how the internal monologues and dialogues of minor characters become constitutive of self-interest, self-promotion, and the extension of self as self-property within the constraints of sociability. Proust created literary forms for this political mode within social striving, and it is precisely this mode of politics that Barthes appropriated in his glossaries of *mondanité*.

In regular columns published in 1978–79 in the popular press (*Le Nouvel Observateur, Magazine littéraire*), Barthes fleshed out the little dramas and memes embedded in expressions used in social situations. In "Politesse," he alights on "how to speak in order to say nothing" ("parler pour ne rien dire").[30] In "Ça prend," he offers up *marcottage* (layering) as a good term for Proust's technique of turning an insignificant detail into the seed of an expansively growing social universe.[31]

---

29 Moretti, *The Bourgeois*, 71.
30 Roland Barthes, "Politesse," *Oeuvres complètes*, vol. 5 (1977–1980), ed. Eric Marty (Paris: Seuil, 2002), 638.
31 Barthes, "Ça prend," *Oeuvres complètes*, 656.

In "Pause," he asks how "nothings" ("des 'riens'"), "trivia" ("cette 'petitesse'"), "small worlds" ("petits mondes") provide life's sweeteners, but also function as conduits of malicious intent, injecting little fits, upsets and hurdles into everyday existence. In "Dîner," the projective fear of speaking like an intellectual and annoying others induces total paralysis:

> If I could have made myself invisible, I would have let myself become interested in their concerns, their personal style, their personalities, in the little standoffs between their social images, in short, in all the rules and shades of difference. But I was paralyzed by fear, a fear that my language (which a premonition told me would be perceived as overly "intellectual") would appear out of place.[32]

Here and in other columns, Barthes tracks the "ding" that nicks the subject in the heat of conversation. In "L'amitié" [Friendship], he remarks on the wound inflicted in passing by a supposed friend, who brags about how he came to Barthes's defense. "That's how I learned I was being attacked."[33] Social discourse of this order pumps little hurts into social interaction and tracks the undercurrents of *Schadenfreude* that, in addition to propelling malice into sociability, train the novice in the martial arts of becoming a militant of the Social.

---

32   Barthes, "Dîner," *Oeuvres complètes*, 646.
33   Barthes, "L'amitié," *Oeuvres complètes*, 648.

Managed Life

The increasing financialization of every aspect of life amid an outburst of astonishing "affluenza" in global capital cities has emerged as an evident symptom of what Wendy Brown, following Michel Feher, diagnoses as the vanquishing of *homo politicus* by *homo economicus.*[1] Brown attributes this political destruction to a "mode of reason" particular to neoliberalism, "boring in capillary fashion into the trunks and branches of workplaces, schools, public agencies, social and political discourse, and above all, the subject."[2] Everyone becomes an entrepreneur overseeing their business selves:

> As Michel Feher argues, homo oeconomicus as human capital is concerned with enhancing its portfolio value in all domains of its life, an activity taken through practices of self-investment and attracting investors. Whether through social media "followers," "likes," and "retweets," through rankings and ratings for every activity and domain, or through more directly monetized practices, the purist of education, training, leisure, reproduction, consumption, and more are increasingly configured as strategic decisions and practices related to enhancing the self's future value.[3]

Brown credits Foucault as the theorist who most presciently analyzed the damaging effects of political rationality as a mode of subjectivation. But Foucault's critique may be usefully supplemented with a

---

1 Wendy Brown, *Undoing the Demos: Neoliberalism's Stealth Revolution* (New York: Zone Books, 2015), 39, 41.
2 Ibid., 35–6
3 Ibid., 33–4.

census of salient tendencies in recent French theory that shift the terms from Foucauldian subjectivation to existentialization in the politics of calculation and the count. I take my cue from a tranche of growing bibliography that includes Alain Badiou's *Mathematics of the Transcendental* (published only in English), Bruno Latour's *Enquête sur les modes d'existence* (An Inquiry Into Modes of Existence), Frédéric Gros's *Le principe sécurité* (The Security Principle), Luc Boltanski's *Enigmes et complots: une enquête à propos des enquêtes* (Enigmas and Conspiracies: An Investigation of Investigations), and Quentin Meillassoux's *Le nombre et la sirène: un déchiffrage du Coup de dés de Mallarmé* (The Number and the Siren: A Decipherment of Mallarmé's Coup de dés).[4] To group these works and thinkers together is a stretch given their discrepant foci and approaches. But, while they differ in genealogy, each may be seen to represent an iteration of French critical thought that continues in the vein of May '68 theory, marked by Althusserian Marxism, structuralism and deconstruction. Latour's latest work follows Foucault in charting fact/value distinctions within distributive spatiotemporal networks. Gros extends Foucauldian biopolitics beyond state security apparatuses to futural subjective investment strategies. Boltanski sees "political metaphysics" in investigative consciousness and the hypervigilance to detail characteristic of detective fiction. In his work there are clear parallels to Foucault's tentacular, paranoid constructions of correctional architectures and postures of subjugation. Meillassoux echoes Badiou in his fascination with the "numerological" Mallarmé, erecting him as the avatar of radical contingency.

These authors diverge to be sure, but what draws them into orbit is their common focus on calculated existence. This harks back to Georg Simmel's calculability of modernity in *The Philosophy of Money* and

---

4   A more comprehensive and comparative consideration of the existentialization of finance would also engage with Bernard Stiegler's "pharmacology of capital" (*What Makes Life Worth Living: On Pharmacology*), Frédéric Lordon's "anthropology of sovereign interest" (*L'Intérêt souverain* as well as *Willing Slaves of Capital: Spinoza and Marx on* Desire), Georg Franck's "mental capitalism" (*Mentaler Kapitalismus*), Peter Sloterdijk's psychopolitical reading of the American construction of "actually existing escapism" (*In the World Interior of Capital*) and Robert Pfaller's economy of "interpassivity" based on fostering a system whereby others consume in your place (*Interpassivity: The Aesthetics of Delegated Enjoyment*).

beyond that (and here I paraphrase Jason Barker glossing Althusser), to the way in which "capitalist reproduction binds humanity to the scourge of calculated interest."[5] Theories of the "count" and punctual-ism converge as existential economies of managed life.

Published after 2005, these texts were written in the context of neoliberalism's global economic crises, whose bleak and familiar scenarios include bank failures and insider trading, a spike in unem-ployment and unequal income distribution, a surge in subprime mortgage debt, the radical downgrading of credit and bond ratings for entire national economies, and extreme economic volatility (Schumpeter's "creative destruction") treated as the natural way market equilibrium is righted. Is there some direct connection, one wonders, between market volatility and the "mathematical turn" in theory? Certainly, the themes of "management," insecurity," and "financial hazard" which underwrite the work of Latour, Gros and Boltanski resonate with the condition of an emergent class that has been dubbed the economic precariat—the class of the socioeconomi-cally insecure—whose rallying movement has been Occupy, and whose galvanizing texts have included Stéphane Hessel's *Indignéz-vous!* (2010), Frédéric Lordon's *Willing Slaves of Capital: Spinoza and Marx on Desire* (2010), David Graeber's *Debt: The First 5000 Years* (2011), Maurizio Lazzarato's *The Making of the Indebted Man: An Essay on the Neoliberal Condition* (2011), Franco "Bifo" Berardi's *The Uprising: On Poetry and Finance* (2012), and Thomas Piketty's *Capital in the Twenty-First Century* (2013). Graeber sees loan payments to rich nations as tribute exacted on a permanently indentured under-class. He references the consistently villainous character of the money-lender in world literature—with Jews the common surrogates—as the expression of a complex western value system that repudiates the creditor while subscribing to "a sense of morality and justice" that reverts "to the language of a business deal."[6] Graeber challenges the myth that money is predicated on primitive barter by arguing that

5   Jason Barker, "Translator's Introduction," Alain Badiou, *Metapolitics* (London and New York: Verso, 2005), xxi.

6   David Graeber, *Debt: The First 5000 Years* (New York: Melville House Publishing, 2011), 13.

"virtual money came first," while the logic of barter or what econo-mists call "the double coincidence of wants" came later.[7] Nonetheless, since Adam Smith, he reminds us, barter has been the prevailing model of thought and discursive interaction: "Even logic and conver-sation," writes Graeber, paraphrasing Smith, "are really just forms of trading, and as in all things, humans will always try to seek their own best advantage, to seek the greatest profit they can from the exchange."[8] Where Graeber analyzes barter as the preeminent form of reason, Maurizio Lazzarato, in *The Making of the Indebted Man*, portrays debt as a mode of being: "Debt becomes a debt of existence, a debt of the existence of the subjects themselves. A time will come when the credi-tor has not yet lent while the debtor never quits repaying."[9] Capitalism, he insists, "has abandoned the epic narratives it constructed around the supposed freedom, innovation, and creativity of the entrepreneur, the knowledge society," and replaced them with narratives of self-servitude: "of poor people charged with managing assistance and menial jobs, and labor conditions that entail greater dependency on institutions."[10]

Graeber debunks economic founding myths that legitimate the debt economy, tracking the depredations of an expended labor force. Lazzarato treats indebtedness as a mode of subjectivation, taking his cue from Deleuze and Guattari's *Anti-Oedipus*:

> The infinite creditor and infinite credit have replaced the blocks of mobile and finite debts . . . Debt becomes a debt of existence, a debt of the existence of the subjects themselves. A time will come when the creditor has not yet lent while the debtor never quits repaying.[11]

Lazzarato's Nietzschean genealogy of indebted man, hobbled by long hours, poor compensation, precarious employment, and diminished life expectancy, reads the debt economy as a form of social subjection

---

7 Ibid., 34.
8 Ibid., 26.
9 Maurizio Lazzarato, *The Making of the Indebted Man: An Essay on the Neoliberal Condition*, trans. Joshua Jordan (Los Angeles: Semiotext(e), 2012), 87.
10 Ibid., 95.
11 Ibid., 87.

and as the expression of a moribund capitalism's desperate effort to stay alive.

These works by Graeber and Lazzarato, alongside David Harvey's many incisive critiques of neoliberalism, are important counterparts to the French texts I listed at the beginning, their impress more significant in the Anglophone world than in France. But they highlight a problem, also engaged with in recent French theory, concerning how financialization—informed by a long history of Marxism and post-Marxist economies of the subject—connects to what Christopher Nealon has described as the desire among key thinkers on the left to reorient a philosophy hitherto "enmeshed in linguistic and literary problems" towards mathematical formalism.[12] Even if one remains skeptical of the hypothesis that the so-called "mathematical turn" effects a clean break with the linguistic turn (where semiotics, deconstruction, and close reading held sway), it seems evident that much contemporary French theory is engaged with reworking the Lacanian matheme and formalist ontology more generally. The harder call consists of working out the relation between numerical subjects and the "quant" subjects of political economy.

Badiou distinguishes clearly between the uses of number in his preface to *Le nombre et les nombres* (Number and Numbers) a book published in 1990 shortly after *Being and Event*. Normally he devotes the big philosophical tomes to formal ontology (*Theory of the Subject, Being and Event, Logics of Worlds, Immanence of Truths*) and the shorter polemical treatises to politics *(Metapolitics, Can One Think Politics?)*. But in *Number and Numbers* he considers them together: "We live in the era of number's despotism," he writes. "Thought yields to the law of denumerable multiplicities; and yet . . . we have at our disposal no recent, active idea of what number is."[13] We don't know what a number is," he reiterates, "so we don't know what we are."[14] Badiou poses the pure mathematical number against "numerical

12   Christopher Nealon, "Value/Theory/Crisis," *PMLA* 127:1, 2012, 104.

13   Alain Badiou, *Number and Numbers*, trans. Robin Mackay (Cambridge, UK: Polity Press, 2008), 1.

14   Ibid., 3.

exegesis," that is, the number that

> governs our conception of the political, with the currency—
> consensual, though it enfeebles every politics of the thinkable—of
> suffrage, of opinion polls, of the majority. Every "political" convo-
> cation, whether general or local, in polling-booth or parliament,
> municipal or international, is settled with a count . . . Political
> "thought" is numerical exegesis.[15]

As Peter Hallward notes, politics for Badiou represents "the impera-
tives of communication and interest, of communal relations or links,
of a mere 'preservation in being.'" The results are nefarious: truth and
thought are reduced to particular interests, interest groups or "subsets
of the oppressed," that defer, as Hallward notes, to the "'false univer-
sality of monetary abstraction,' the undivided rule of capital . . . culture
takes the place of art, technology replaces science, management
replaces politics, and sexuality replaces love. The resulting cluster,
culture-technology-management-sexuality, is perfectly homogenous
with the market it feeds."[16]

The grip of particularism and partitive identity may be impossible
to escape, but it cannot entirely foreclose the idea of what Badiou
calls "a subject to truth . . . counted as one." The "count as one" (the
English term commonly adopted to translate "Il y a de l'Un") is an
"inexistent," that is, a non-appearing subject whose presence is registered as a "void in the situation." Hallward explains it this way in relation to Badiou's arguments in *Being and Event*: "The subject is inexistent, and yet, it is a one or part of a group of ones that are made to
be: 'L'un n'est pas' – There is no be-ing of the one – but 'Il y a de
l'Un'"—a statement whose meaning might be best rendered, says
Hallward, as "There is a One-ing."[17] The one is not, but there is an
operation that "one-ifies" or makes one. There is no one; there is only
an operation that counts as one. Badiou's "count as one" is qualified

15 Ibid., 1–2.
16 Peter Hallward, *Badiou: A Subject to Truth* (Minneapolis: University of
Minnesota Press, 2003), 25.
17 Ibid., 61.

as a situational inconsistency that ensures that multiplicity can be, even if projected only as an invisible force field awaiting appearance. One can think of this "count as one" as a manifestly unaccountable or non-accounted-for subject. In Badiou's *Mathematics of the Transcendental: Onto-logy and Being-There* (a text conjoining two works published previously in neither French nor English, *Topos, or Logics of Onto-logy: An Introduction to Philosophers*, and *Being-There: Mathematics of the Transcendental*), the theory of the subject is even more explicitly grounded in set theory and logic. Badiou, according to A. J. Bartlett and Alex Ling, subtracts "being itself" from ontology, referring to a discourse

> which prescribes the rules by which something can be presented or 'counted' as one—its sole operation being that of the count—and the 'one' thing that necessarily fails to be counted is nothing other than inconsistent multiplicity, or being itself.[18]

From *Number and Numbers* (2008), to *In Praise of Mathematics* (2016), where Badiou heralds, as a fulcrum of philosophy, the "Mathematicians' Internationale"; from the seminars of the mid-1980s on "the Infinite" in Aristotle, Spinoza and Hegel, to a pamphlet on "The Metaphysics of Real Happiness" (2016)[19]—mathematics is cast as a perseverant path to the true life (incomparable *bonheur*). This "life" is conceived as theatrical embodiment, as experiment in the formation of a subject who overcomes the conservative self's life-conserving instinct for risklessness and the bounded existence of finitude. Badiou suggests that "happiness is fundamentally egalitarian," because it integrates the question of the other, whereas "satisfaction, tied to the egoism of survival, ignores equality" . . . it is a restricted figure of subjectivity, a figure of "success" as measured by worldly norms. When the Stoic says "Be satisfied with being satisfied," she or he participates in a "syndical" vision of social life circumscribed by the normative claim (*la*

---

18 A. J. Bartlett and Alex Ling, Translator's Introduction, Alain Badiou, *Mathematics of the Transcendental* (London: Bloomsbury, 2014), 5.

19 The pamphlet is built around the legend that "Tout bonheur est une jouissance finie de l'infinie" (Every happiness is a finite pleasure of the infinite).

revendication). By contrast, happiness poses another order of demand, in line with Lacan's "Do not give up on your desire." This translates into Badiousian language as "Do not give in to living the way of the society of calculation . . . il vaux mieux un désastre qu'un 'désêtre'" [Better disaster than to dis-exist].[20] For Badiou, "happiness" yields the larger project of defining unalienated Number. For Eleanor Kaufman, this leads to "to a latent messianism embedded in Badiou's consistent preoccupation with questions of number" comparable to the mystical element in Agamben's state of exception.[21]

Subtractive, multiple, inalienable, the subject is an unaccountable number divorced from politics as usual. Extrapolating here, one could say that Badiou's metapolitics (which presupposes an unaccountable subject) stands against metadata, the newest currency of capital, fully congenial to the regime of capitalo-parliamentarianism. Badiou long ago named this regime "Thermidor," or "the long Restoration," with reference to sequences characterized by the equation of interest and property; or more precisely, as Badiou puts it, "the idea that every subjective demand has an interest at its core."[22]

While Badiou and Foucault are rarely compared, one could say that Badiou's notion of the "society of calculation" is not incompatible with Foucault's disciplinary chronometries. In addition to religious orders, deemed by Foucault to be "the great technicians of rhythm and regular activities," there was the army's "chronometric measurement of shooting" and the labor management of a wage-earning class that necessitated a "partitioning of time"—techniques of "time-management that optimized production and minimized time wasted."[23] This temporal micro-physics and its complement, a comparable spatial micro-physics, are constitutive of "cellular power."[24] Raymond Depardon's 2004 film *10e chambre, instants d'audience* (The Tenth

---

20   Alain Badiou, interviewed by Nicolas Truong, "La leçon de bonheur d'Alain Badiou," *Le Monde*, August 8, 2015, lemonde.fr.

21   Eleanor Kaufman, "The Saturday of Messianic Time (Agamben and Badiou on the Apostle Paul)," *South Atlantic Quarterly* 107:1, 2008, 37, 39.

22   As cited in Hallward, *Badiou: A Subject to Truth*, 28.

23   Michel Foucault, *Discipline and Punish*, trans. Alan Sheridan (London: Penguin Books Ltd., 1977), 154.

24   Ibid., 149.

Judicial Court: Judicial Hearings) gives filmic form to this chrono-metrics; its medium consists in the timing of the law, and its very title scores the pacing of temporal intervals in judicial protocols. What also comes through palpably is how juridical subjects are constituted out of statistical metrics of crime and punishment—percentages of alcohol over the limit, fines in relation to salary or days out of work, determinations of moral character coordinated to degrees of positive or negative comportment on the stand. A male defendant shows contrition, accepting culpability for driving under the influence, keeping his gaze respectfully lowered when the judge addresses him. By contrast, a grandmother charged with a similar offense resists the terms of the prosecution's evaluation of her behavior. Desperately trying to impose her own sense of fairness on the law, speaking out of turn, she throws her case disastrously off course. Her miscalculation of judicial timing earns a sentence disproportionately high for the infraction.

This micro-chronometry of timing in the context of the law is easily extended to matters of timing in politics, something on which Latour places great emphasis in *An Inquiry into Modes of Existence*: "The principal infelicity condition of the political," he states, "is to have its course interrupted." Latour goes on to examine politics as a complex set of systems of calibration: notably, of enunciation (the "crab-wise moves of the political mode associated with the Machiavellian 'Prince of twisted words'); and of fluctuation (according to the temperature of "passionate interests," and the "astonishing immanence of organizations" in all facets of existence and expression).[25] In one chapter Latour identifies "a mode that asks what it means to act and to speak organizationally." Management-speak is not business lingo but rather a direct expression of calculative techne. The word "stock-ticker," preserved in English in the French text, becomes a prime example of a material object that transcribes "economy with a small e." It belongs to a class of objects

---

25 Bruno Latour, *An Inquiry into Modes of Existence: An Anthropology of the Moderns*, trans. Catherine Porter (Cambridge, MA: Harvard Univeristy Press, 2013), 388–9.

through which economics transits: account books, balance sheets, pay stubs, statistical tools, trading rooms, Reuter screens, flowcharts, agendas, project management, software, automated sales of shares, in short, what we can group together under the expression ALLOCATION KEYS, or under the invented term VALUE-METER (valorimètre).[26]

The stock ticker is the quintessential evaluative instrument, a "measuring measure," a universal key "with the function of distributing both what counts and those that count."[27] It goes to the heart of the proprietary drive in possessive individualism ("This is mine") and points to

an entangling of scripts and projects [that are] measurable, accountable, quantifiable, and thus calculable: how are we to allocate, distribute, share, coordinate? The scripts are still there, but equipped with devices that will necessarily produce quantitative data, as the stock ticker example shows. Without equipped scripts, such interweaving would be impossible: we are too numerous, there are too many quasi-objects and quasi subjects to put in series. . . . We would get lost.[28]

Adhering to his principled refusal to divide the worlds of things and humans, discrete objects and processual phenomena ("without an apparatus for calculating, no capacity for calculation"), Latour treats the stock ticker as a timer of the new existent—part subject, part object:

The stock ticker does not measure prices in the sense of reference: it gives them rhythm and pace, it visualizes the, arranges them, accelerates them, represents them, formats them in a way that brings to light both a new phenomenon—continuously fluctuating prices—and new observers and beneficiaries of these prices, new exchange "agents," new entities "agenced" or "agitated" by these new data. And

---

26   Ibid., 406.
27   Ibid.
28   Ibid., 408.

with each apparatus we see the emergence of both new (quasi) objects and new (quasi) subjects.[29]

Latour's metrics of agency, his vision of stocks as a measure of modes of existence, complements Frédéric Gros's notion of "shareholder existence." A political theorist who has edited Foucault's Collège de France lectures, Gros argues in *Le principe sécurité* that "techniques of protection and control have put into motion logics of permanent solicitation, in contrast to the ancient ideal of interior stability." Gros maintains that "biosecurity presumes constant vigilance, proper to maintaining the system at maximum tension, like a body that in order to stay alive must remain hyper-sensitive to its milieu."[30] American neoliberalism, with its history of organizational complexes, has ushered in a new ontology, "une managerisation des existences" (a managerialization of existences). This brings in its train an even more specialized form of subjectivation that Gros dubs "share-holder existence":

Each subject is called on to report to him or herself as one might to a business, constructing a life like a series of investments that one counts on to make a profit. Finance capitalism encourages a share-holder-like existence [une actionnarisation de l'existence]. Each entity, every individual becomes a financial agent [un actif finan-cier], in a supporting role for speculation. The problem is no longer knowing one's price, but anticipating the arc of one's value. The secu-ritization of identities, institutions, and businesses involves continu-ous processes of evaluation. At every moment there must be an accounting of the future in order to determine values and decisions in the present. This alienation of the present in the future may be found in inverted form in indebtedness. Whether it is household or state debt that is stake, indebtedness is the reverse of financial specu-lation insofar as the present engulfs the future . . . The future serves to pay down the expenses of the present . . . Individuals no longer

---

29   Ibid.
30   Frédéric Gros, *Le principe sécurité* (Paris: Gallimard, 2012), 232. Translation my own.

have aquisitions, they define themselves instead by their capacity to alienate their future.[31]

Gros, like Graeber, Lazzarato (and, more recently Ivan Ascher, who elaborates a risk-management theory of the "portfolio society" based on "the capitalist mode of prediction"), situates debt, indebtedness and credit default as conditions of contemporary life pervading every small transaction and facet of thinking, inclusive of but not restricted to hedging, leveraging, and derivating as financialized modes of existence.[32] Debt goes hand in hand with a market model in which you trade in futures (your own future) to cash out the present. There is a dramatic reshuffling of the progressive temporal blocks that divide the life span into past, present and future. The future takes precedence over the past, and the present is either indebted to the future or part of its debt. Either way, life is financialized, whether as deficit, or as "pay it forward." For Gros, "shareholder existence" makes experience fungible like an investment, stock option or credit swap. In this case, we are well beyond the familiar notion of the self-interested individual who is constantly on the lookout to extract money, social capital or power through politic maneuvering. The shareholder exceeds the character of the Machiavellian schemer, à la Frank Underwood in *House of Cards*, who, by dint of cunning and calculated risk, becomes lethally adept at turning political setbacks to personal advantage. Shareholder existence is modeled on the well-managed investment portfolio, in which the subject is at once the resource to be invested (the abstract unit of asset appreciation and market speculation) and the accounts manager of the resource.[33]

Roland Barthes identified a complementary subjective mode with "the daily grind" in *Preparation of the Novel*, complaining that the writing subject had been reduced to "his own manager" and that life

---

31   Ibid., 236.

32   Ivan Ascher, *Portfolio Society: On the Capitalist Mode of Prediction* (New York: Zone Books, 2016). See, in particular, how Ascher casts the risk management expert or invester, as this "neoliberal *Homo probabilis*, this 'entrepreneur of the self' . . . on which today's capitalist mode of prediction depends" (106).

33   On the financialization of existence in a smiliar vein, see Michel Feher's "Self-Appreciation; or the Aspirations of Human Capital," *Public Culture* 21:1, 2009.

tailored to the "ready-made box" involves "counting against the tide," which is to say, remaining hyper-conscious of "the use of Time Before Death" or "Doing Time."[34] Like Barthes, Gros emphasizes "managerization" as a kind of totalized subjectivity. Passing over the French *gérance*—which implies a top-down administrative style characteristic of CEOs rather than existential optimization—Gros aligns his "security principle" with time management treated as no mere organizational best practice, but as a way of thinking "actuarily" (through performing risk-assessment) and non-stop (by always remaining open for business). As Jonathan Crary observes in *24/7*,

> Markets and a global infrastructure for continuous work and consumption have been in place for some time, but now a human subject is in the making to coincide with these more intensively . . . *24/7* announces a time without time, a time extracted from any material or identifiable demarcations, a time without sequence or recurrence. In its peremptory reductiveness, it celebrates a hallucination of presence, of an unalterable permanence composed of incessant, frictionless operations.[35]

There is a parallel concern with managed life in Luc Boltanski's *Enigmas and Conspiracies: An Investigation into Investigations*, but with a big difference: capitalism, as it emerges in the nineteenth century, is pitched against the nation-state. The "volatility of fortunes" linked to the financial fluctuations of the stock market and the career meritocracy's shake-up of class entitlement destabilizes the normative hierarchies that keep "reality" in place.[36] The ascendance of detective and spy fiction in the nineteenth century is attributed by Boltanski to the nation-state's need to reassert control over capitalism by extending reason's mastery over the "plasticity" of the external world.[37] The state

34   Roland Barthes, *The Preparation of the Novel*, trans. Kate Briggs (New York: Columbia University Press, 2010), 6.
35   Jonathan Crary, *24/7* (London and New York: Verso, 2013), 29 and 3—4, respectively.
36   Luc Boltanski, *Enigmes et complots: une enquête à propos des enquêtes* (Paris: Gallimard, 2012), 48.
37   Ibid., 49.

tamps down anxiety around the "reality of reality" by subjecting the unknown to a mass of fact-checking, mathematical calculation, and scientific analysis (and we must not forget that it is during Thermidor, year eleven of the Republican Calendar, that the numeration of French society acquires bureaucratic momentum, buoyed later by Napoleon I's introduction of numbered addresses and Louis-René Villermé's statistics on mortality rates in Paris).[38] For Boltanski, investigative procedures, and the paranoid psychic disposition that can be fostered by them, belong to a larger process of securitization and management. The representation of crime-solving also bolsters the state's desire to stimulate national *Bildung* and national conscience. For Boltanski, the *roman policier* and the *roman d'espionnage*, along with the journalistic *forme affaire* and *forme scandale* (which elicit strategies of spin and damage control) are constitutive of a political metaphysics that neutralizes the revolutionary side effects of capitalism by making the enigma accountable to reality.

In isolating the enigma as both symptom and target of investigative consciousness, Boltanski provides an associative bridge to Quentin Meillassoux's *The Number and the Siren: A Decipherment of Mallarmé's Coup de dés*, a text that on first reading comes off as a set of the puzzle-game Enigma, or a spy-worthy exercise in code-breaking. Meillassoux is, of course, not theorizing the enigma as part of capitalism's threat to the society of control or nation-state. Neither Marx nor Foucault casts a shadow. The enigma grows out of the mysterious numbers that Mallarmé encrypted in *Le Livre* (The Book) and his poem *Un Coup de dés* (A Throw of the Dice) of 1898. For Meillassoux, the enigma matters because it helps to resolve the question of how to make pure Chance possible, a problem of "divine inexistence" tackled in his as-yet unpublished 1997 thesis, which contained the sentence: "One can thus compare the free act to a throw of the dice. A throw of the dice never guarantees chance, but is that alone which makes chance possible."[39] Meillassoux's goal, at least at one level, is to free Number from

---

38   Ibid., 41.

39   Quentin Meillassoux, *Divine Inexistence*, as translated by Graham Harman as an excerpted appendix in *Quentin Meillassoux: Philosophy in the Making* (Edinburgh: Edinburgh University Press, 2011), 216 (cited on 111).

Calculation, and to this end he sets out to rescue the "advent ex nihilo" from frequential law; from necessitarianism and the causal overdeterminism of the Principle of Sufficient Reason.[40]

Meillassoux argues that decoding Mallarmé's poem is a condition of elucidating the workings of its "Unique Number," which in turn proves that "Mallarmé never renounced—in principle, anyway—the calculative project of the Book."[41] The code of *Un Coup de dés* is demonstrably indebted to calculations found in Mallarmé's notes on *Le Livre*, an unfinished lifework commenced in 1855, projected as a five-volume project in 1866, then slimmed down to a volume of verse and prose poems in 1867. Hailed by Barthes as a premier example of the "Book-as-Guide" ("the unique, possibly secret book that directs the life of a subject"), it contains an array of opaque computations, including instructions for the seating chart at spirit-channeling séances that Mallarmé planned for posthumous communications with his friends.

Meillassoux locates part of the key to *Coup de dés*'s secret calculation in the poet's program for "an absolute Literature of elementary arithmetical operations concerning all possible aspects of the publication and the public reading of the Book" that would have "a purely symbolic rather than utilitarian meaning."[42] The Master of the poem "infers" the advent of Number in the Master's hesitation to throw the dice—an expression of the "expectation of a unique Number potentially contained in the situation of shipwreck."[43] The looming prospect of "radical disaster" is deciphered as "a superior metrical necessity."[44]

Meillassoux sets out to determine whether there is a Meter intrinsic and specific to *Un Coup de dés*, and if so, what it numbers. Soon the

---

40   On the abandonment of "real necessity" and the irruption ex nihilo of an immanent metaphysics, see Quentin Meillassoux, "Potentiality and Virtuality," in *The Speculative Turn: Continental Materialism and Realism*, eds. Levi Bryant, Nick Srnicek and Graham Harman (Melbourne, Australia: re.press, 2011), 233–6.

41   Quentin Meillassoux, *The Number and the Siren: A Decipherment of Mallarmé's Coup de dés*, trans. Robin Mackay (New York: Sequence Press, 2011), 6, 9.

42   Ibid., 6.

43   Ibid., 20.

44   Ibid., 37.

number seven comes up ("medium term between the classical metric and pure chance") embarking us on a numerological adventure.[45] In Mallarmé's "punctilious calculations" in notes for *Le Livre*, he discovers the equation 12-5=7: "The Number internal to the Book will be the reciprocal of 5 to obtain 12."[46] This is interpreted as a formula for Mallarmé's sacrifice to pure poetry, a sacrificial subtraction that allows Meillassoux to associate the decapitated head of the Master (whose "head and crest [are] alone left floating above") with the word "Si" ("perhaps") typographically set off in capital letters, and thus a singularized "majuscule" or floating head.[47] "Si" also corresponds to the musical note that sits at place number seven on the "sol-fa" scale. Meillassoux treats this as the "metaphor of 'essential Song' deposed 'into the lap of poetry' and deployed 'in silence', as it is written, making of it a mental and no longer an instrumental melody."[48]

Meillassoux's road to Damscus leads to the number 707. It is construed as "the Number of the demon"; "an encircling structure for the abyss of O"; a "cyclopean Number whose central eye, but an empty socket, is the source of all beauty"; a negation that figures a secret of poetics; a scale model of the Number's relation to the Poem; and the heralding of a new sacred (he notes that the word *sacré* is the 707th word of the poem).[49] Taking stock of the metric count in several octosyllabic sonnets often clustered with *Un Coup de dés*—*Salut* (Toast/Salvation), *A la nue accablante tu* (Beneath the Oppressive Cloud), *Sonnet en -x*—and calculating that the odds are that they share a common count ("there is one chance in nine that a Mallarméan sonnet has, merely by chance, 77 or 70 words"),[50] Meillassoux bets the store on the chance that *Coup* hews to the same "premeditated" numerological code as the sonnets.[51] They all, as it were, get with the program; which is to say, they identify 707 as the incomparable number, synonymous with infinite Chance.

---

45   Ibid., 45.
46   Ibid., 48.
47   Ibid., 61.
48   Ibid., 65.
49   Ibid., 76–80.
50   Ibid., 86.
51   Ibid., 113.

One way to take the code's gesture is as "a nihilist version of Christ's Passion." Meillassoux maintains:

> The *Coup de dés* would then reveal, with a calculated delay, the discreet drama of a man ready to sacrifice himself for the nullity that he knew was the foundation of his art. And the reader could be shaken by this proof of extreme love—heartrending love—for a Literature whose central vanity would have been symbolized by the prosaic operations of a pointless code.[52]

This idea of sacrifice to "pointless code" is intended quite literally: the Mallarméan negation defaults to the "the count," and to the computing of ones and zeros that are themselves dumb numbers of the algorithm. On another level though, the "calculated delay" imbues the count with meaning, giving rise to a "quavering number" keyed to Igitur's hesitation. The delay registers mathematically as a plus or minus one.

What is Number doing here exactly? Coding a premeditated 707 or decoding a meter with unaccountable feet? In a perverse act of table-turning, having spent the whole book proving that 707 is the unique Number, Meillassoux reveals in the appendix that to arrive at a word count of 707 he has had to cheat, counting "quelqu'un" as two words rather than one. There's much equivocating in this finale; we're told that the number one is duplicitous, and thus counts for two, though it would seem to count only for one.

What Meillassoux affirms with this "one that is not one" is his faith in the bifid siren (or "si-ren," who conflates the subjunctive, conditional "if" with the musical note "si," or note seven on the scale). This is an amphiboly that, as he puts it, "unfetters Meter from its arithmetical truth."[53] Meillassoux wagers on the compound word "peut-être," whose hyphen instigates uncertainty in the count-as-one, while serving as an index of "other lines" (dashes, punctuation marks, strokes), all of which unsettle the perfect count. He also wagers on the futural condition embodied in the phrase "ne jamais abolira le hasard":

---

52 Ibid., 125.
53 Ibid., 193.

The title does not affirm that a throw of dice cannot abolish Chance, but that it can never abolish it again ... Everything is necessarily contingent except contingency itself and the unique act of the Poet who incorporates himself into it—once, once only, and forever.[54]

"Once, only once and forever"; this dictum bespeaks an incantatory, militant adherence to numerological convictions.

Standing back, we might take away from this reading a mental theater doubling as a house of cards, itself geared towards accounting for "divine inexistence" by projecting a subject that is unaccounted for. Where Latour, Gros and Boltanski are interested in the critique of accountability, associating it with forms of managed life (or shareholder existence) coincident with specific historical iterations of finance capitalism, Meillassoux identifies unaccountability with pure number, with the discipline of mathematical ontology. And lest one assume that there is nothing political about this philosophical numbers game, Meillassoux builds into his theory a politics of Adventism irreducible to the kind of prognostics that is by now familiar in discourses either of "capitalist modes of prediction" (Ascher) or of a Badiousian "communism to come" (in which the field of capitalist financialization is effectively leveled). Meillassoux elaborates, rather, a probabilistic aesthetics reliant on the clairvoyance of numbers. They are numbers that encrypt life in poetic meter and gesture towards a possible repunctuation.[55] An otherworldly metrics, a book on Mallarmé that goes crazy with numbers; all this may incline you to think you are wasting your time on frivolous calculations, but you just might be considering how to think another count: a mode of existence in which the meter is not always running.

---

54   Ibid., 166.

55   On the aesthetics of punctuation, see Peter Szendy's *A coups de points: la ponctuation comme expérience* (Paris: Minuit, 2013). In tying his notion of punctuated experience to the graphemic trace, Szendy follows through on a Derridean impetus, treating onomastics as the source of *différance* and as a site of the subject's encounter with his own death.

Occupy Derivatives!

We don't want someone who governs anymore.
 — Alice Creischer, untitled poem, fall 2016[1]

As a diffuse force field of political actions (as opposed to a politics of party or unified movement), the Occupy movement trained our eyes on the problem of finance capital as invisible entity and abstracted zone of *agiotage*.[2] Christopher J. Arthur echoes a common argument that "capital does in reality constitute itself through abstraction and the march of abstract forms."[3] For his part, Fredric Jameson, in *Representing Capital*, underscores the non-visible and non-localizable character of the contemporary finance form, comparable to the state form in its elusiveness as an "untheorizable singularity":

---

1   Original German: "Wir wollen keinen mehr, der regiert." Alice Creischer, untitled poem, trans. Karl Hoffman, "Post-Election Artists Dossier," supplement, *Grey Room* 65, 2016.

2   *Agiotage*, an eighteenth-century term for stockjobbing and speculation that acquired currency after the South Sea Bubble of 1720, seems appropriate to revive at this juncture because of its association with new cultures of economic risk. In today's context it would refer to insecurity, financial whales and black swans.

3   Christopher J. Arthur, "Contradiction and Abstraction: A Reply to Finelli," *Historical Materialism* 17, 2009, 172. See also, Roberto Finelli, "Abstraction versus Contradiction: Observations on Chris Arthur's *The New Dialectic and Marx's 'Capital*,'" *Historical Materialism* 15, 2007, 61–74. The debate between Finelli and Arthur over "real abstraction" is a complex one involving the question of how or whether, in Marx's *Capital*, the concrete stands in for an invisibility of mediation. Finelli makes the interesting case that Marx, read against the grain of his humanism and historical materialism, becomes the premier theorist of real abstraction for a definition of wealth today.

Economics posits invisible entities like finance capital on the one hand, and points to untheorizable singularities like derivatives on the other. And as for political theory, the traditional question—what is the state?—has mutated into something unanswerable with its postcontemporary version, where is the state?—while the former thing called power, as solid and tangible, seemingly, as a gold coin, or at least as a dollar bill, has become the airy plaything of mystics and physiologists alike.[4]

Is it impossible to visualize derivatives, credit default swaps, leveraged buyouts, or what the business reporter Eduardo Porter calls "liar loans" (described as the housing bubble's "most toxic, no-doc, reverse amortization" loans)?[5] The parlous effects of such economic transactions are modeled in relief in the non-abstract guise of foreclosures, despoiled pensions, income disparity, wage deflation, and spiking poverty rates, but economic decisions as such, taken by unseen technocrats, *responsables*, and algorithms, remain moving targets.

With OWS, it would seem, there was an attempt to confront finance capital's disappearing act—its vastly inventive arsenal of techniques for dissembling or disappearing evidence of insider trading, illicitly hedged debt, predatory lending, tax shelters, hostile takeovers, dummy corporations, interest-rate fixing, money laundering, and political lobbying of every stripe disguised as public interest. While obviously unable to reverse the damage of vulture capitalism, OWS experimented with ways to respond to Wall Street in kind. Anonymous intervention, hacking, leaks, flash mobs, decentered leadership, viral imaging; such tactics gave new life to the impassive politics of civil disobedience, non-cooperation, abstinence from action, and what Roberto Esposito has associated with the "impolitical"—a "mode of seeing politics," or "way of looking" politically.[6] Shows like *No*

---

4 Fredric Jameson, *Representing Capital* (London and New York: Verso, 2011), 4–5.

5 Eduardo Porter, "The Spreading Scourge of Corporate Corruption," *New York Times*, July 11, 2012, newyorktimes.com.

6 Esposito states in an interview: "I prefer to call the impolitical, more so than a category, let us say, a perspective, a way of looking, a mode of seeing politics; and I do not call it a category because the latter already gives the idea of something complete and definite, something like a concept, whereas in this case it is in fact rather a question of a tonality, of a way of looking." Roberto Esposito, "L'impolitico,"

Comment, organized by the Loft in the Red Zone art collective at the J. P. Morgan building near the New York Stock Exchange (which boasted a burning of a flag made of one dollar bills), or *This Is What Democracy Looks Like*, curated by Keith Miller at NYU's Gallatin School, drew on the agitprop theatrics, cheap print and Internet media flowing out from Zucotti Park.[7] The year 2012 saw OWS, in alliance with the NYC District Council of Carpenters, extend the concept of "art" to protests against the London-based Frieze Art Fair's employment of non-union labor. A small group calling itself Occupy Museums staged demonstrations at New York City museums—the Frick, MOMA, the New Museum of Contemporary Art—to publicize its objections to the rampant financialization of art and to the cozy relation between the 1 percent and nonprofits. The idea of a post-market barter economy animated the "Free Art for Fair Exchange" event that took place on the sidewalk in front of the March 2012 Armory Show. On February 24, 2012 an open letter denounced the Whitney Biennial for preying on the willingness of economically vulnerable young artists to indebt themselves in order to produce work for the exhibition. Another action took the form of a fake press release (under the domain whitney2012.org), declaring that the Whitney Museum had renounced financial backing for the Biennial from Deutsche Bank and Sotheby's on the grounds that these sponsors had committed "reckless and even fraudulent financial speculation" (and, in the case of Sotheby's, locked out unionized art handlers).[8]

---

in *Encylopedia multimediale delle scienze filosofiche*, 1993, emsf.rai.it. Translated by Bruno Bosteels and cited in his "Politics, Infrapolitics and the Impolitical: Notes on the Thought of Roberto Esposito and Alberto Moreiras," *New Centennial Review* 10:2, 2010, 207.

7   For a census of OWS art, see Yates McKee, *Strike Art: Contemporary Art and the Post-Occupy Condition* (London and New York: Verso, 2016). See also, Joshua Clover, *Riot, Strike, Riot: The New Era of Uprisings* (London and New York: Verso, 2016), 180–2.

8   "We love art and art exhibitions. But the art system as it is currently organized is unjust and unsustainable, and we are confident that new alternatives will emerge based in principles of inclusion, mutual aid, and collective creativity . . . as we all begin to imagine the possibility of art institutions being unshackled from the interests of the 1%." As cited in Matt Seaton, "The Whitney Biennial Web Occupation," *Guardian*, February 28, 2012, theguardian.com.

In each of these interventions, some related directly to OWS, others not, the idea was to match Wall Street's business-as-usual procedures of non-transparency with concealed methods of running interference that sometimes entailed, paradoxically enough, making an appearance—just where Wall Street least desired attention drawn, paper trails uncovered, or premises breached. It qualifies as "smallest p" politics, which is to say, politics that is promissorily effected by flash trades, hedged risk-management, and the invisible bonds of contract established by securitized instruments like derivatives.[9]

"*We are the 99 percent* remains a great slogan because it's not only about income and taxation but also about representation and influence."[10] This phrase, taken from an OWS diary, reminds us that "smallest p" politics relies on ways of seeing politics rather than on a concept-driven program. Art practice and critique prove crucial, even though OWS-related art practice cannot be pinned down to a specific art form. If it is often associated with low-budget, low-tech, DIY, ephemeral, recyclable, and performative mediums, it remains an inchoate movement without standing in Art History. Let it be thought of as an impolitic *regard* on financial sector injustice: finance capital's intangibility surrenders a significant measure of its immunity once it is refracted as the "look" of the 1 percent through an OWS lens. As banks and wealth management corporations, or nonprofits dependent on institutions engaged in unfair labor practices and resource exploitation, "appeared" as sites ripe for occupation, so the representational modes of luxury and patrician social life at a time of acute economic recession emerged as loci of politicized spectatorship. Ways of viewing gave rise to new areas of institutional and conceptual occupation, and in this spirit, to the series "Occupy Museums" and "Occupy Theory, Occupy Strategy" (*Tidal*'s watchword) we would add "Occupy Derivatives!"

T. J. Clark plumbed this politics of the aesthetic in his reading of the "fulsome materialism," and "madness all around" discerned in

---

9   See Arjun Appadurai on "the logic of promissory finance" and "charismatic derivatives" in *Banking on Words: The Failure of Language in the Age of Derivative Finance* (Chicago, IL: University of Chicago Press, 2016).

10   "The Intellectual Situation: A Diary. Song for Occupations," *n+1* 13, 2012, 9.

Gustave Courbet's paintings at their most Second Empire. "Matter can, and regularly does, press in on us and give us no room to breathe. A painter whose view of the world begins from an actual realization of this closeness and fulsomeness is a materialist to be reckoned with."[11] Clark's description of Courbet's world, as projected in *Les Demoiselles au bord de la Seine*, is worth quoting at some length as a form of "smallest p" politics defined through the phenomenology of visual perception. In it, we see

two tired, blowsy women, out for a row up the river, who have moored their boat and spread themselves and their petticoats on the grass. They are pinned unconvincingly to the ground like shopsoiled butterflies in someone's collection. And the lack of a felt relation between them and the earth they rest on matters not at all. They and their underskirts are a territory. We go exploring. We smell the sweat and loosen the corset . . . This is a version of materialism . . . if it is possible to say of Courbet . . . that in his art the world becomes all one body, perceived as so many extensions of self, then it is equally true that the qualities of the object-world we find most alien to our vitality—its heaviness and slowness and hard-edged resistance to change—are taken into the body, and give it a strange new consistency.[12]

This "strange new consistency," this practico-inert of corporeal "placidity" has, Clark insists, "something to do with Courbet's politics." While most art critics are content to deflate the myth of Courbet the revolutionary at the level of content by noting his paintings of soft porn nudes and Second Empire patrons, Clark discerns politics at the level of techne and facture.[13] He maintains that

---

11   T. J. Clark, "The Special Motion of a Hand: Courbet and Poussin at the Met," *London Review of Books* 30:8, 2008, 5.

12   Ibid, 6.

13   See Paul B. Crapo, "The Problematics of Artistic Patronage under the Second Empire: Gustave Courbet's Involved Relations with the Regime of Napoleon III," *Zeitschrift für Kunstgeschichte* 58, 1995, 240. Crapo is interested in investigating what the imperial regime gained from courting "an unpredictable, vainglorious painter, who professed radical politics," emphasizing that "contrary to accepted opinion, which portrays Courbet as a staunchly democratic painter standing aloof

Courbet's great moments of matter-of-factness tend to happen when the social material he is working with touches him – above all, touches his class position – most intimately and confusingly . . . The deeper the political undertow in Courbet, the more untroubled – the more completely empirical his picture of matter.[14]

Matter, registered in the heaviness and pallor of flesh, is treated here as a politics of sensation associated with Courbet's subterranean compromise with an imperial aesthetics of materialism, no less suasive for its being embedded in the impasto of paint.

French Second Empire style fused repressive governance and state functionalism is associated by Clark with Courbet's late realism. Indeed, the very fact that Courbet, in Clark's estimation, is all about style at this careerist juncture of his trajectory indicates the workings of "smallest p" politics as an aesthetic of materialism imbued with clientism.[15] Arguably, something like Second Empire realism, now in the guise of capitalist realism, flourishes anew as *the* grand style of finance capital in the work of an artist like John Currin. In Currin's paintings figurative realism is marshaled for social scenes celebrating hilarity and high spirits. There is a full-on appeal to the senses: you can hear the laughter and clink of glasses (as in *Park City Grill*), or revel in the jubilation of meal-sharing before a cornucopia of rich meats and sauces. And of course the painting surface affords the ultimate commodity sheen, with its tongue-in-cheek nod to Old Master technique. Beyond his reliance on allegorical emblems typical of seventeenth-century Dutch scenes of wealth and worldliness, Currin adapts a nouveau riche, Second Empire, pornotopic salon sensibility—fleshy, densely material, surface-driven—for a patron portraiture of today. Together with his partner and muse, the artist Rachel Feinstein, Currin has perfected an

---

from an authoritarian Second Empire, the artist carried on a complex relationship with Napoleon III's regime throughout the two decades of its existence." For a political reading of Courbet's nudes, see Petra ten-Doesschate Chu, "Gustave Courbet's Venus and Psyche: Uneasy Nudity in Second-Empire France," *Art Journal* 51:1, 1992, 38–44.

14   Clark, "The Special Motion of a Hand," 6.

15   "Clientism," or its variant "clientelism," is used here as a politically marked term with reference to how the patron-client relationship leaves its trace on the painting medium and on the artist's choice of subject.

aesthetic for the finance class; one that fully recuperates the "fulsome materialism" perceived by Clark in Courbet's nudes and in his expensively accoutered bourgeoise.[16] Feinstein and Currin deliver the American imperial aesthetic fully capitalized as a luxury form, marketing their own celebrity images as natural extensions of the art that they produce and the spaces they inhabit.

Anticipating the mobilization of *ressentiment* by OWS, Silvia Kolbowski in her 2004/5 photo essay *With What Should the Artist be Satisfied?* included Feinstein's image from a 2004 Marc Jacobs ad in which she appears swathed in the designer's fur, jewelry and dark glasses. In her accompanying text, Kolbowski quotes Melania Trump from a 2005 *Harper's Bazaar* "Luxury Report" (where she is billed as "wife of developer and television personality Donald Trump, and owner of a $1.5 million engagement ring"): "For some, luxury shopping is about creativity . . . It is like you are buying art. It isn't necessary for survival, but it makes the journey more beautiful." Kolbowski shines a light on the ludicrous appropriation of the myth of artistic freedom and creativity for "a marketable image of *high bourgeois* bohemianism," while pointing to the still more troubling evidence, typified by Feinstein's Marc Jacobs ad, of the "Faustian bargain" struck by artists with luxury labels.[17] There may be nothing inherently radical about exposing either the unabashed embrace of self-marketing by artists, or the present-day acceptance of art's complicity with commercial branding; yet, seen through Kolbowski's editorializing frame, Feinstein's glamourous portrait becomes a visual indictment of life in the 1 percent lane.

Where Kolbowski subjects capitalist realism's luxury look to an infrared glare that unsettles the complacent symbiosis between wealthy sponsor and wealthy celebrity artist, William Powhida

---

16   See Thomas Michl's review of Gérard Duménil and Dominique Lévy's *The Crisis of Neoliberalism*, "Finance as a Class?," *New Left Review* 70, 2011, 121. The authors track how the managerial elite, working for its shareholders, has "effectively disincentivized investment in favor of shareholder value."

17   Silvia Kolbowski, *With What Should the Artist be Satisfied?*, in *The Artist as Public Intellectual*, ed. Stephan Schmidt-Wulffen (Vienna: Schlebrügge.Editor, 2008), 52. Original emphasis. First presented as a slide projection during the symposium of the same name, sponsored by the Academy of Fine Arts and the Friends of the Secession, Vienna, October 16, 2004.

hammers the art world's grand sellout to Wall Street with charts, diagrams and manifestos that amount to a veritable "J'accuse" of the 1 percent. Even before OWS Powhida was experimenting with political satire in ways that had him compared by critics to William Hogarth, Honoré Daumier and the caricaturists of *Punch* and *Private Eye*. An installation in February 2008 at the Schroeder Romero gallery titled *The New York Enemy/Ally Project* was an electoral parody that arranged framed caricatures of power players on a scale of "Equivocal" to "Absolute" depending on how "voters" cast their ballots. In *Cosmology Number 1*, a mixed media work from 2010, the heads of critics, curators and collectors, arrayed on a wheel of fortune, were assigned a symbol (or hex sign) designating their status as "Saintly Benefactors," "Rebels and Cynics," "Dominators Diabolical" or "Destroyers Demonic." Larry Gagosian, Jeff Koons, Jeffrey Deitch, Lisa Phillips and Maurizio Cattelan face off against the gallerist Elizabeth Dee (a "dealer angel"), artist Michael Waugh (whose works include "The Wealth of Nations," "The Accumulation of Capital," and "The Inaugurals,"), and the critic Ben Davis (dubbed a "World-class badass"). Davis's "9.5 Theses on Art and Class" had gained particular notoriety: they charged art criticism with the task of critiquing the conditions "of middle-class creative labor in a capitalist world"; discrediting art institutions that extract free labor from aspiring artists; challenging "art's current definition as a luxury good, or the primary concern of a specific professional sphere"; and militating for projects that surmount the paralyzing "critique of the art market paradigm."[18] Powhida annexed their content in a show co-organized with Jennifer Dalton at the Winkleman gallery (March 2010), posting them on the gallery vitrine. The installation, *#class*, featured a classroom, chalkboard, and panels on topics like "Success," "Access," "The System Works," and "Bad Curating." It mined the double meaning of class as scene of instruction and socioeconomic category. And it provided a space for experimenting with attitudes and tactics that became prevalent during OWS, as in the case of Mira Schor's lecture on failure and anonymity as political resources, or the Fine Art Adoption Network's proposal of "care of the object in the place of

18   Ben Davis, "9.5 Theses on Art and Class," *Idea* 33, 2009.

A PHILOSOPHY[1] OF THE **SUPER** WEALTHY

(or the 1%)

We are CAPITALISTS and we have a long-term[2] plan.[3]
It's like we are   .[4] It's AMAZING![5]
We realize working is the stupidest way to make money.[6]
We already have 40% of the country's wealth, BUT...
We won't feel SAFE until we have ███, ███, ███, 93%[7]
YOUR problems are not OUR problems.[8]
You couldn't *possibly* understand NEVER having enough,
When you have almost NOTHING, *peasant*.[9]
You smell like bacon to us.
We like your subSTANDARD of living.
But, OUR tides are rising and we will loan[10] you our boats.
Unless we turn off the fucking TAP. *"Water carriers!"*[11]
What is good for US, is good for US.[12]
Actually, there is no "us." There SHOULD only be *I*
As in **THE** 0.0000003257259%[13] ObjectivISM. *Say it.*
Get a job, sir. Your revolution is over![14]
and "GIVE ME MY FUCKING MONEY!"[15]

---

1. We read Atlas Shrugged AND The Fountainhead at Yarvard.
2. By long term we mean yesterday.
3. It's obviously not a conspiracy. That would require secrecy.
4. Seriously, it's like having another super power besides having TONS of money.
5. No, really we can go anywhere, do anything. It's like people UNsee us.
6. We don't really count income, that's not fair.
7. There is some internal disagreement on the duration of subsistence living.
8. No income? No employment? You're a high-yield, high-risk investment vehicle.
9. Please, continue to argue about making more or less of yourselves while we take your homes.
10. The variable Annual Percentage Rate is 21.99% or higher.
11. LOL! We are SO proud of the Tea Party.
12. We just call it enlightened self-interest or greed, for short.
13. Fuck Ayn Rand, it's not an ISM. That implies other people.
14. Jeffrey Lebowski IS an achiever and a hero, even without the use of his legs.
15. While this is an article of faith, I BELIEVE Lloyd Blankfein said this to the FED.

William Powhida
The 1%
2011
letterpress on paper
20 x 16 inches
edition of 25 + 3 AP
Courtesy the artist and Postmasters Gallery, New York

ownership."[19] Interviewed in *Idiom* about #*class*, Powhida had recourse to a statistical language of class that, once again, would seem to foretell the use of what I call a "quant aesthetic" by OWS: "As artists, if we feel uneasy with selling work, I think it's because we feel uneasy being so isolated from other social interests and dependent on 1% of society."[20] In the midst of the OWS groundswell, Powhida would produce *The 1%*, a set of propositions grouped under the banner title "A Philosophy of the Super Wealthy (or the 1%)," among them: "We won't feel SAFE until we have 20%, 40%, 80%," "We read Atlas Shrugged AND the Fountainhead at Yarvard [*sic*]"; "Seriously, it's like having another super power besides having TONS of money"; "No income? No employment? You're a high-yield, high-risk investment vehicle"; and "GIVE ME MY FUCKING MONEY!" qualified by the footnote, "While this is an article of faith, I BELIEVE Lloyd Blankfein said this to the FED." Formally a cross between a ransom note and a broadside for a protest rally with its mix of fonts, exclamation marks, obscenities and blacked out words, the document unleashes explosive affects.

Though Powhida may be for some a problematic artist on account of his pseudo-Warholian publicity stunts (to wit, his *Art Newspaper* cover lampooning Art Basel Miami Beach with the fake headline "MARKET CRASH: Collectors Abandon Miami," and *POWHIDA*, his spoof on artist-centric installations, staged at Marlborough Contemporary in 2011), he excels at the "art" of the financial derivative, staging and reproducing what a derivative does by bundling, packaging and redistributing images.[21] *Dear Art World (Derivatives)*, produced during the full sway of Occupy in December 2011, makes

---

19   "Interview with William Powhida and Jennifer Dalton," *Idiom*, July 13, 2010, idiommag.com.

20   Ibid.

21   Ken Johnson seems amused by *POWHIDA*, but what comes through in his review is a certain fatigue with yet another attempt to deflate the cult of the artist-genius: "Who is Powhida, the artist whose name is spelled on the gallery wall facing the street? For one thing, he is a jerk. He is here in aviator sunglasses and a black suit sitting on a black leather sofa drinking beer all day and verbally abusing the staff . . . Powhida is a fictional character played by an actor hired by William Powhida . . . Mr. Powhida, as distinct from Powhida the lout, is a quixotic gadfly. It is unlikely he will ever topple the windmills of vanity, mendacity and gullibility that power today's art world. But he will never lack targets for his idealistic ire." Ken Johnson, "POWHIDA," *New York Times*, August 4, 2011, www.nytimes.com.

ample and amusing use of trademark, copyright and hashtag symbols, underscoring how corporate entities have succeeded in privatizing every facet of existence, branding concepts, beliefs, and speech, and turning every act of creative expression into a test of the right to ownership:

I mean, everyone ALREADY has the Answer, it's just that every ELSE ~~just~~ has 'it' all wrong. It's really simple, apparently, to fix everything by applying some JESUS™, REGULATION®, or CONSTITUTION™ to it. If only we'd just free the Market, convict some bankers, spiritually channel the Founding Fathers, regulate derivatives, STOP eating GM corn syrup, spend more . . . time with your Family OR LEGALIZE DRUGS.

EXCEPT WE don't do shit*, because this is AMERICA, Land of the Mr. Softee® and home of the BRAVES® where we are FREE to ARGUE about the CAUSES of social and ECONOMIC inequalities until the grass-fed cows come home. We argue in comment threads, on Facebook™, and twitter™. AND, when we aren't arguing, We agree with our favorite 'experts' on FOX®, CNBC™, and CNN™ as we slide into RECESSION 2.0.

One of the OBVIOUS conclusions I've arrived at is that a very FEW people LIKE it that way. WHILE SHIT is bad for MOST of us—9%+ unemployment, $14 TRILLION+ debt, and a perpetual War on Terror®—*THEY* hope we'll all just pull a lever next fall 'PROBLEM SOLVED' and argue some more about the INTENTIONS of the CLIMATE, BECAUSE the 1% is doing fine.

The only FACTS worth stating are that 20% of the population controls 85% of the net worth and earned 49.9% of the income last year. IN the AMERICAN SPIRIT™ of BLAME and recrimination I'm going to point the finger at . . . deREGULATED CAPITALISM®! IT is in the very spirit of Capitalism to ACQUIRE MORE CAPITAL. To quote @O_SattyCripnAzz, fellow citizen and member of #Team #1mmy, "Money is money no matter how u get it."
[. . .]

So, in my useless capacity as a ~~tool~~ artist, I've made some pictures about this SHIT that are FREE to look at**, and they're ALL DERIVATIVES.

Sincerely,
[signed William Powhida]
*#OWS?
** Bring a chair[22]

In addition to repurposing the "art" of the logo (in a way reminiscent of *Adbusters*'s "Corporate America Flag," where the stars are replaced by the logos of Citi, Visa, CNN, Exxon, Pfizer, Google, and others), Powhida mobilizes the outlaw ethics of hacking, piracy and depropriation. By making pictures of "derivatives" "free to look at," the work comes off as an affront to the logic of profit and exclusive access, treated as sacrosanct in the financial industry. *Dear Art World (Derivatives)* delivers its punches without any subtlety whatsoever, but this does not prevent it from denaturalizing the workings of a financial instrument that enriches itself through other people's debt and posits its own speculated value as economic sufficient cause.

Powhida uses economic statistics and the lexicon of finance capital as raw materials of aesthetic practice. For instance, *A Painted (Revised) Guide to the Oligopoly Market* literalizes the pyramid scheme. Inside the pyramid in a variety of graphics and colors are the names of market-hyped artists like Jeff Koons, Damien Hirst and Takashi Murakami, followed by those of major commercial galleries. Outside the pyramid, and continuing the "bite the hand that feeds you" politics of ingratitude, palimpsests of critical journals like *Artforum*, *Frieze* and *Flash Art*, and academic institutions known for art programs (Columbia, RISD, Yale, Cranbrook), vie for space with descriptive statements about the buyer's market. *What Can the Art World Teach You* (2012) employs similar put-downs: a trompe l'oeil rendering of a sheet ripped out of a spiral notebook contains a cynical glossary of art business terms (for example, "Flipping," defined as "the ugly opposite

---

22   William Powhida, *Dear Art World*, 2011, graphite on paper, from his solo show *Derivatives*, Postmasters gallery, Miami, 2011.

of collecting where gamblers, speculators, colluders, investors desperate people sell 'their' art for a profit essentially telling the artist to go
fuck themselves"). *Griftopia* (2011) carefully diagrams targets that
were singled out for excoriation by Matt Taibbi in his book *Griftopia:
Bubble Machines, Vampire Squids, and the Long Con that is Breaking
America.* Here Powhida adapts Mark Lombardi's "connect the dots/
follow the money" technique (on display in Lombardi's large-scale
drawings of various banking and Savings and Loan scandals from the
1970s through the 1990s), with paths connecting caricatures of the
heads of America's most wanted financial miscreants and corporate
lobbyists. This is "smallest p" politics insofar as the selected subjects
approximate a rogue's gallery of contemporary American political
culture. It is as if Powhida were saying that if it is impossible to make
convincing art that allows you to see a "cap," a "floor," a "collar," a
"swaption," a "put," a "call," "a tranch," a "PAC" (Planned Amortization
Class), or an "SMBS" (Stripped Mortgage-Backed Securities)—all
jargon for financial instruments in the derivatives market—at the very
least you can out the names and faces of the players manipulating
those hidden transactions or make use of tactics for visualizing capital
that may not be new to OWS but that are energized by it. By tracking,
plotting, counting, and graphing finance operations, Powhida mobilizes a "quant aesthetic" for OWS. His work is set off from OWS-related
actions—it is after all highly produced and contextualized as art—but
it is arguably part of an OWS continuum inasmuch as it derives political charge from the relocation of statistical measurements of class and
income inequity (99 percent, 1 percent) from the boardroom (or
laptop) to the public façade (or Tumblr).[23] His sardonic perception of

---

23   Tumblr's "wearethe99percent," has been credited with helping to generate a
real-time archive that raises class consciousness: "The creation of an archive or
memorial, even in real time, doesn't by itself constitute resistance and it may be that
the 99-percenters represented by the Tumblr will be viewed by future historians as
the necessary fallen of the Great Adjustment, or whatever name they give our present
moment of wracking socioeconomic realignment. At the same time, by writing "I
am the 99 percent" or in some cases "We are the 99 percent" at the end of their
litanies, the individuals who post their miseries on the web are doing something that
Americans of recent generations have been averse to doing. They are actually creating
class consciousness, for themselves and those around them. It's not just a gesture but
a speech act, in the way that declaring Jesus Christ your savior makes you a Christian.
When an individual follows the instructions of wearethe99percent.tumblr.com—*Let*

William Powhida
Griftopia
2012
print on paper
44 x 88.5 inches
edition of 13 + 2 AP
Courtesy the artist and Postmasters Gallery, New York

the 1 percent as a culture driven by ratings and bids to "occupy" top percentiles complements Jameson's vision of a "repressed" phenomenality of distinct "qualities of work" that elude quantitative expression:

> Labor here orients the exploration of quality in a new and unexpected direction: the quality of work involved as an existential or phenomenological activity. "Digging gold, mining iron, cultivating wheat and weaving silk are qualitatively different kinds of labour." ([Marx, *Capital*,] 29): and this is why their qualities must be repressed from the quantitative, or better still, why they must fall out of its frame, remain undetected on its screens of measurement. This absent persistence of the body, of the existential quality of physical work and activity, will inform the text [*Capital*] throughout.[24]

It would take another discussion to adumbrate Jameson's politics of persistent bodies—his phenomenology of work, unemployment, and the labor form more generally. Suffice it to say that elements of this political aesthetic appeared in OWS adventures in anticapitalist representation and "media as direct action."[25] Some involved a politics of deregulated *espacement*, a reformation of public and private space through bodily assembly. Some relied on poster art that returned to public view the faces of historic activists, from proponents of the general strike (Georges Sorel, Rosa Luxembourg) to the grand examples of non-cooperation (Mahatma Gandhi). And still others deployed guerilla efforts to "Occupy Art History," redolent of the way in which *Guernica* served as flashpoint of contested censorship after the United States, preparing to announce the Iraq invasion of 2003, insisted that a reproduction of it hanging in the anteroom of the UN Security Council be placed behind a curtain:

---

us know who you are. Take a picture of yourself hodling a sign that describes your situation. Below that, write 'I am the 99 percent'—he or she writes a letter of resignation from the American Dream and pledges allegiance to the 99 percent movement, the goals of which remain undefined." "The Intellectual Situation: A Diary. Song for Occupations," 6–7.

24 Ibid., 25–6.

25 See Katie Davison, "Media as Direct Action," *Tidal* 2, 2012, 26–7.

The episode became an emblem. Many a placard on Piccadilly and Las Ramblas rang sardonic changes on Bush and the snorting bull. An emblem, yes – but, with the benefit of hindsight, emblematic of what? Of the state's relentless will to control the minutiae of appearance, as part of—essential to—its drive to war? Well, certainly . . . Did not the whole incident speak above all to the state's *anxiety* as it tried to micromanage the means of symbolic production—as it feared that every last detail of the derealized décor it had built for its citizens had the potential, at a time of crisis, to turn utterly against it?[26]

In the wake of the pepper spray incident at UC Davis[27]—which prompted Nathan Brown, at the time an assistant professor of english and critical theory at Davis, to call for Chancellor Linda P. B. Katehi's resignation in the name of "faculty and students who are well trained *to see through* rhetoric that evinces care for students while implicitly threatening them"—the old pitched battle between authoritarianism and revolution was comparably restaged at the scale of image micromanagement and the "minutiae of appearance."[28] Drafted for the medium of Tumblr and in the guise of what Roberto Esposito calls

---

26 Ian Boal, T. J. Clark, Joseph Matthews and Michael Watts (Retort), *Afflicted Powers: Capital and Spectacle in a New Age of War* (London and New York: Verso, 2005), 16.

27 Jennifer Doyle narrates an account of the incident in *Campus Sex, Campus Security* (South Pasadena, CA: *Semiotext(e)*, 2015), 13. In her analysis of the incident, Doyle emphasizes how Chancellor Katehi played on associations between race and sexual assault—Occupy Davis could turn into Occupy Oakland if "outside violators" were allowed to mingle with campus protestors—to justify her actions:

"Let us begin with the image of a man at work. The image of a campus scandal.

A police officer waters demonstrators with a jet of pepper spray.

A policeman and his pepper spray: students with their hoods up, stunned and slumped forward; a crowd of people watching. Recording.

On November 18, 2011, during the season of the Occupy Movement, the University of California Police Department at UC Davis assembled its troops to break up a camp recently established by students protesting endless increases in college tuition. A psychology student at Davis took this photograph of Sergeant John C. Pike at work. She was close enough to get pepper spray on her jeans. She posted the image on Facebook. It had explanatory power: it migrated to Reddit and went viral."

28 Emphasis mine. Nathan Brown, "Open Letter to Chancellor Linda P. B. Katehi," November 18, 2011, available at ucdfa.org.

"the implant" (the pathogen of biopolitical autoimmunity), an insurgent micropolitics ("smallest p" politics) became fleetingly visible in the insertion of the Lt. John Pike meme—a viral memorial to the pepper spray attack and to moments of solidarity within OWS—inside major tableaux of the art historical canon, including Delacroix's *La liberté guidant le peuple*, Manet's *Déjeuner sur l'herbe* and Picasso's *Guernica*.[29]

Pepper-spraying John Pike inside Eugène Delacroix's *Liberty Leading the People*

peppersprayingcop.tumblr.com

---

29 Roberto Esposito, *Immunitas: The Protection and Negation of Life*, trans. Zakiya Hanafi (London: Polity Press, 2011), 145–77.

Serial Politics

Televisual series have emerged as one of the most effective media for communicating the inner workings of obstructionism, imparting not just fluency in the lingo of K Street, the niceties of back-channeling, and the finer points of parliamentary procedure, but also obstruction's seriality, its endless reconfiguration into disparate modalities of existence. Confronting obstructionism can lead to "philosophies of defeat," as considered in Bruno Bosteel's *Philosophies of Defeat: The Jargon of Finitude*; but it can equally well provide grist for entertainment, attested to by the immense global popularity of the American *House of Cards* along with its counterparts and spin-offs such as *Borgen* in Denmark, *1992* in Italy, or *Snakes and Ladders* in Canada. These serials, whose hallmark is the imbrication of sexual and institutional politics, invite definition of what is extra to statecraft by means of the measure of the *extra time* produced by the serial format. Viewers quite literally make time, extracting it from busy days of labor, or, in a more financialized mode, banking and hoarding time for credit hours of watching. Thibaut de Saint-Maurice notes that the series' extended duration allows viewers to experience the undramatic texture of the everyday, the slow unfurling of the non-event, the possible worlds of infinite situations. And Sandra Laugier suggests that the exorbitant amount of time expended watching a character works like a pleasurable form of school, instructing audiences in the philosophy of judgment as they are prompted over time to hone their skills as judges of moral character.[1]

---

1   See Thibaut de Saint-Maurice, *Philosophie en séries—saison 2* (Paris: Ellipses, 2011), 11; and Sandra Laugier, "Les séries télévisées: éthique du care et adresse au public," *Raison publique* 11, 2009, 277—88, as cited by Marjolaine Boutet, "Philosopher avec *The West Wing*," *TV/SERIES*, 2015, tvseries.revues.org.

The political series equips the spectator with tools to decode the dynamics of dysfunctional moves and successful scoring, both within and outside the circumference of political institutions, as if the screen were a form of game space for calculating an act's proportional importance to a situation. Among these game spaces, the ubiquitous surveillance monitor plays a major role, as Elisabeth Bronfen notes in her article "Shakespeare's Wire." Here the monitor refracts the isomorphism and imbrication of overlapping worlds—those of criminal networks, the police, and Baltimore politicians:

> The computer screens transform the police into the audience of schemes and movements they can only partially understand. Recorded by hidden microphones, photo and video cameras, individual scenes of the game are rendered visible as snippets of coded dialog, as freeze frames or silent movie footage . . . the gangsters, cognizant that they are being watched, explicitly perform for the police, play to their expectations or ludically thwart their reconnaissance efforts.[2]

Political serials specialize in similar game spaces that erase the lines between politics and non-politics at the very seat of power. Arenas such as the White House, the Houses of Parliament, or government offices emerge as stages of containment for the uncontainable, entropic energies of politics in its daily emissions. Ophir Levy, writing about *The West Wing*, and in particular, about hallway chat ("Do you mind if I talk to you while we walk?"), locates this entropy in the "frantic activity" of extras, who flit across the screen like projectiles, mobilizing a positive yet ever-changing spatial field:

> *The West Wing* is famous for its long single steadicam shots in which characters walk along the West Wing of the White House. Symbolizing continuity, these shots methodically reveal a space characterized by the frantic activity of the people who seem to cross it in all directions. It can be the diverse trajectories of the numerous anonymous bodies of extras (assistants, secretaries, interns) who seem to cross the screen

---

2   Elisabeth Bronfen, "Shakespeare's Wire," 2015, paper circulated online at academia.edu.

in less than a second, like projectiles, and then disappear, caught up in what they are doing. It can be the continuous trajectories of the main collaborators of the president, or of the president himself, sustained by the continuous dialogue which seems to fuel their movement. It can be the repetitive trajectories of words themselves, darting like projectiles in the martial arts of speech. What does the coextensivity between walk and talk suggest in *The West Wing?* The continuous steadicam takes make the physical dimension of speech palpable, underlining the constant exertion and the virtuosity of characters, the vertigo of speech or, on the contrary, its utmost performativity. They probably also allow access to the very essence of politics: speech is indeed an actual act in the series, used to convince, legislate, rule—not just some inconsistent rambling.[3]

The "physical dimension of political speech," experienced materially in serially produced, stochastic real time may be associated with the realism of what Marx termed *real abstraction*.[4] David Cunningham,

---

3 Ophir Levy, "Projectiles: de l'usage du plan-séquence dans *The West Wing*," *TV/Series*, 2015, tvseries.revues.org.

4 My critically ambivalent approach to "real abstraction" in relation to the mimesis of unexceptional politics in political fiction and TV serials is comparable to the one developed by Leigh Claire La Berge in her book *Scandals and Abstractions: Financial Fiction of the Long 1980s* (New York: Oxford University Press, 2015), which argues for a less abstracted abstraction in relation to the periodized genre of "financial print culture." Reviewing the book, Nicholas Dames eloquently summarizes La Berge's recuperation of financial representation: "La Berge is careful to avoid nostalgia for the Marxist theory that came under fire in the 1980s, but she wants to signal the blindnesses of the insights that supplanted it. Primarily, the emphasis on the 'abstraction' of finance, a term that echoed the sublime aporias of poststructuralist theory in its pomp, slid unhelpfully into a sense of finance as 'unrepresentable'. La Berge is canny in the way she shows how an acute recognition of the abstractions of post-regulatory capital flows became a (rather aestheticized) capitulation to the self-serving obscurantism of a financialized economy. The abstraction of finance from production, when it is, rightly or wrongly, understood as an abstraction that has always already escaped definition—and, not coincidentally, regulation—becomes a kind of literary-theoretical admonition that whereof one cannot speak, thereof one must be silent. Against this elision of abstraction and unrepresentability—part of the intellectual history of 'the long 1980s'—La Berge wants to recover a particular representational history in the abstractions of finance." Nicholas Dames, "Fictions of Capital," *New Left Review* 99 2016, 152. See also, La Berge's article "Fiction is Liquid: States of Money in *The Sopranos* and *Breaking Bad*" (*Journal of American Studies* 49:4, 2015) where she develops the thesis that fiction may be seen as a kind of

writing about New Italian Epic and referring to Roberto Saviano's novel *Gomorrah*, together with the immensely popular Italian film and TV serial spun off from it, applies the idea of real abstraction (as mediated by Hegel and Lukács) to the socially totalized objective reality of commodity exchange, and to the conditions of their exchangeability as such: the idea that "the specific set of circumstances of capitalist modernity come to have an actual (and thus paradoxically concrete) objective social existence."[5] Cunningham identifies the representation of real abstraction with the "critical mimesis of capital's own global 'incursions,'" citing Saviano's observation that

> it's not hard to imagine something, not hard to picture in your mind a person, gesture, or something that doesn't exist. It's not even complicated to imagine your own death. It's far more difficult to imagine the economy in all its aspects: the finances, profit percentages, negotiations, debts and investments . . . You may be able to picture the impact of the economy, but not its cash flows, bank accounts, individual transactions.[6]

Cunningham sees *Gomorrah* as exemplary in making manifest the internal politics of sabotage or the intricate business transactions of an organized crime network. And, borrowing from Enzo Paci, Alberto Toscano argues in a similar vein, underscoring that abstract drive and structure assume "the explicit contours of a matter of fact, of a state of affairs . . . [of the] universal capable of reality."[7]

I would, however, reorient this reading of real abstraction, arguing that the realism at issue here represents, first, a totalizing retrospect, or an abstracted "real" of capital, rendered in the production

---

liquidity, a form taken by capital through money laundering, or the conversion of a criminal economy (based on "toxic assets") into its double, the so-called legitimate economy.

5   David Cunningham, "Capitalist Epics: Abstraction, Totality and the Theory of the Novel," *Radical Philosophy* 163, 2010, 16.

6   Ibid., 19. Cunningham cites Roberto Saviano, *Gomorrah,* trans. Virginia Jewiss (London: Pan Macmillan: 2006), 282.

7   Enzo Paci, as cited by Alberto Toscano in "Real Abstraction Revisited: Of coins, commodities and cognitive capitalism," 2005, circulated online, available at www2.le.ac.uk.

rhythm of serial narrativity (what Joshua Clover dubs *retcon*, or *retroactive continuity*:"an annealing of logical fissures in a given backstory after they have cracked open into system-threatening incoherence"); and second, a real that defies abstract theorization, which is to say, that remains true to the untidy, incoherent maze of interactions, calculations, and structures of psychopower diffused within distributed systems of institutional power in and beyond the sphere of *nomos* or Reason of State. From this infrapolitical perspective on realism, we derive a picture of politicians thinking politically in economic metaphors (following Clover's argument that metaphor is essentially an equation, making it the most financial and mathematical of literary figures), as well as a picture of politics—substantialized in random willings rather than exceptional, individual acts—that is never something "the people" can have or to which universals can lay claim.[8]

Whether deadly or satirical (or both), political serials—considered as the aesthetic form of serial politics—rely on a tradition of political fiction harking back to Benjamin Disraeli's *Coningsby or, The New Generation* (1844), often classed the first political novel in literary history and the first of the "Young England" trilogy that included the more famous *Sybil, or, The Two Nations* (1845).[9] A turgid chronicle about Parliament in the era of cabinet shake-ups following the Reform Act of 1832 (an act that enlarged the enfranchised electorate, bolstered representation of industrial cities in the House of Commons, and diminished seats in the House of Lords), *Coningsby* maps the protean geography of political crisis:

> At present the world and the confusion are limited to St James's Street and Pall Mall; but soon the boundaries and the tumult will be

---

8 See Joshua Clover, "*Retcon*: Value and Temporality in Poetics," *Representations* 126:1, 2014, 14, 9. The opposite of "*Retcon*," in Clover's scheme, is "*Hysteron proteron*," associated with the "epistemological shudder of causality's collapse" (15).

9 I have considered the parliamentary novel in the French nineteenth century tradition using Zola's *Son Excellence Eugène Rougon* as central example. It should be mentioned that there is a robust tradition of Italian parliamentary fiction. See Alessandra Briganti's *Il parlamento nel romanzo italiano del secondo Ottocento* (1972); Carlo Madrignani's *Rosso e nero a Montecitorio*; and Giovanna Caltagirone's *Dietroscena: l'Italia post-unitaria nei romanzi di ambiente parlamentare* (1993).

extended to the intended metropolitan boroughs; to-morrow they will spread over the manufacturing districts. It is perfectly evident, that before eight-and-forty hours have passed, the country will be in a state of fearful crisis.[10]

An orphaned aristocrat, Coningsby is based on the real-life politician George Smythe, undersecretary to Prime Minister Robert Peel. A Tory Romantic, advocate for social justice, and opponent of the utilitarian, "whatworks" political style of Peel, Smythe faced off against the cynical utilitarian operative John Wilson Croker. The Croker character in the novel is Rigby, the yes-man of choice to ministers, the ultimate party insider and proxy, ghosting the man of power even as he himself is ghosted by ghostwriters. Rigby represents the legions of flunkies whose actions provide the filler of serial politics:

> The world took him at his word, for he was bold, acute, and voluble; with no thought, but a good deal of desultory information; and though destitute of all imagination and noble sentiment, was blessed with a vigorous, mendacious fancy, fruitful in small expedients, and never happier than when devising shifts for great men's scrapes . . .
>
> After a struggle of many years, after a long series of the usual alternatives of small successes and small failures, after a few cleverish speeches and a good many cleverish pamphlets, with a considerable reputation, indeed, for pasquinades, most of which he never wrote, and articles in reviews to which it was whispered he had contributed, Rigby, who had already intrigued himself into a subordinate office, met with Lord Monmouth.
>
> He was just the animal that Lord Monmouth wanted, for Lord Monmouth always looked upon human nature with the callous eye of a jockey. He surveyed Rigby; and he determined to buy him. He bought him; with his clear head, his indefatigable industry, his audacious tongue, and his ready and unscrupulous pen; with all his dates, all his lampoons; all his private memoirs, and all his political

10   Benjamin Disraeli, *Coningsby or, The New Generation* (Bungay, Suffolk: Penguin Books, [1844] 1983), 52.

intrigues. It was a good purchase. Rigby became a great personage, and Lord Monmouth's man.[11]

Disraeli's Rigby is familiar as the Machiavellian advisor to the Prince, a formulaic figure to be sure. But the adjectives and qualifiers attaching to his persona—"desultory information," "mendacious fancy," "small expedients," "small successes," "small failures," "cleverish speeches," "subordinate office"—bring more attention to the microphenomenology of politics than to the particular traits of an individual character within a web of dramatic action. What Disraeli invents is serial politics as a literary order of discursivity, as in this spectacular run-on sentence, which plunges the reader into a welter of syntactic imbrications and insider references:

> The startling rapidity, however, of the strange incidents of 1834; the indignant, soon to become vituperative, secession of a considerable section of the cabinet, some of them esteemed too at that time among its most efficient members; the piteous deprecation of 'pressure from without,' from lips hitherto deemed too stately for entreaty, followed by the Trades' Union, thirty thousand strong, parading in procession to Downing-street; the Irish negotiations of Lord Hatherton, strange blending of complex intrigue and almost infantile ingenuousness; the still inexplicable resignation of Lord Althorp, hurriedly followed by his still more mysterious resumption of power, the only result of his precipitate movements being the fall of Lord Grey himself, attended by circumstances which even a friendly historian could scarcely describe as honourable to his party or dignified to himself; latterly, the extemporaneous address of King William to the Bishops; the vagrant and grotesque apocalypse of the Lord Chancellor; and the fierce recrimination and memorable defiance of the Edinburgh banquet, all these impressive instances of public affairs and public conduct had combined to create a predominant opinion that, whatever might be the consequences, the prolonged continuance of the present party in power was a clear impossibility.[12]

---

11   Ibid., 39–40.
12   Ibid., 90–3.

Even Disraeli's readers, knowledgeable in British history, would have had considerable difficulty parsing the sequencing of political events from this passage, which describes the fallout of the Reform Act that precipitated Lord Grey's retreat from government in 1834.

In developing a mode of narration that is archly allusive, hard to follow, and riddled with innuendo, Disraeli anticipates Anthony Trollope, and particularly the Trollope of the Palliser novels where the minutiae of national domestic politics, policy-making, and power-jockeying are overlaid on the family romance. As Adam Gopnik observed,

> The faceless bureaucrats of large organizations are his great love . . . Trollope, were he alive today, would be in Brussels, writing comedies about the European Parliament . . . In Trollope's fiction, even the most small-scale and homely stories have as a background this special crisis of modernization—not the crisis of industrialization and mass immiseration, seen by Dickens, but a crisis of institutions, produced by reform and standardization.[13]

The prosaic business of the society of calculation highlighted by Trollope arguably carries over to the serial, defined as anti- or mock-epic, the opposite of the historical novel, which traces the arc of an epochal event.

Serial politics enters the political brain and translates it into the scripts of political serials, often through a repertoire of phrasal refrains and hooks. This is especially apparent in the British *House of Cards*, where Chief Whip Francis Urquhart marks out the beat of his compulsive scheming through repeated expressions: "You might well think that. I couldn't possibly comment"; or "I'm the chief whip. Merely a functionary. I keep the troops in line. I put a bit of stick about. I make 'em jump"; or "Me? Well, I'm just a backroom boy."[14] The American *House of Cards* contains comparable bons mots: Frank Underwood's "Power is a lot like real estate. It's all about location, location, location. The closer you are to the source, the higher your property value"; "Democracy is overrated"; "A great man once said, everything is about

---

13 Adam Gopnik, "Trollope Trending," *New Yorker*, May 4, 2015, newyorker.com.
14 *House of Cards*, IMDB Quotes, imdb.com.

sex. Except sex. Sex is about power." But the series achieves even an stronger holding effect with sensory cues, embedding seriality in sequences that relay the mood poetry coming off traffic lights on Washington streets at early morning, the metric beat of oars on a rowing machine, the sound of footfalls on a cemetery path, the oppressively coordinated earth tones of formfitting outfits, the luxury finishes of home furnishings and state-of-the art appliances.

Though based on the 1990s British mini-series, the American *House of Cards* belongs to a larger set of American TV series: *Hail to the Chief* (a 1985 sitcom featuring Patty Duke as woman president), *Tanner '88* (a brilliant mockumentary made by Garry Trudeau and Robert Altman), *The West Wing*, *Wag the Dog*, *K Street*, *Madam Secretary*, *Scandal*, *Spin City*, *Alpha House* and *Veep*. It is also the distant heir to Britain's *Yes, Minister*, a sitcom about public choice politics, as well as to Armando Iannucci's *The Thick of It* (the basis for the film *In the Loop*, which brilliantly dissects the workings of political back-channeling). Both Iannucci productions featured an incompetent cabinet minister who is manipulated by a cynical press officer, played by Peter Capaldi and based on Tony Blair's former Press Secretary Alastair Campbell. Iannucci, it is worth noting, spent some years at Oxford writing a thesis on Milton. In a TV special on Milton, he suggested that Satan's ability to "make a Heaven of Hell and Hell of Heaven" transferred directly to the art of spin because the "operatives who employed such 'meaningless nonsense' were 'literally doing the Devil's work.'"[15] *In the Loop* fully exploited this demonic energy. Jamie—one of the hardcore Scots brought in to do damage control after the minister has let drop in an interview that the prospect of war with Iraq was "unforeseeable"—showers the fey, Oxbridge-educated handlers with violent imprecations, stomping on the fax machine. This ritual performance of "killing the object" is not just a display of rage against the fact that the actual speed and traffic in information is impossible to control; it also comes off as a fit of frustration at the utter lack of meaning or constancy of any political gesture. Serial politics reads in this instance not just as a comedy of manners, or as social

15 Ian Parker, "Expletives Not Deleted: The Profane Satire of Armando Iannucci's 'Veep,'" *New Yorker*, March 26, 2012, newyorker.com.

satire of the hypocrisy and mendacity of politicians, but as a protest against the performance of repetitive exercises in political futility.

Serial politics shows the *matter* of politics: the zingers that anchor political discourse and mark the turning-circle of an episodic cycle, the sensorial cues and physical objects that provide the ambience in which a political maneuver is hatched. Nowhere is this non-totalized, unexceptional aspect of serial politics more effectively rendered than in Robert Altman and Garry Trudeau's mockumentary *Tanner '88*. Hailed as "guerilla filmmaking" in its mix of improvisation and script, true-life politicians and fictive ones, it tracks the peregrinations of Democratic hopeful Jack Tanner, an obscure liberal representative from Michigan, on the campaign trail in the lead-up to the primaries. Since the film was made during the American election season of 1988, we see Tanner crossing paths with real-life candidates Gary Hart, Bob Dole, Bruce Babbitt, and Pat Robertson. Linda Ellerbee, an actual news anchor, conducts a fictional debate with Tanner, Jesse Jackson and Michael Dukakis that splices in real debate footage of Dukakis and Jackson. Mario Cuomo, Martin Scorsese and Kitty Dukakis, playing themselves, each have cameos. Lee Hamilton, Ralph Nader, Gloria Steinem and Art Buchwald, nominated by Tanner as cabinet picks, are shown in mock televised interviews commenting on the prospects of a Tanner administration. The hall of mirrors effect between reality and fiction is compounded by filmic reality effects. *Tanner '88* draws on Rielle Hunter–style videography of life on the campaign circuit, as well as reaction shots of focus groups screening campaign ads; scenes that are filmed being filmed; scenes of chaos in the campaign war room; stock footage of Democratic convention halls; long pans of phone banks, food cartons, and messy desks; and recordings of tech failures and transportation glitches. All this is recorded with vérité technique: roving handheld camera movements and jump cuts. The informal camera work, coupled with the real-time duration of these inside views of campaign work, serializes the ethos of a particular moment. It also communicates the uneasy commingling of image curation and technological improvisation that defined politics at the dawn of a new media matrix in the 1980s. As Matt Bai, writing about Gary Hart's crash-and-burn at the hands of the media, observed, by the late 1980s "a series of powerful, external forces in the society were colliding, creating a dangerous vortex on the edge of our politics. Hart didn't create that vortex. He was, rather, the first to wander into its path."[16]

Tanner '88 zeroes in on visual technologies of power brokerage, focusing on how media stagecraft supplants statecraft. It confronts the viewer with the spectacle of unexceptional politics in all its granular detail—in particular, in its aspect as a process dependent on the infrastructural contingencies and random social encounters that get factored into political strategy. This unexceptionalism carries over to the candidate's personal character. Tanner is the unexceptional sovereign, the "man who carries his own bag." His handlers deem this a weakness: It sends "the wrong symbol at the wrong time. It says that you either can't, or won't delegate. It says Jimmy Carter."[17] Tanner rails against the pressure to remake his image, invoking the name of Daniel Boorstin, a University of Chicago legal scholar who, in his bestseller *The Image: A Guide to Pseudo-Events in America* (1961), championed the idea that America was in the vise of the "pseudo-event." He defined it as "not spontaneous, but planted or incited"; as governed by the promotion of newsworthiness and typified by statements that never really mean what they say.[18] The pseudo-event was epitomized by the leak:

> A clue to the new unreality of the citizen's world is the perverse new meaning now given to the word "leak." To leak, according to the dictionary, is to "let a fluid substance out or in accidentally: as this ship leaks." But nowadays a news leak is one of the most elaborately planned ways of emitting information. It is, of course, a way in which a government official, with some clearly defined purpose . . . makes an announcement, asks a question, or puts a suggestion. It might more accurately be called a "*sub rosa* announcement," an "indirect statement," or "cloaked news."[19]

---

16   Matt Bai, "How Gary Hart's Downfall Forever Changed American Politics," *New York Times Magazine*, September 18, 2014, nytimes.com.

17   As cited in Nancy Franklin, "Tanner Revisited," *New Yorker*, October 11, 2004, newyorker.com.

18   Daniel Boorstin, *The Image: A Guide to Pseudo-Events in America* (New York: Harper & Row, 1961), 11.

19   Ibid., 30–1.

In *The Image*, Boorstin claimed that Americans, as victims of "diplopia" (a blurring of image and reality, fact and value), were no longer able to maintain control over the real. As if wholly in tune with the book's message, Tanner watches in horror as his realness becomes grist for the campaign slogan *"Jack Tanner, 'For Real.'"* The situation worsens when footage of Tanner's heartfelt soliloquy on the moral calling of politics—an anamophosis of parrhesia filmed on the sly from underneath a glass table by his videographer—is co-opted for a campaign clip.

If *Tanner '88* is first and foremost a mockumentary about politics as pseudo-event and artifact of image management, it also works as a documentary of the most tedious aspects of politicking: empty hours, dreary pit stops, endless bus rides, glad-handing, stumping, debriefing, along with the succession of petty humiliations that candidates and their staff routinely endure. The spectacle of political boredom is enhanced by attention to institutional protocols: the "how it's done" aspect of parliamentary procedure and delegate roll call. In the concluding episode, captioned "The Boiler Room," shot on location at the Democratic National Convention, we are treated to real-life Chairman Jim Wright and Convention administrator Dorothy Bush tediously intoning the roll call rules, followed by the roll call itself. The monotony breaks only when Tanner's wily campaign strategist T. J. Cavanaugh feeds a news anchor the story that a "minority report" has been filed by the Tanner campaign challenging the superdelegate vote count. Wagering correctly that the fictive report will not be fact-checked and will take fire, T. J. maneuvers to alter the course of presidential history. As in *Coningsby* (where anonymous "'slashing reports' . . . passed off as genuine coin" succeed in diminishing a party's standing), word of the report ripples through the phone channel, passes directly into the nightly news, and erupts on the Convention floor, where it is taken to a vote.[20] Something is generated out of nothing: the specious report, like the planted rumor or the use of massaged data in a poll, mobilizes the inexistent as a critical device of political machination.

---

20 Disraeli, *Coningsby*, 57.

In the end, not even the manic energies of Billy Ridenour, the testosterone-pumped delegate-harvester brought in to perform some backroom magic, can overcome the forces of the political machine in Ohio, the rogue course of the Jesse Jackson campaign, or the specter of defeatism that has dogged the Tanner campaign throughout. The series comes to a close with a long pan shot of detritus: obsolescent candidate buttons and pennants, overflowing ashtrays, and silent telephone banks.

Tanner '88 capitalizes on gritty cinematography and the settings of cramped hotel rooms, noisy bars, and disorderly campaign headquarters to communicate the most mundane workings of ordinary politics. By contrast, the American *House of Cards* is a slickly produced political fantasia. Directed by David Fincher and Beau Willimon, it ran for five seasons on Netflix between February 2013 and May 2017. The show was put together on the basis of an algorithm culled from marketing metadata on viewers' genre preferences, suggesting that each plot turn or character device reflects an invisible factor of statistical outcome-modeling. Kevin Spacey as Francis (Frank) Underwood is a Democratic congressman from South Carolina and house majority whip. The formula is *The Prince* crossed with *Richard III, Macbeth*, and a dash of *King Lear*. Like its British forbearer, *House of Cards* presents politics as an agon of monster egos, with fights to the death, contests of will, dangerous games of entrapment, blackmail, and cover-up, all mired in the desiderata of administration and political management (how to get a bill passed, how to get rogue players lined up for a vote). "Chapter 6," an episode from season 1 of *House of Cards*, explores a moment of Shakespearean vulnerability where the hero, normally unstoppable, is hoisted on his own rhetorical petard. A teachers' strike has broken out, put into motion by Marty Spinella, who opposes Frank Underwood's reforms to the teachers' unions. Under pressure to drop his entire education bill, Frank arranges for a brick to be thrown through the window of his townhouse so he can blame it on Spinella's protesters. He plans to shame Spinella during a televised debate, thereby garnering enough PR ammunition to ram through his bill: "I'm ready for battle," he confides right before the debate; "Watch me put the final nail in Spinella's coffin."

Frank: You know what I'd like . . . an apology, [for] when that brick
    came through the window.
Spinella: Are you serious? Ok . . . I am sincerely sorry that you had to
    go through that ordeal, it sickens me what you had to go through
    in your home. But what sickens me more [he turns to face Claire
    who is looking on from the newsroom floor] is that your husband
    is using you as a prop on national TV to win a debate.[21]

Furious and thrown off guard by the address to his wife, Frank takes a
wrong turn into the alphabet. He crosses the letters I, O, U with the
vowel series A,E,I,O,U, losing track of the errant E of "Education"
along the way. There is a moment of panic as he tries to rectify cognitive dissonance—perhaps, the viewer wonders, he is trying to eradicate the specter of what the strikers feel they are "owed" (or "O'ed").
But Frank runs aground in the confused positioning of the U and the
I, losing his own subject position in the process and committing a
horrendous lapsus: "defecation" for "education." He effectively shits
himself on national TV.

Frank: You've got this wrong, there is no "you" nor "I" but education
    with a capital E, you know what I'm talking about. You and I in
    education.
You want to play the vowel game with me . . .
Y O I am . . . you left out E for education, defecation
Spinella: You like Sesame Street so much . . .
Frank: What I'm trying to say about education . . . I guess you
    schooled me there Marty.[22]

Of particular interest here is the way in which the vocables of uncontrolled speech disturb the airbrushed screen of televised debate,
revealing the sheer vacuity of phatic political utterance. We are in
reverse mode here from, say, Peter Sellers as Chauncey Gardiner in
Being There (1979, adapted from the 1970 novella by Jerzy Kosiński,

---

21   "Chapter 6," *House of Cards* (US), season 1, episode 6, dir. David Fincher
and Beau Willimon (Los Angeles: Netflix, 2013).
22   Ibid.

who also wrote the screenplay), where the character's gnomic pronouncements are taken by the public as the coin of a political metaphysics dealing in sacred truth-saying (à la Ben Carson). Frank's brain freeze is closer to the real-life cases of Rick Perry, who forgot several branches of government in a debate on national TV in 2008, and Gary Johnston, the independent libertarian running for president in 2016 who didn't know what "Aleppo" was, and failed to come up with the name of a single national leader in the entire world. His slip of the tongue (education/defecation) resembles Warren Beatty's performance in *Bulworth* (1998) where the controls of the superego are blown off their axles as the presidential candidate starts to rap his fund-raising speech, letting fly what he really thinks about big oil, big pharma, banks, and corporate ownership of elections. As in *Bulworth*, this episode in *House of Cards* exposes phatic speech and political patter to ridicule. Rote sound bites and point-scoring are exposed as flimsy rhetorical contrivances, vulnerable to deconstruction.

If my first *House of Cards* example emphasized the alphabet soup in which politicians discursively swim and occasionally drown, my second focuses on how (as in *Tanner '88*) parliamentary procedure is conscripted televisually as an expressive medium of unexceptional politics. A scene in the third chapter of season 2, in which senators are dragged into the Senate chamber in handcuffs, is based on a real-life event in 1988, in which Republicans left the Senate chamber, meaning quorum could not be reached, and Senate Majority Leader Robert Byrd ordered them back. Senator Robert Packwood of Oregon was found hiding in his office and carried into the chamber.

The *House of Cards* episode starts with Frank's efforts to avoid a government shutdown. He extends an olive branch to the Republicans, figuring that in return for his support for their desire to raise the retirement age, he will pass an omnibus bill with bipartisan support. Everything seems on track, with Frank arriving at a compromise with Republican Senate Majority Leader Hector Mendoza, until Tea Party leader Curtis Haas balks and takes his caucus with him. The Republicans' absence means that the Senate will no longer have the quorum necessary for a vote, so Frank uses an arcane parliamentary measure to compel the absent senators to appear under threat of arrest. After six of them are handcuffed and hoisted bodily into the chamber, the vote passes. This prompted one *House of Cards* commentator to observe wryly, "It's actually a rather interesting episode, if you enjoy the inner workings of the Senate. However . . . there are two things in the world you never want to let people see how you make 'em—laws and sausages."[23]

Cloture, quorum call, filibuster, "medieval" maneuvers that involve recognizing a minority leader's motion to compel the attendance of senators; this is the stuff of political serials that treat parliamentary procedure as the matter of politicking. Obstructionism takes on the character of a political kind of materialism that sublates human agency and ideological telos. We move well beyond what Claude Lefort identified as the "malefic logic" of Machiavellianism, which aligns ruse with intention and affirms the persona of the serenely perverse sovereign who hews to his objectives. *House of Cards* portrays political ends, even when they are realized, as mired within arcane procedures and non-events—occurrences that, examined in close-up, appear as befuddling as Frank Underwood's vowel game.

If TV political serials—the branded form of serial politics—have emerged as a preferred medium, rival to as well as continuous with American world literature in the stream of cultural artifacts for export, we can perhaps explain their appeal, at least in part, by the way in which they perform a pageant of the destruction of political entelechy communicated not through exceptional characters but by means of epic unexceptionalism, what I have characterized throughout as microscaled, "small p" politics. Here, I approach the recouping of ordinariness that Lauren Berlant is after when, in *Cruel Optimism*, she argues on behalf of "the situation as a genre of unforeclosed experience." For Berlant, "the situation" (as opposed to the high-stakes "event"), in affording a "historical sense of the present as immanence, emanation, atmosphere or emergence," proves capable of "releasing subjects from the normativity of intuition and making them available for alternative ordinaries."[24] At its most "optimistic," this micropolitics

---

23   Andrea Reiher, "'House of Cards' Season 2 episode 3: Doormats and matadors, laws and sausages," *Screener*, February 18, 2014, screenertv.com.

24   Lauren Berlant, *Cruel Optimism* (Durham, NC: Duke University Press, 2011), 5, 6.

of adjustment, incoherent narrative, and unmanageable contingency promises some modicum of relief from the feeling of "stuckness with relation to futurity."[25]

My own reading of political serials as serial politics is not so optimistic: it stays in the thick of obstruction and a kind of bleakness that comes with seriality, itself associated with the compulsion to repeat— all while making a (serial) killing on the political market, where the death drive appears in its most prosaic guises. Political serials provide a guilty pleasure; they permit wallowing in stuckness or political impasse; they produce *Schadenfreude* at one's own expense.

My impetus to think politics as the serial representation of unexceptional politics was concluded in the saga of "Bridgegate," which erupted in 2013 and thwarted Chris Christie's political ambitions. The scandal, which seemed to have flowed seamlessly from a systematic policy to defund public transportation and abet stuckness as a modus vivendi, involved the New Jersey governor's presumed hand in orchestrating a monster traffic jam on the bridge connecting Fort Lee to Manhattan in retribution for the Fort Lee mayor's refusal to support Christie in the gubernatorial election. Like "the whip," a metaphor used for a political position in Congress (incarnated by the character "Jackie Sharp" in *House of Cards*, who takes malicious pleasure in disciplining the flock towards a vote count), the "jam," as I noted in the introduction, is a quite literal expression of the "small p" politics of obstruction. The unfolding sequence of events as reported in the *New York Times* read like a script outline for a TV series that could be titled "Profiles in Pettifoggery."

This script is punctuated by phrases—"Time for some traffic problems," "gridlock," "lane closings," "access," "odd and wrong," "take it to Trenton," "humiliated," "withhold money," "denial"—composed of leaks and verbal accusations that turn into a menu of memes, cataloging the action of political jamming and orchestrated obstruction even as it serializes the sequence of micro-events unfolding in real time. In this case, serial politics acquires definition as a paratactic series, with every "and then this happened" engendering the next. In addition to

25   Ibid., 13.

foregrounding the way impolitic political utterances inflect the narrative accounting of "small p" politics, serial politics pulses and fluctu-
ates like a human drive. In this sense, it is committed like serial murder,
which is to say, like a ritual of sacrificial savagery and victim-targeting,
linked to psychogenic and environmental factors that are causally
tethered to infinite regress and beyond the pale of political theory.

Serial politics, like the political serial, is long-form (infinite),
episodic in rhythm, and structured by the compulsion to repeat. It
traces a political unconscious in the outcomes of calculation and
provides a CAT scan of political intelligence, revealing the cognitive
solutions and workarounds to hurdles, the insurmountability of
obstruction, the instrumentalism of political reason, and the fatigue
produced by incrementalism—the build-up of infinitesimal stresses
and pressures, be they breakdowns in the cabinet of a ruling party,
setbacks preceding comebacks, or the snowballing of *mesquineries*
that culminate in vaporized political careers.

In the contemporary period, televisual political serials, much like
Disraeli's *Coningsby* or Trollope's Palliser novels in the nineteenth
century, strike a nerve; they offer a high-definition picture of an era in
which personal trivia and technical point-scoring, often conjugated
together, exert a strange fascination. There may be nostalgia for
American exceptionalism and grand narratives of triumphalism—to
wit, Trumpism—but the nostalgia ultimately dissipates into the effluvia of social media. What we are left with is an inchoate morass of
political reality-effects that suffuse the atmosphere. Their units are
nanoscale and unaccountable; they are as imperceptible as high-
frequency stock trades, bits of metadata or Twitter messaging, stealth
infusions of Internet-borne fake news, or trace-free instances of back-
channeling that will never figure in the annals of diplomacy. If this
layer of "smallest p" politics is hardly perceptible, it makes all the more
visible evidence that the state has waned, that the demos is undone,
and that political parties have become an anachronism, fully
supplanted by donor networks. The political serial as premier form of
serial politics deflates the myth that a superstate like "America" or a
transnational cultural imperium might still really exist. From *Tanner
'88* to *House of Cards*, we may go looking for sovereign allegory, or
"the Political" in a story, a narrative arc, a tragedy, a melodrama. But

what we discover is that the plot eventually sputters and flatlines; what remains is a nonstop flurry of bait and switch. Political serials refract the deathly seriality of "smallest p" politics, offering no escape from the reiterability of politics, no relief from the oppression of its modes of self-exposition (essential to the constitution of what Mark Seltzer dubs "official worlds").[26] Political serials are condensations of official worlds that self-depict the flat earth of serial politics, in micro-phenomenologies of obstruction, impasse and the impolitic.

---

26 Mark Seltzer, *Official Worlds* (Durham, NC: Duke University Press, 2016).

Acknowledgements

This book went through multiple iterations over the years, changing shape from Bush II to Trumpism. For permission to publish sections of the book that have appeared in different journals I thank *October*, *Romanic Review*, *Textual Practice*, and *Political Concepts*, as well as *Understanding Rancière, Understanding Modernism* ed. Patrick M. Bray, Bloomsbury Academic for permission to reprise part of my essay "*The Hatred of Democracy* and 'The Democratic Torrent': Rancière's Micropolitics." Many interlocutors offered insight and forbearance along the way. I would like to express special thanks to Étienne Balibar, whose philosophically acute theorizations of politics have been a constant source of inspiration. Alain Badiou and Bruno Bosteels, with whom I've had the privilege of collaborating on several projects, will continue to forge the adventure in aesthetics and politics, and Ayman El-Desouky, who provided an illuminating opportunity at SOAS to learn about Arabic terms for political agency. I thank Denis Hollier for his encouragement to write about French political fiction; Adi Ophir, Ann Laura Stoler, Jay Bernstein, Jacques Lezra and Stathis Gourgouris for their collaboration on "political concepts"; Bernard Harcourt and Jésus R. Velasco for the occasion to present on Fanon at Columbia; Vincent Kaufmann for giving me the opportunity to do a dry run on "micropolitics" at the Universität St. Gallen, Switzerland; Gisèle Sapiro for conversations about microsociology in Bourdieu; Benjamin Conisbee Baer for his illuminating remarks on Marx, Benjamin and Derrida when we taught together at Princeton and NYU; Ben Kafka, Diane Rubenstein, Martin Crowley and Nicholas White for their thought-provoking responses to the construct of "small p" politics; Ken Reinhard and Ron Clark for giving me indispensable and ongoing forums at UCLA and the Whitney Independent Study Program;

and David Cunningham, Elisabeth Bronfen and Joshua Clover for their insights into the critical stakes of political serials. New York University generously provided research support and a fulfilling year as a fellow at the NYU Institute for the Humanities. To Sebastian Budgen, my appreciation for laconic prompts and tips on what to read. Gratitude to Duncan Ranslem for help with production details and thank you to Dominik Zechner for assisting with German and Greek references. My dad, David Apter, gave me the taste for arguing about politics at an early age and this book owes its impetus to the memory of his lifelong political engagements. Anthony Vidler, as always, has been my truest reader, best friend and greatest love.

Index

1 percent, 120, 233, 234, 237, 238, 243–6
99 percent, 234, 243

Adbusters (magazine), 242
Adorno, Theodor, 133n57
aesthetics, 4, 5, 132, 180, 230, 236
affluenza, 213
Africa, 41, 123
Agamben, Giorgio, 1, 5, 23, 34, 48, 220
  bare life, 79
  Bartleby, 116, 124, 129, 130n47
  Coming Community, The
    (Agamben), 28
  Homo Sacer, 2
Ahmed, Sarah, 5
Akin, Todd, 84
Alaska, 169
Algeria, 54, 129, 160
alienation, 22, 49, 53, 75, 108, 223
Alliez, Eric, 191n44
Althusser, Louis, 109, 140, 205, 214, 215
Altman, Robert, 6n9257, 258
amāra, 111–12
Andler, Charles, 68
Anidjar, Gil, 11
Anonymous, 9
Antelme, Robert, 129
anticapitalism, 108, 120, 205, 246
Antifa, 123
apartheid, 69, 141

aporia, 5, 31–4, 87, 112, 118, 122–4, 129
Apprill, Olivier, 47n30
Arabic (language), 107, 108, 111, 112
Arab Spring, 27, 109, 123
d'Arboussier, Gabriel, 67
d'Arcais, Paolo Flores, 13
architecture, 40, 47, 49, 54, 119, 214
Arendt, Hannah, 1, 4, 23, 30–31, 34, 140
Aristotle, 2n2, 30, 83, 86, 140, 219
Arnaud, Claude, 203–4
Artforum (journal), 242
Arthur, Christopher J., 231
Art Newspaper (journal), 240
Ascher, Ivan, 224, 230
Athanasiu, Athena, 64
Athenian democracy, 102, 103
Athens, 24n12, 121–2
Atlantic (magazine), 120
Augst, Thomas, 125
Attica Prison, 40
austerity, 14, 65, 123, 201
à-venir, 32, 34
Avicenna, 129–30

Babbitt, Bruce, 258
Bachelard, Gaston, 109
Badawi, ElSaid, 111
Badiou, Alain, 4, 9, 10, 25–8, 34, 109–12, 123, 187, 193–4
  mathematics, 214, 217–20, 230
  Plato, 90, 91

Baguley, David, 170–72
Bai, Matt, 6, 258, 259n16
Balibar, Étienne, 9, 16, 22n2, 23, 34, 35n53, 87, 140, 153
Baltimore, 250
Balzac, 4, 156, 164, 180, 210
bare life, 68, 79, 119
Barker, Jason, 215
Barthes, Roland, 185, 199–212, 224, 225, 227
Bartleby, 48, 91, 114–35
Bartlett, A. J., 219
Bataille, Georges, 87, 132, 205
Baudelaire, Charles, 200
Beatty, Warren, 263
Beaud, Stéphane, 61
Beck, Ulrich, 13–14
Beckett, Samuel, 50, 132, 134
Belgium, 62, 63
Belle Époque, 4, 200
Bellos, David, 105
Belmessous, Hacène, 123
Benjamin, Walter, 106, 168, 169
Bennett, Jane, 133n57, 174
Bennington, Geoffrey, 29–34
Bentham, Jeremy, 85, 86, 140
Bergounioux, Pierre, 189n39
Berlant, Lauren, 16, 17n27, 264
Berlusconi, Silvio, 13, 16
Berlusconismo, 13, 16
Berna, Serge, 90
Bernard, Anne-Marie, 199
Bignall, Simone, 42n14
Bildungsbürgertum, 211
biopolitics, 42, 68, 79, 125, 140, 214
biopower, 39
biosemiosis, 190
de Biran, Maine, 190
Bismarck, 15
Black Lives Matter, 68, 134
blackness, 67–8, 75
Blair, Tony, 257

Blanchot, Maurice, 132, 134
Blum, Hester, 121
Bodin, 30
Boehner, John, 84, 102
de la Boétie, Étienne, 65
de Boever, Arne, 35, 125
Boltanski, Luc, 59n16, 161, 214, 225–26, 230
Boorstin, Daniel, 259, 260
Bosteels, Bruno, 88, 98, 249
Bourdieu, Pierre, 185, 201
    micropolitics, 10
    microsociologies, 53–60, 62, 65
Bowie, Malcolm, 207–8
Braudel, Fernand, 38
Brazilian Democratic Movement Party, 98
Brecht, Bertolt, 50
Brewster, Ben, 108
Brexit, 9
Briganti, Alessandra, 253n9
Bronfen, Elisabeth, 250
Brown, Nathan, 247
Brown, Wendy, 125, 129, 213
Bruni, Frank, 84
Brussels, 7, 256
Buchanan, James, 127
Buchwald, Art, 258
Burke, Edmund, 85
Bush, Dorothy, 260
Bush, George W. See Bush administration
Bush administration, 8, 92, 169, 247
Butler, Judith, 5, 64, 114, 124, 128, 129
Byrd, Robert, 263

Cacciari, Massimo, 99
California, 48
    Oakland, 108
    UC Davis, 247
Campbell, Alastair, 257
Canada, 249

Canetti, Elias, 87
Canguilhem, Georges, 109
Capaldi, Peter, 257
capillary politics, 37
Carbon Liberation Front, 48
Carrier, 14
Carson, Ben, 263
Carter, Jimmy, 259
Cassin, Barbara, 12, 104, 105, 110
Castronovo, Russ, 120
casualization, 59, 65
Cattelan, Maurizio, 238
Cavanaugh, T. J., 260
Caws, Mary Ann, 113
Ceaucescu, 13
Cellular power, 220
CERFI (Le Centre d'études, de
     recherches et de formation insti-
     tutionelle), 42
CGT (General Confederation of
     Labor), 62
Chakrabarty, Dipesh, 67
Char, René, 110
Châtelet, Gilles, 169, 181
Chiapello, Ève, 59n16
Chirac government, 177
Christian, Margareta Ingrid, 194n51
Christie, Chris, 265
Cicero, Marcus Tullius, 35
Citizens United, 8
civil disobedience, 90, 104, 114, 119,
     123, 232
Clark, T. J., 234–7
class
   association, 58
   Bourdieu, 56
   domination, 53
   struggle, 5, 24
clientism, 236
Clover, Joshua, 233n8, 253
Cobb, Richard, 38
Coleman, Ornette, 132n54

colonialism, 27, 73, 123n30
Comay, Rebecca, 113, 118
communism, 10, 26, 29, 91, 110, 112,
     140, 153, 230
communitas, 5, 87, 88
Comte, Auguste, 188
Congress. *See* US Congress
Conrad, Joseph, 192–3
Coupat, Julien, 48
Courbet, Gustave, 235–7
Crapo, Paul B., 235n13
Crary, Jonathan, 225
Creischer, Alice, 231
Croker, John Wilson, 254
Crouse, Timothy, 6n8
Cruz, Ted, 84
Cultural Revolution, 109–110
Cunningham, David, 251–2
Cuomo, Mario, 258
Currin, John, 236–7
Curtis, Adam, 127–8

Dada, 50
Dagognet, Francois, 190n43
Dalton, Jennifer, 238
Dames, Nicholas, 251n4
Dardenne brothers, 62, 63
Darwin, Charles, 188
Daumier, Honoré, 238
Davis, Ben, 238
Davis, Kim, 114
Davison, Katie, 246n25
debt, 123, 215–17, 223, 224, 232, 241,
     242
decolonial struggle, 68
Dee, Elizabeth, 238
Deitch, Jeffrey, 238
Deleuze, Gilles, 69, 116, 133n57, 146,
     200
   Anti-Oedipus (Deleuze/Guattari),
     205, 216
   Bartleby, 125, 132

Guattari, 46, 78, 206, 216
Lines of Flight, 46
micropolitics, 4, 206
Nietzsche, 73
Denmark, 249
Depardon, Raymond, 220–21
Derrida, Jacques, 1, 5, 11, 23, 34, 69,
    103, 116, 133n57, 206
aporia, 31, 32
death penalty, 102
Plato, 101, 104
Rogues (Derrida), 15, 33
Der Spiegel (magazine), 13
Descartes, René, 190
des Forêts, Louis-René, 113, 129–34
desire, 44, 46, 54, 69, 71, 199, 208
Desouky, Ayman El-, 111, 112
deterritorialization, 45, 46, 140
Deutsche Bank, 233
Dewald, Jonathan, 180–81
dialectics, 5, 67, 70, 72, 146
Dickens, Charles, 141, 256
Diès, Auguste, 103
Diogenes, 95
discursivity, 43–5
disentrenchment, 97–100
Disraeli, Benjamin, 141, 253–6, 260,
    266
Dole, Bob, 258
Doyle, Jennifer, 247n27
Dreyfus affair, 202, 208
drones, 6, 156, 157, 161, 162
Dukakis, Kitty, 258
Dukakis, Michael, 258
Duke, Patty, 257
Duras, Marguerite, 132
During, Simon, 64
Durkheim, Émile, 190n42

Eastern Europe, 108
education, 57, 101, 104, 124, 183, 213,
    262–3

Edwards, Brent Hayes, 132n53
Egyptian Revolution, 111
Ellerbee, Linda, 258
Ernaux, Annie, 56
Esposito, Roberto, 86–9, 124, 232,
    248
European Union, 108
exceptionalism, 1, 5, 6, 16, 32, 116,
    125, 266
state of exception, 1, 6, 34, 79, 116,
    118, 140
extraordinary politics, 87n13

fake news, 30–31, 266
Fanon, Frantz, 67–79
fascism, 13, 46
Feher, Michel, 213
Feinstein, Rachel, 236–7
feminism, 91, 108, 204
Ferry, Jules, 188
Fincher, David, 261
Fine Art Adoption Network, 238–40
fixing, 39
Flash Art (journal), 242
Flaubert, Gustave, 4, 54, 141, 142, 155,
    180, 185, 193
Florida, 84
Fore, Devin, 38n2
Forestier, Alexis, 49
Foucault, Michel, 42, 54, 55, 109,
    213–14, 220, 223, 226
Collège de France, 39, 43, 199, 203,
    223
micropolitics, 4, 10, 37–45, 206
foundationalism, 43, 44
Fraisse, Rémi, 107
France, 9, 39, 48, 53, 146, 165, 177,
    178, 203, 217
banlieues, 59, 123n30
Bordeaux, 164
French Resistance, 132
May '68, 110, 115, 130, 200, 220

Paris, 29, 53, 58, 59, 149, 156, 165, 167–8, 202–3
    Second Empire, 164, 169, 172–77, 179, 184, 235, 236
    Versailles, 164, 189
Franck, Georg, 214n4
François, Anne-Lise, 132n52
Franklin, Nancy, 259n17
French (language), 9, 15, 21, 60, 69, 89–90, 95, 102, 103, 104, 107, 188, 225
French National Assembly, 15
Frick (museum), 233
friendship, 69
Frieze (journal), 233
Frieze Art Fair, 233

Gabriel, Kay, 103
Gagosian, Larry, 238
Gandhi, Mahatma, 246
Garfinkel, Harold, 53
Gavriilidis, Akis, 121–2
genocide, 73, 141
Gerima, Haile, 77
Germany, 86, 181
Geuss, Raymond, 28
Giddens, Anthony, 92
Ginzberg, Carlo, 38
Glucksmann, André, 205
Goffey, Andrew, 45
Goffman, Erving, 53, 190n41
Google, 30, 242
Gopnik, Adam, 142n6, 256
Gourgouris, Stathis, 2–3
Graeber, David, 215–17, 224
grammar, 4, 44, 45, 92, 103, 130
Greece, 14, 123
Greek (language), 31, 102–5, 107, 108, 117
Greek referendum, 121, 123
Greenberg, Jonathan D., 120
Grendi, Edoardo, 38

Grieve, James, 210
Griffith, D. W., 77
Gros, Frédéric, 214, 215, 223–5, 230
groupuscules, 46, 50
Guantánamo Bay, 41
Guattari, Félix, 54
    Deleuze, 46, 78, 206, 216
    micropolitics, 4, 10, 37, 42–8, 206
Guernica (painting), 246, 248
Guiradet, 163
Guizot, M., 111, 142, 165, 188

habeas viscus, 69, 74, 76, 78–9
habitus, 53, 54, 90, 185
Hagel, Chuck, 84
Hallward, Peter, 218–19
Hamilton, Lee, 258
Harcourt, Bernard, 39, 67, 71
Hardt, Michael, 23
Harmon, Graham, 226n39, 227n40
Harney, Stefano, 132
Hart, Gary, 258–9
Harvey, David, 217
Hebrew, 48
Hegel, Georg Wilhelm Friedrich, 16, 30, 139, 191, 219, 252
Heidegger, Martin, 23, 30, 61, 205
Herder, Johann Gottfried, 188
Hessel, Stéphane, 215
Hewlett, Nick, 26–7
Hibou, Béatrice, 7n10
Hinds, Martin, 111
Hirst, Damien, 242
Hobbes, Thomas, 1, 30, 63, 64, 73, 139, 140
Hochschild, Arlie Russell, 61
Hogarth, William, 238
Holder, Eric, 73–4
House of Cards (television), 224, 249, 256, 257, 261, 263–4, 265, 266
Hughes, Edward, 210

Iannuci, Armando, 6n9, 92, 257
Imaginary Party, 50
impolitic, 9, 10, 14, 83–96, 97, 98, 103,
    234, 266, 267
Indiana, 14
informal politics, 1, 37
informatics, 45
infrapolitics, 37, 98
inscription, 33, 45, 64, 76, 100
insecuritization, 58, 59. *See also*
    securitization
interference, 101–112
Invisible Committee, 47, 48, 49
Iran, 8
Iraq, 5, 92, 246, 257
Italy, 14, 164, 189, 249
    Turin, 107, 172
    Venice, 99

Jackson, Jesse, 258
Jameson, Fredric, 4, 5, 12, 231, 246
Janet-lange, Ange-louis, 170
janking, 14–16
Jaspers, Karl, 75
Jay, Antony, 127
Johnson, Ken, 240n21
Johnston, Gary, 263
Jonck, Michael, 121
Jones, Chuck, 14
Joyce, James, 48, 106
J. P. Morgan, 233
Judy, Ronald A. T., 75
justice, 15, 32, 102–3, 142, 156, 162,
    215
    Bartleby, 128–9
    social justice, 63, 114, 254

Kalyvras, Andreas, 87
Kamuf, Peggy, 102
Kant, Emmanuel, 10, 28, 30, 33
Katehi, Linda P. B., 247
Katrina, Hurricane, 170

Kaufman, Eleanor, 220
Keats, John, 97
Kelley, Wyn, 119
Kentucky, 114
Khalifa, Jean, 75n20
Kiev uprising, 107
Kluge, Alexander, 11, 37, 38n2, 118,
    134
Kolbowski, Silvia, 112n23, 237
Koons, Jeff, 238, 242
Kosiński, Jerzy, 262–3
Krasner, Stephen, 141
Kristeva, Julia, 133n57, 200n2, 207

Labam, Rudolf von, 192n46
La Berge, Claire, 251n4
La Borde, 42, 47, 49
labor time, 3, 194
Lacan, Jacques, 104, 217, 220
Lacoue-Labarthe, Philippe, 28, 34,
    205–6
LaFarge, Paul, 50
La Fontaine, 15
Laing, R. D., 53
Lalopoulos, Sofia, 121–2
Lamb, Charles, 85
Lancaster, John, 141
Lane, Edward, 111
Latour, Bruno, 7–8, 10, 34–5, 45, 139,
    140, 214, 215, 221–3, 230
Laugier, Sandra, 249
Lawless, Joseph F., 73
Lazarsfeld, Paul, 53
Lazerges, Jean Raymond Hippolyte,
    170
Lazzarato, Maurizio, 215–17, 224
Lefort, Claude, 1, 163, 264
Leibovich, Mark, 6
Le Nouvel Observateur (magazine),
    130, 211
Les Indigènes de la République, 123
Lévy, Bernard-Henri, 205

Levy, Ophir, 250
Lezra, Jacques, 11, 105
LGBT, 108
libido, 42, 46, 175
Ling, Alex, 219
Locke, John, 64, 140
Loire valley, 170
Lombardi, Mark, 243
Lombardo, Patrizia, 188n37
London, 141, 233
London Review of Books (journal), 105
Lordon, Frédéric, 62, 63, 65, 128,
    214n4, 215
Louis, Édouard, 57
Lukács, Georg. *See* Lukács, György
Lukács, György, 4, 139n1, 141, 208,
    252
Lula da Silva, Luiz Inácio, 98
Luxembourg, Rosa, 246
Lyotard, Jean-François, 133n57

Maastricht Treaty, 28, 205
Machiavelli, Niccolò, 22, 89, 140, 149,
    163, 164, 221, 224
Machiavellianism, 1, 13, 163, 164, 165,
    264
MacPherson, C. B., 140
Madame Bovary (Flaubert), 192
Madrignani, Carlo, 253n9
Madrid, 108
Magazine littéraire (magazine), 211
Maidan, 1, 107, 108, 123
Malabou, Catherine, 35. *See also*
    plasticity
Mallarmé, Stéphane, 187, 214, 226–30
managed life, 17, 42, 213–30
Mann, Heinrich, 83
Mann, Thomas, 83, 86
Mao Tse-Tung, 109, 140
Marchart, Oliver, 21–2
Marc Jacobs, 237
Markmann, Charles Lam, 75

Marlow, Christopher, 193
Marx, Karl, 22, 108, 118, 140, 180, 226,
    246, 251
Marx, Leo, 121
Marxism, 22, 57, 214, 217
Mascolo, Dionys, 129
materialism, 45, 153, 174, 181, 234–7,
    264
materialities, 27–8, 180
Mayer, Arno, 201
Mbembe, Achille, 41, 68–74
McKee, Yates, 233n7
McKibbin, Ross, 2
McQueen, Steve, 77
Mead, George Herbert, 53
Meillassoux, Quentin, 214–30
Melville, Herman, 48, 114–32
Merkel, Angela, 13–14
Merkiavellianism, 13–14
Merleau-Ponty, Maurice, 133n57
Merton, Robert, 53
metapolitics, 194, 220
Miami, 240
Michl, Thomas, 237n16
micro-aggression, 69, 73, 114, 121, 134
microhistory, 38, 56
micro-physics, 38, 39, 40, 42, 220
micropolitics, 3, 9, 17, 37–51, 107, 162,
    193, 203, 248, 264
  anti-psychiatry movement, 53
  Bourdieu, 54
  civil disobedience, 123
   exceptionalism, 1
  Fanon, 69, 78
  Foucault, 4, 10, 37–45, 206
  ostinato, 113, 115, 129–34
  plasticity, 36
  psychopower, 84
microsociological research, 39, 53, 54,
    61, 61
microsociology, 53–65
Milan, 43

military, 40, 155, 159, 171
Miller, Keith, 233
Milner, Jean-Claude, 96n29, 125–6, 129
Milton, John, 257
Missouri, 84
Mitterrand, François, 58, 65, 151, 204
Moby Dick (Melville), 119
molecular politics, 10, 17, 45, 46, 48, 50–51, 53
MOMA (Museum of Modern Art), 233
Moreiras, Alberto, 98–99
Moretti, Franco, 4, 200, 210, 211
Morin, Edgar, 129
Moten, Fred, 132n53
Mother Jones (magazine), 84
Mouffe, Chantal, 23, 24, 34, 140
Müller, Heiner, 50
Murakami, Takashi, 242
Musset, Alfred, 210
Musil, Robert, 48
mutism, 129–30

Nadar, Paul, 199, 201, 202
Nader, Ralph, 258
Nancy, Jean-Luc, 28, 34, 124, 205–6
nanoracisms, 67–79
Napoleon I, 146–51, 165, 169, 171–3, 207, 226
Napoleon III, 158, 165, 169, 173, 202
nationalism, 70, 74, 108
National Security Agency, 6
Naughton, John T., 129
Nazism, 84
Nealon, Christopher, 217
necropolitics, 41–2
Negri, Antonio, 23, 28, 140, 153, 154
négritude. See blackness
Negt, Oskar, 11, 37, 38n2, 118, 134
neoliberalism, 11, 24, 35, 64, 110, 213, 217

America, 4, 65, 223
Bartleby, 120, 123, 125, 129
economics, 100, 215
Europe, 4, 59, 179, 206
Netanyahu, Benjamin, 102
Netflix, 261
neuroscience, 26
new Confederacy, 67, 69, 73
New Jersey, 265
New Museum of Contemporary Art, 233
New Orleans, 170
New York, 119–21, 233, 238, 265
    Wall Street, 119, 232, 234, 238
    Zucotti Park, 108
New Yorker (magazine), 120
New York Review of Books (journal), 107
New York Stock Exchange, 233
New York Times (newspaper), 114, 265
New York University, 233
Nicolas, Ariane, 63
Nietzsche, Friedrich, 67–75, 87–8, 89, 90, 99, 145–8, 216
    retournement, 68, 70
Nixon, Rob, 3n5
NYC District Council of Carpenters, 233

Obama administration, 8, 73–4, 84, 103
Obamacare, 84
object-oriented ontology, 45
obstinacy, 4, 11, 113–35
obstination, 1, 128, 130, 132–4
obstructionism, 8, 91, 104, 249, 264
Occupy, 1, 107, 108, 215, 231–47
    Occupy Museums, 233
    Occupy Wall Street (OWS), 118, 120, 121, 123–4, 232–43, 248
Odysseus, 102
oedipal organization, 42, 46

Ohio, 261
ontology, 46, 75, 123, 162, 200, 217, 219, 223, 230
Oregon, 263
ostinato, 113, 115, 130–35
Oury, Jean, 47, 49
Oxford University, 257

Paci, Enzo, 252
Pangle, Thomas, 83
Parker, Ian, 257n15
Parker, Nate, 77
Parsons, Talcott, 53
Pascal, Blaise, 31, 60
Paul, Zakir, 190
peasant, 49, 56, 194
pedagogy, 103, 104, 112
Peel, Robert, 254
Pentagon Papers, 30–31
Pericles, 102
Peugeot auto plant, 61, 62
Pfaller, Robert, 214n4
pharmakon, 103, 116
phenomenology, 4, 28, 61, 89, 235, 246, 255
Phillips, Lisa, 238
philology, 105, 108, 110–12, 180
phronesis, 83, 100
Picasso, Pablo, 246, 248
Pike, John, 248
Piketty, Thomas, 215
Planat, Isidore, 180
plasticity, 11, 35, 191, 192n46, 225
Plato, 10, 22, 30, 86, 119, 194, 140
   Gorgias (Plato), 24
   Laws (Plato), 101–2, 105
   Republic (Plato), 90, 102, 103, 104, 217
   Socrates, 90, 91, 101, 103, 104, 119
Platonism, 26
pluralism, 21, 23, 25, 28
Podemos, 123

Political, the, 1, 2, 12, 13, 34, 85, 87, 140, 205, 206
   meaning of, 9, 10, 28
   Occupy, 118, 123, 124
   politics, 21–5
   ressentiment, 72
   translation, 103
political fiction, 4, 6, 10, 12, 139–43, 148, 155, 156, 164, 253
   Machiavellianism, 94
political theory, classical, 1, 2, 9, 27, 84
Politics (big P). *See* Political, the
politics (small p), 2, 9, 10, 17, 21–36, 58, 98, 166, 174, 264–6
   Foucault-Guattari, 42
   Lacoue-Labarthe and Nancy, 206
   Negri, 153
   political fiction, 143
   Unger, 100
   warfare, 157
la politique. See politics (small p)
le politique. See Politics (big P)
Poore, Jonathan, 120, 121
Porter, Eduardo, 232
postmodernism, 12
Powhida, William, 6, 237–45
precarity, 47, 53, 58, 59, 61, 62, 64, 65
Prendergast, Christopher, 105–6
Pre-Socratics, 104
prisons, 40–41, 54, 119, 194. *See also* Guantánamo Bay
privatization, 40, 46, 128, 140, 241
Proust, Marcel, 4, 199–212
psychoanalysis, 45, 54, 74, 104
psychopolitics, 10, 68, 69, 72, 117, 145–54, 208
psychopower, 84, 149, 159, 253
Pussy Riot, 90
Putin, Vladimir, 90, 108
Putnam's (magazine), 119

Queneau, Raymond, 129, 132

Rancière, Jacques, 4, 24, 25, 34, 122,
    140, 177–80, 185–8, 191–4, 200
Rankine, Claudia, 134
Rawls, John, 140
real abstraction, 231n3, 251–52
Realpolitik, 1, 139, 156
Reason of State, 94, 118, 162, 253
Reed, Naomi C., 120
Reform Act (1832), 211, 254
refugees, 14, 168
relativism, 26, 73, 104
ressentiment, 67–72, 90, 121, 146, 147,
    237
Restoration, 4, 9, 155, 156, 220
Reynaud, Philippe, 21
Rhone valley, 170
rhythm, 38, 49, 132, 186, 191, 208,
    220, 222, 253, 266
Ricoeur, Paul, 21–3, 34
Robertson, Pat, 258
Robertson-Lorant, Laurie, 119n16
Robillard, André, 50
Rodin, Auguste, 191
Romero, Schroeder, 238
Romney, Mitt, 84
Rousseau, Jean-Jacques, 30, 139, 140,
    152, 159
rupture, 10, 28, 44, 123, 130, 193
Russell, David J., 85
Russian (language), 107

de Saint-Maurice, Thibaut, 249
Salmon, Christian, 61
Samoyault, Tiphaine, 203–4
Sarkozy government, 27, 48, 177
Saro-Wiwa, Ken, 40–41
Sartre, Jean-Paul, 67, 115, 154, 187
satire, 6, 92, 127, 141, 238, 253, 258
Saunders, Trevor J., 102, 105
Saviano, Roberto, 252

scatter, 29–34
Schadenfreude, 199–212, 265
schizo-language, 45, 54
Schmitt, Carl, 1, 5, 10, 21, 22n2, 23, 34,
    68, 69, 86, 87, 140
Schor, Mira, 238
Scorsese, Martin, 258
Scott, Felicity, 47, 48
Scott, Walter, 208
security, 39, 74, 161, 223, 225
securitization, 46, 68, 70, 92, 226, 234.
    See also insecuritization
Sellers, Peter, 262
Seltzer, Mark, 267
Senate. See US Senate
shareholder existence, 223–24
signification, 44, 195
Simmel, Georg, 190n41, 214–15
Simondon, Gilbert, 45
singularity, 33, 43–5, 106, 231
Situationists, 48, 90
slavery, 27, 70, 77–8, 119, 123, 140–41
Sloterdijk, Peter, 95–96, 214n4
Smith, Adam, 216
Smythe, George, 254
Snyder, Timothy, 107
Solnit, Rebecca, 3n5, 9n14
society of calculation, 220
sophistry, 30, 36, 104
Sorel, Georges, 126, 246
Sorel, Julien, 147, 194
Sotheby's, 233
South African Truth and
    Reconciliation Commission, 11
South Carolina, 84, 261
sovereignty, 5, 22, 24, 32–5, 39, 67, 78,
    79, 90, 141, 156, 161
Spacey, Kevin, 261
Spillers, Hortense, 77
Spinoza, Baruch, 62, 128, 140, 148,
    152–4, 219
Spitzer, Leo, 192n46

Spivak, Gayatri Chakravorty, 11
squatting, 107, 119
Steinem, Gloria, 258
Stendhal, 4, 94, 141, 145–54, 164, 186, 194, 208
Stirner, Max, 118
Stockholm, 48
stock ticker, 222
Stoics, 219
Strauss, Leo,
subjectivation, 38, 44, 45, 61, 74, 75–6, 78, 214, 216, 223
subjectivity, 1, 42, 78, 200, 211, 219, 225
Syntagma Square, 108
syntax, 4, 44, 92, 130, 132
Szendy, Peter, 230n55

Taga, Shigeru, 42
Tahrir Square, 108, 111, 112
Taibbi, Matt, 243
Taine, Hippolyte, 4, 139, 177n1, 179–80, 185, 188–95
Taksim Square, 108
Tarantino, Quentin, 77
Taylor, A. E., 102
Tea Party, 8, 84, 263
techne, 30, 83, 99, 221, 235
terrorism, 48, 103, 108, 168
thermocracy, 10, 163–75
Thibaut de Saint-Maurice, 249n1
Thoreau, Henry David, 119–21
Thucydides, 102
Toscano, Alberto, 252
translation, 21, 45, 90, 102, 103–12
Trollope, Anthony, 142
Tronti, Mario, 91
Trott, Adriel, 194n49
Trudeau, Garry, 257, 258
Trump, Donald, 15, 16, 237
Trump, Melania, 237
Trumpism, 8, 14–16, 266

Tumblr, 243, 247
Turkey, 14
Twitter, 14, 241, 266

Ukrainian (language), 107–8
Unger, Roberto Mangabeira, 3, 97–100, 140, 142
ungovernables, the, 37
United Steelworkers Local 1999, 14
University of Chicago, 259
UN Security Council, 174, 246
unpolitical, the, 99
untranslatables, 83, 104–6, 110, 111, 129
US Congress, 8, 102, 265
US Senate, 8, 84, 174, 263, 264
utilitarianism, 85–6, 100, 227, 254
utopianism, 1, 49, 50, 99

Valéry, Paul, 106
Venuti, Lawrence, 105
Vienna Congress, 207, 208
Vietnam War, 122
Vigny, Alfred de, 210
Villermé, Louis-René, 226
violence, 4, 46
  Balibar, 16
  Bourdieu, 53, 58, 60
  Fanon, 76, 77–9
  Lordon, 62
  Mbembe, 68, 70, 72
  Ricoeur, 22
  Sorel, 126
  Žižek, 123
  Zola, 168

Wallace, David Foster, 141
Wark, McKenzie, 48, 50
War on Terror, 70, 92, 116, 241
Waugh, Michael, 238
Weber, Sam, 106
Weheliye, Alexander G., 69, 74, 76–9, 132n53

Weil, Simone, 86, 87
Wellek, René, 188
West Wing, The (television), 250–51, 257
White, Hayden, 38
white supremacism, 68
Whitney Museum, 233
Wikileaks, 9
Willimon, Beau, 261
Wilson, Joe, 84
Wittgenstein, Ludwig, 96
Wood, Michael, 105
Woolf, Virginia, 192–3
World War I, 201

Wright, Jim, 260
Wynter, Silvia, 76

Yancy, George, 76
Yes, Prime Minister (television), 126–7, 257
YouTube, 30

Zakim, Michael, 125
Žižek, Slavoj, 5, 50, 51, 112, 122, 123, 129
Zola, Èmile, 4, 141, 164–75
zombification, 42